British Officials and British
Foreign Policy
1945-50

British Officials and British Foreign Policy 1945-50

Edited by
John Zametica

Leicester University Press
(A division of Pinter Publishers)
Leicester, London and New York.

©Editor and Contributors 1990

First published in Great Britain in 1990 by Leicester University Press
(a division of Pinter Publishers Ltd)

All rights reserved. No part of this publication may be reproduced, stored in a retrieval system, or transmitted, in any form or by any means, electronic, mechanical, photocopying, recording or otherwise, without the prior permission of the Leicester University Press.

Editorial offices
Fielding Johnson Building, University of Leicester,
University Road, Leicester, LE1 7RH

Trade and other enquiries
25 Floral Street, London, WC2E 9DS and P.O. Box 157, Irvington, New York.

British Library Cataloguing in Publication Data
A CIP cataloguing record for this book is available
from the British Library
ISBN 0-7185-1270 7 hardback

Library of Congress Cataloging-in-Publication Data
British officials and British foreign policy, 1945-1050/edited by
  John Zametica.
      p.   cm.
  ISBN 0-7185-1270-7
     1. Great Britain—Foreign relations—1945- 2. Great Britain—
  Officials and employees—Foreign countries. I. Zametica, John.
  DA588.B645 1990
  327.41—dc20   90-5664
                                                                    CIP

Typeset by Witwell Ltd, Southport
Printed and bound in Great Britain by
Billing & Sons Ltd, Worcester

Contents

Introduction
Raymond Smith   1

1 Roger Makins: 'Mr Atom'
Jill Edwards   8

2 Three letters to Bevin: Frank Roberts at the Moscow Embassy, 1945-46
John Zametica   39

3 Duff Cooper and the Paris Embassy, 1945-47
John W. Young   98

4 Sir Alec Kirkbride and the Anglo-Transjordanian alliance, 1945-50
Ilan Pappé   121

5 Robin Hankey
Victor Rothwell   156

6 Oliver Franks and the Washington Embassy, 1948-52
Peter G. Boyle   189

7 William Strang and the Permanent Under-Secretary's Committee
Ritchie Ovendale   212

8 Development diplomacy: Sir John Troutbeck and the British Middle East Office, 1947-50
Wesley K. Wark   228

Index   250

Editor's Acknowledgements

I am very grateful to Alec McAulay of Leicester University Press and to the contributors for their remarkable patience in awaiting the completion of editorial work on this volume.

Dr Michael Stenton provided valuable comments on my essay. Richard Aldrich and Anthony Gorst were, as always, very helpful with their criticisms. I am also grateful to Edward Petraitis and Jill Stuart for their support. I am particularly grateful to Dr Raymond Smith on whose vast knowledge of the 1945–1948 period in British foreign policy I was able to draw many times. The views expressed in my essay are, however, my own. I should also like to thank Sir Frank Roberts for his kindness in granting me an interview.

Robert Gibbs provided invaluable help in the final preparation of the manuscript.

John Zametica
Cambridge 1990

List of Contributors

Peter Boyle is a lecturer in American History at the University of Nottingham. He has published many articles on aspects of relations between Britain, the United States and the Soviet Union, 1945-55. He is currently editing *The Churchill-Eisenhower Correspondence, 1953-55*.

Jill Edwards read Modern European History at the University of Reading, and gained a doctorate there in 1977. She is the author of *The British Government and the Spanish Civil War, 1936-1939* (Macmillan 1979). She has taught at Reading University and at Queen Mary College, University of London, where she was also Visiting Fellow in the Centre for Contemporary Spanish Studies, 1985-87. Between 1981 and 1984 she was engaged in research on international affairs at the Centre for Policy Studies. She presently teaches at the American University in Cairo and is currently writing *Anglo-U.S. Relations with Spain, 1945-1955* for Oxford University Press.

Ritchie Ovendale is a Reader in the Department of International Politics, University College of Wales, Aberystwyth. He holds degrees from the University of Natal, McMaster University, and Oxford, and is a Fellow of the Royal Historical Society. His publications include *'Appeasement' and the English Speaking World. Britain, the United States, the Dominions and the Policy of 'Appeasement', 1937-1939* (1975); *The Origins of the Arab-Israeli Wars* (1984); and *The English-Speaking Alliance: Britain, the United States, the Dominions and the Cold War 1945-51* (1985). He has also edited *The Foreign Policy of the British Labour Governments, 1945-1951* (1984). Forthcoming works include *Britain, the United States and the End of the Palestine Mandate, 1942-1948*.

Ilan Pappé is a lecturer in the Department of Middle East History at the University of Haifa, Israel. He gained a doctorate from the University of Oxford (St Antony's College) in 1984. He is the author of *Britain and the Arab-Israeli Conflict, 1948-1951* (Macmillan 1988). He has written extensively on British policy towards the Middle East and the history of Jordan and the Palestinians.

Victor Rothwell is Reader in History at the University of Edinburgh. He obtained his Ph.D. at the University of Leeds. His publications include *British War Aims and Peace Diplomacy 1914-1918* (1971), *Britain and the Cold War 1941-1947* (1982), and several articles on international history.

Raymond Smith gained his Ph.D. at the University of Liverpool in 1983. He co-authored, with John Zametica, The Cold Warrior: Clement Attlee reconsidered, 1945-7, *International Affairs*, **61**, no.2, Spring 1985, and he is the author of A Climate of opinion: British officials and the development of British Soviet Policy, 1945-7, *International Affairs*, **64**, no.4, Autumn 1988.

Wesley Wark is Assistant Professor of History, University of Toronto. He has taught at McGill University and the University of Calgary. He received his Ph.D. in International History from the London School of Economics in 1984. His *The Ultimate Enemy: British Intelligence and Nazi Germany, 1933-1939* was published in 1985 by I.B. Tauris and in 1986 in paperback by Oxford University Press. He has written numerous articles on British and U.S. intelligence subjects. He is now at work on an authorized biography of Field Marshal Lord Ironside.

John Young is a lecturer in International History at the London School of Economics. Born in Whitehaven in 1957, he studied at Nottingham and Cambridge Universities and is the author of *Britain, France and the Unity of Europe* (1984) and *France, the Cold War* and *the Western Alliance, 1944-49* (1990), and editor of *The Foreign Policy of Churchill's Peacetime Administration* (1988).

John Zametica was born in Yugoslavia. He gained his M.A. in International History at the London School of Economics, and his Ph.D. at Corpus Christi College, Cambridge. He is currently completing *British Strategy in the Cold War* for Routledge.

Introduction
Raymond Smith

There is a type of memoir written by former British diplomats which seeks to reinforce the view of their role as facilitators of ministerially driven policy initiatives. Typically, these memoirs hide behind the aspect of confidentiality in revealing very little, if anything, of the role of officials in the formulation of British foreign policy.[1] Fortunately, some officials have been less discreet in the diaries they maintained during their period of service; and using these sources, together with the official documents released at the Public Record Office historians have started to develop a clearer picture of the manner in which immediate post-war British foreign policy was formulated and executed.

If, initially, historians tended to highlight the political actors in this process then this tendency in some measure had its roots in the reputation of the Attlee government. People spoke at the time and subsequently of the 'Big Five' of the Labour Cabinet — Attlee, Bevin, Dalton, Morrison and Cripps. In particular, Bevin commanded attention. Lord Bullock, Bevin's biographer, has recalled how Sir Orme Sargent, Permanent Under Secretary at the Foreign Office from 1946 to 1948, was prompted to contact him to stress that his former political master 'understood more about Europe' than any Foreign Secretary since Salisbury, 'and I do not exclude Salisbury'. Sargent was speaking from experience, having served under every Foreign Secretary from Salisbury onwards.[2] Even Bevin's biographer, however, has acknowledged the strength of the Foreign Office official team which served Bevin during his tenure as Foreign Secretary.[3] But at no stage would Bullock accept that Bevin had become a tool of these officials. Indeed, despite Bevin's reliance on oral communication and possible greater dependence on the information and appreciation of that information supplied by the Foreign Office, Bullock has concluded that Bevin 'played as decisive a part in shaping policy as any Foreign Minister in modern times'.[4]

Yet this has not stifled the debate on the role of officials and their impact on the development of policy. The views which surfaced at the time about the power of permanent officials have inevitably attracted historians now better able to judge from the state papers the strength of the case. The availability of Hugh Dalton's diary has shown that he felt very early on that Bevin had 'become more devoted than any of his predecessors for a generation to the Career Diplomats and all the Old Boys in the F.O.'[5] In these terms there is a certain irony that a number of people including Francis Williams and Dick Crossman had used what influence they had to get Bevin rather than Dalton at the Foreign Office because they thought the latter would be too 'orthodox' particularly with regard to the personnel of the Foreign Office, whereas they thought Bevin would make tremendous personnel changes and clear out all the 'old gang'.[6] There is some evidence that this view was not wholly mistaken. As Anthony Adamthwaite has pointed out, by the end of 1947 the foreign service had been considerably restructured and of 147 members of the foreign service of senior rank in 1943, nearly half had left by the end of 1947, including seventeen forced retirements.[7]

It would be idle, however, to pretend that this proved that Bevin was 'firmly in the saddle'.[8] Such a conclusion requires a far closer look at the personnel of the Foreign Office than such a statistical exercise allows — it certainly says nothing about the staff that remained. One set of personnel changes which took place at the beginning of 1946 is particularly instructive in this respect. In February 1946 Orme Sargent had replaced Alexander Cadogan as Permanent Under Secretary. One official noted privately at the time that Sargent represented 'the F.O. of say 1910...He laughs at the United Nations as he did the League, and the Southern and Northern departments which with Reconstruction are the kernel of the F.O. take their lead from him. He may not last long but may do infinite harm in that time'.[9] Equally, Christopher Warner's promotion to Superintending Under Secretary of the Northern and Southern Departments was of some significance given his close working relationship with Sargent and his developing views on the Soviet threat.[10] The appointment of Maurice Peterson as Ambassador to Moscow also took place at this time. The *New Statesman* saw the shuffle of personnel as designed to frustrate the implementation of a socialist foreign policy.[11] Later Warner was to recognize the extent to which this could damage British policy and standing in the world:

We have foreseen that the Russians would pretty soon realise how clumsy they have been in the last few months, and would attempt to pull a velvet glove over their iron hand; and that public opinion and many important people both here and in America might well be misled into thinking quite erroneously that the iron hand had been discarded, or even that it had been a figment of the imagination of wicked Foreign Office and Foreign Service officials.[12]

Warner may well have reflected that this was the inevitable fate of the senior Foreign Office official. Had he looked back to the period before and during the First World War he would have found a similar controversy about the role of Foreign Office staff. As Paul Kennedy has noted, 'radical journalists and politicians claimed that far from being the neutral advisers and executors of the elected government's wishes, these officials had sought to influence and even to direct policy contrary to the wishes of the Liberal Cabinet and party.'[13] There are now few defenders of that view of official control of policy before and during the First World War. Equally there is a significant body of historians that takes exception to the suggestion that foreign policy during Bevin's time was anything other than under the control of the Cabinet. 'Bevin's policy was not invented by a phantom army of Sargents, Warners, Furlonges and Troutbecks . . . Bevin's foreign policy was vividly his own', is the robust view of one historian of Labour's period in power.[14] A.J.P. Taylor in equally robust mood has commented on an early assessment of Britain's role in the Cold War drawn from official documents: 'At best it is a competent precis of "what one clerk said to another clerk" during a period when great events were happening a long way from Whitehall'.[15] Taylor's willingness to see all officials of the Foreign Office from the Permanent Under Secretary down as clerks suggests more than a disagreement as to the role of officials in developing policy. And indeed there are those who quite readily criticize officials for aspects of policy while apparently adhering to the view that policy is the creation of ministers rather than officials. The intellectual attitudes of the top diplomats in this period have been said to 'resemble nothing so much as Montaigne's apes – the higher they climbed the more they displayed their posteriors.'[16]

Yet for all the hesitancy in ascribing great policy influence to the officials of the Foreign Office, there has been an increasing willingness amongst historians to look more closely at the process of policy formulation and to highlight the role of permanent officials of the Foreign Office and Foreign Service in that process. And indeed some former officials have been more forthright in suggesting the influence they have had in that process. Nicholas Henderson, for instance, has written illuminatingly on the powerful position of the Principal Private Secretary to the Foreign Secretary.[17] Nor has the ministerial view always sought to contradict this interpretation of the power of officials. George Brown has reflected that 'the Foreign Office is equipped to give the best information, the best briefing on any international issue . . . But what bothered me . . . was . . . that it was they who were deciding the areas I should be briefed about, and I quickly became aware that, unless I was very determined, I would inevitably become the purveyor of views already formed in the office.'[18] Certainly there has been a tendency to look at the nature of the foreign policy-making elite in Britain in a way which addresses the 'why' of official action rather than the 'how' officials determined policy. So Hugh Thomas has described the shortcomings of the British Foreign Office in the following terms: 'Most . . . were conditioned by their backgrounds. It was thus as difficult for them to judge Stalin as it had been Hitler for, in both of those men's motives, ideology, a most uncertain element (and scarcely considered in English public schools) played a real part.'[19] Yet several of Bevin's team of officials were from middle class rather than upper class origins.[20] And in many cases it is almost impossible to use an absolute social origins theory to interpret or help understand why a particular policy was developed by officials.

Indeed it may be that historians will benefit more from analysing how officials ensured that a particular policy was adopted rather than in investigating their motives for doing so. The wealth of documentary material available at the Public Record Office has tended to move investigation in this direction, though some would argue that this can lead to viewing the files 'too literally and unreflectively'.[21] This danger undoubtedly exists. It is for the historian to make his or her case and to be judged on the results. It should not be assumed, however, that close analysis of the process of policy formulation leads by its very act to a blinkered view of the origins of a foreign policy line. It is not necessary to argue that officials were superlatively purposeful in pressing their own line to see ways and means by which officials manipulated foreign policy. The very fact that many of the critical aspects of British foreign policy were developed outside the Cabinet room points to the opportunities for the official line to have a direct influence on the adoption of policy. Even members of the Cabinet's Defence Committee were not always privy to the discussions which led to the adoption of policy.[22]

Where then does this leave any assessment of the role of officials in the development of British foreign policy in the immediate postwar period? It seems clear that groups of officials, and on occasion individual officials, can not only have an impact on policy but can actually determine its main lines. Sometimes a small group of senior officials can in effect push a line which has not received ministerial sanction.[23] As this present collection of essays shows, the impact of individual officials within their specialist fields can often be important in safeguarding British interests. Throughout this period there is a degree to which officials, despite Britain's weakened position in the world, felt that they could influence the direction of world events by superior statecraft. In the main this meant convincing the Americans that the main aims of British policy should be their own. Inevitably, there were times when this proved almost impossible to achieve. Yet, as the careers of both Roger Makins and Oliver Franks during this period indicate, there was an extent to which officials of sufficient calibre could and did effect something of a damage limitation exercise on Anglo-American relations. And it is at least arguable that their quiet persuasiveness was more influential than any number of ministerial *démarches*. There is also a large body of evidence which suggests that Britain's impact on western Cold War policy was the greater because of the push from Foreign Office and Foreign Service officials to reassess Soviet intentions at the beginning of 1946. The close working relationship which developed between the British and American embassies in Moscow can be seen as part of this process.

If this set of essays raises the view of officials from that of simple clerks it will have performed a singular service to diplomatic historiography. It will unquestionably have achieved one of its major aims if historians take more care in assessing the roots of British foreign policy and hesitate before subscribing to a view of purely ministerially or Cabinet driven policy. It should not be necessary to follow the vulgar view of official power to pursue this line of historical investigation. The *Sunday Express* captured that view in October 1952 when it questioned: 'How is it that when the Government changes the blunders go on just the same? Largely because the senior officials . . . continue to make policy'.[24] It would, of course have been uncomfortable for the leader writers of the *Sunday Express* to have taken a more positive view of the permanent officials of the Foreign Office. The evidence, in fact, is that far from being unfeeling and faceless bureaucrats, the senior officials of the Foreign Office were very often sophisticated, dedicated and hard-working analysts and observers of the world scene. No one, for instance, could but fail to be impressed by the quality of the despatches written by Frank Roberts in the early months of 1946 commenting on the Soviet Union's aspirations and intentions in the critical regions of the world. It is hardly surprising that in this process officials should develop strong views on the policies which would best serve Britain's interests. Nor indeed that they should work to see them adopted. Rather than question the constitutional proprieties of such action, historians would best set their efforts to determining how far and when such a process took place.

Notes

1. Consider, for instance, Sir Maurice Peterson's memoirs, those of Lord Strang and those of Sir Ivone Kirkpatrick.
2. *The Guardian*, 7 November 1983.
3. Alan Bullock, *Ernest Bevin: Foreign Secretary*, 1983, 98.
4. ibid, 102.
5. Hugh Dalton Diary, The British Library of Political and Economic Science, entry for 25 February 1946.
6. ibid.
7. Anthony Adamthwaite, Britain and the World, 1945-9: the view from the Foreign Office, *International Affairs*, **61**, no.2, Spring 1985.
8. ibid.
9. Charles Webster Diary, The British Library of Political and Economic Science, entry for 3 February 1946.
10. Raymond Smith, A climate of opinion: British officials and the development of British Soviet Policy, 1945-7, *International Affairs*, **64**, no. 4, Autumn 1988.
11. 8 February 1946.
12. Public Record Office, Kew, FO 181/1023, File 2 [504], Warner to Roberts, 1 May 1946.
13. Paul Kennedy, *The Realities Behind Diplomacy*, 1981, 61.
14. Kenneth O. Morgan, *Labour in Power 1945-1951*, 1984, 236.
15. A.J.P. Taylor's review of Victor Rothwell's *Britain and the Cold War 1941-1947* in *The London Review of Books*, 18 February-13 March 1982.
16. *The Times*, 4 March 1982. Piers Brendon's review of Rothwell.
17. Nicolas Henderson, *The Private Office*, 1984.
18. George Brown, *In My Way*, 1971, 129.
19. Hugh Thomas, *Armed Truce: The Beginnings of the Cold War 1945-46*, 1986, 201. There can be little doubt that nearly twenty-five years after its original publication D.C. Watt's *Personalities and Policies* is still playing a part in determining the shape of writing on twentieth-century diplomatic history. See, also, Peter G. Boyle, The British Foreign Office View of Soviet-American relations, 1945-46, *Diplomatic History*, **3**, (3), Summer 1979. Writing about the officials in the Washington Embassy and the North American Department of the Foreign Office, Boyle comments: 'These officials were a homogeneous group and had little disagreement in their general world views or in their views of the reasons for the breakdown in relations between Russia and the West. Their social and educational backgrounds were very similar.'
20. Bullock, 98.
21. Morgan, 236
22. Shinwell complained in November 1946 that Cabinet ministers 'who were not members of the Defence Committee were not ... fully informed of all the strategic considerations which were being taken into account in the formulation of foreign policy'. Public Record Office, CAB 128/8: CM(46)97, no circulation record, 18 November 1946.

23. Smith.
24. Quoted in Anthony Adamthwaite, Overstretched and overstrung: Eden, the Foreign Office and the making of policy, 1951-5, *International Affairs*, **64**, no.2, Spring 1988.

1 Roger Makins: 'Mr Atom'
Jill Edwards[1]

'So far as I'm concerned we ought to pull the plug on the bastards,' one visiting American senator remarked to colleagues during a discussion of Britain's financial problems. Ever conscientious, Sir Roger Makins, who had been about to leave the meeting took off his coat, resumed his seat and began again.[2] The episode exemplifies Harold Macmillan's description of his former aide's 'rapier like brain combined with that almost monastic devotion to duty', which made Makins, he said, 'such a unique figure in the public service'.[3] But just how much did such evident ability and determination count in the formative years of British post-war foreign policy? What effect if any on the course of policy formulation could the input of any one official have? This essay examines Roger Makins's role in the development of British policy in two highly specialized areas — atomic energy and economic policy — over the relatively short period from the end of 1945 to the beginning of 1948, in an attempt to establish where influence in those areas lay and how it was achieved.

During the course of foreign policy planning in the summer of 1945 it had been suggested Britain should

> not be afraid of having a policy independent of our two great partners and not submit to a line of action dictated to us by either Russia or the United States, just because of their superior power or because it is the line of least resistance or because we despair of being able to maintain ourselves without United States support in Europe.[4]

The dismal reality of peacetime, however, soon swept away this lotophagous mood. Roger Makins's was not the only powerful voice to be heard in the ongoing reappraisal, but of the limited choices which faced the British Government from 1945 it was his brand of Atlanticism which came to prevail. That his views carried weight was due to personal qualities, to expertise, and to the degree of chance which placed him in the three key areas from which his influence derived.

Indeed it is clear that only someone of exceptional abilities could have come to dominate to the degree Makins did the threefold axis of British foreign policy: atomic energy (as it was then called), economic aid, and, commanding both these, Anglo-American relations. The importance of the latter to all aspects of British overseas policy, not only East-West relations but also Dominions and Commonwealth, can scarcely be overstated. Moreover, his unique position astride both economic and atomic energy worlds added force to his views in broader areas of policy formulation where many colleagues were in the dark. Even Ernest Bevin, the incoming Foreign Secretary, had been briefed on atomic energy at the end of July 1945 only because it was thought '. . . it would be odd if the Minister in charge of a Department had no knowledge of the existence of a subject in which members of his department were engaged'.[5] Makins's career encompassed a wide spectrum of British foreign policy formulation at a high level for over a decade, but this chapter concentrates on the years in which the direction of his career was set, and in particular on British atomic policy formulation leading to the momentous Modus Vivendi of January 1948, and the economic negotiations surrounding the Marshall Plan with which atomic policy became enmeshed.

That atomic energy has tended until recently to be placed outside the main stream of historical analysis is partly due to the excellence of the official histories of its development, and to the prolonged unavailability of records.[6] For example, at the time of writing, many of Makins's own Foreign Office papers relating to atomic policy are still closed. But it also reflects the blinkered attitude adopted after Hiroshima to a topic which, as one historian has remarked, was too clumsy an instrument for diplomatic exchange.[7] Nevertheless, though shunned in diplomatic discourse, the bomb became a silent influence, and the secrecy imposed on the narrow circle of initiates in the craft of atomic energy intensified this factor. During the war Churchill had declined to inform Clement Attlee on the subject; and when Bevin became Foreign Secretary in July 1945, it was clear that his participation in atomic policy would be little more than a formality. Moreover, by 1947, with atomic issues shunted into the maw of the United Nations, public interest had lapsed, one American journalist observed, into 'bored apathy'. Yet at neither government nor official level was it possible to divorce what Attlee in August 1945 had called 'the major factor' from the whole range of politico-economic problems, and most notably the panoply of policy leading up to the European Recovery Programme (ERP), more commonly known as the Marshall Plan.[8]

The scope of Makins's work was vast, but by late 1944 he was particularly well qualified for the trinity of tasks he was to undertake. A lawyer by training, his first Foreign Office posting in 1931 took him to Washington where he married the daughter of Senator Dwight F. Davis. Thereafter, even in wartime, he travelled frequently to the United States establishing an invaluable network of American diplomatic, political and family friends.[9] A potential set-back came in 1940-1 while he was at the Belgium desk of the Foreign Office and fell foul of Labour ministers for supporting the Belgian Government — many of whose members he knew well — and whom Labour regarded as defeatist. That year, accompanying Clement Attlee, then Lord Privy Seal in the wartime coalition government, to the International Labour Organization (ILO) Conference in New York, he championed the candidacy of M. Paul van Zeeland, the ex-Belgian Premier and Foreign Secretary for chairman of a special ILO post-war planning commission. Attlee, who regarded van Zeeland as an extreme reactionary, was reportedly very angry with Makins whom he felt had exceeded instructions.[10] This seems not to have affected Makins's career, however, and the Belgian connection, useful in later dealings over the uranium agreements, was further developed in 1942 when Makins was seconded to the Treasury to supervise the control of raw materials in French West Africa and the Belgian Congo.[11]

In 1943 he joined the staff of Harold Macmillan, Minister Resident in north-west Africa, and remained with him until September 1944. He spent 1945 and 1946 in the British Embassy in Washington, where he took charge of atomic energy matters, but from March 1945 he became in addition Minister in charge of Economic Affairs. He returned to the Foreign Office in February 1947 as Assistant Under-Secretary supervising the economic departments. During that year, for example, Makins worked not only on the Marshall Plan and the atomic energy negotiations, but on reparations and the host of post-war problems with which his departments dealt. He also contributed to the Russia Committee, the forum into which all Foreign Office departments fed information relevant to Anglo-Soviet policy. As the Foreign Office representative at the Treasury he was instrumental in setting up the Colombo Conference of 1950 which investigated the broad needs of the Commonwealth. In 1953 he became British Ambassador in Washington, returning to become Joint Permanent Secretary of the Treasury in 1956, and chairman of the United Kingdom Atomic Energy Authority in 1960. It is therefore in analysing the dual atomic and economic background to Britain's relations with the United States that the role played by Roger Makins comes most clearly into focus.

During his time with Macmillan, Makins had worked closely with Field Marshal 'Jumbo' Sir Henry Maitland Wilson, C.-in-C. Middle East, and joined up with him again in Washington in January 1945. Macmillan had been most reluctant to lose Makins whom he found invaluable: 'absolutely tireless, very scrupulous, and a splendid draftsman. He really is a great help. He also has a keen sense of humour'. In Makins he felt he had lost not only 'a most agreeable companion and friend', but an exemplary assistant: 'the inspiring thing about him is his standard of work . . . *never* satisfied with second best. And this goes through the office and inspires others'.[12]

However, Lord Halifax, the British Ambassador in Washington, prevailed then, and although in February 1945 when the Foreign Secretary Anthony Eden wanted Makins for Cairo, Halifax, due to staff shortages, had to agree to Makins filling both atomic and economic posts, he was keen to keep Makins and confident of his ability to cope 'I have been very much impressed', he wrote, 'with the importance of having someone who will readily secure American confidence. This Makins would certainly do . . . I am sure I shall not think of anyone I shall like better than Makins.'[13] Thus Makins became Minister for Economic Affairs and in July 1945 Joint Secretary of the Combined Policy Committee on atomic energy (the C.P.C.) on which 'Jumbo' Wilson, as head of the British contingent at the Joint Staff Mission, represented Britain. Initially, knowing little of scientific matters, he had access to the most eminent scientists in the field and quickly familiarized himself with the complex and arcane world of atomic energy. During the spring of 1945, in his alternate role, he toured the Midwest, lecturing that congressionally influential bastion of isolationism on Britain's post-imperial international policy — an experience he found as useful to the lecturer as the lectured.[14]

On his return to Washington where he took over the British side of atomic energy negotiations, the secrecy shrouding atomic research proved something of a double-edged weapon from the British point of view. The bomb was nearing the experimental stage. Its use would end public ignorance, and a whole range of problems would transfer atomic energy from the military, economic and scientific to the diplomatic sphere. It would be difficult, for example, to reveal the full extent of British involvement without also acknowledging the part played by French scientists who in early 1945 were trying to re-establish France's claim to certain atomic patents. French threats to turn to the Russians merely confirmed Churchill's opposition to French participation. They were to be fobbed off with promises of 'fair treatment' after the war, and the President was advised not to make any commitment to the French, and no disclosure to the Russians, although the Foreign Office believed that the longer the revelation was postponed the more 'resentful and suspicious' the Russians were likely to be.[15]

The two wartime written agreements delineating Anglo-American cooperation on atomic energy were the Quebec Agreement of August 1943 (clause 2 gave Britain right of veto on use of the bomb) and the Hyde Park Aide Mémoire of 18 September 1944.[16] Of these the second, reinforcing post-war collaboration, was the product of a brief, less formal meeting between Roosevelt and Churchill and knowledge of its existence strictly limited. After Roosevelt's death it emerged that the Americans had lost their copy of it. Makins advised sending all relevant documents directly to Stimson who was already briefing Truman. He also urged colleagues in London to use the opportunity to remind the Americans of a conversation at Yalta during which Churchill had extracted from Roosevelt a verbal promise to waive clause 4 of the Quebec Agreement under which Britain's post-war commercial atomic development — already *the* central issue for the British — would be dependent on American consent.[17]

By May 1945, as the need to plan for international reaction grew more pressing, the Foreign Office saw that atomic energy policy, previously with no precise departmental demarcation, though under the supervision of Sir John Anderson, then Lord President of the Council, was fast becoming essentially a diplomatic problem.[18] To speed up discussions before the atomic test, Henry L. Stimson, Secretary for War, proposed bypassing the CPC: he would talk directly to Halifax. Similarly, Stimson's 'mouthpiece' and 'altar ego', Harvey Bundy, conferred with Makins, his opposite number on the CPC. Between them they agreed an announcement on the bomb should be made as soon as possible. Fearing the moment might be missed, Makins urged colleagues in London to sort out their policy, before American ideas crystallized. The British, however, seemed mainly relieved that American colleagues had acknowledged the obligation to consult them. Returning from San Francisco via Washington, Eden consulted Halifax and Makins, and in London the next day, 17 May, prepared to meet the War Cabinet and the chiefs of staff to discuss the bomb.[19]

At the end of the month the Americans set up their own informal 'advisory' group of five to consider problems posed by the imminent testing of the bomb, but assured Makins the group intended to consult the British on matters of all but domestic concern, which now centred on international reaction. The British Chiefs of Staff were 'anxious to see it put to a practical test of that sort as soon as possible'. So was Churchill, though he was concerned to remind Marshall of the second provision of the Quebec Agreement on the shared right to veto its use. He also reserved the right to discuss the matter further at Potsdam. The Russians would be told, reported Makins, that 'if we succeed as we think we shall, we plan to use it against the enemy'.[20]

This period proved pivotal in Makins's career. He had played a key role both as the leading British representative in negotiations with the Americans, and as the informed intermediary between Field Marshal Wilson and the British Ambassador. They relied on his evaluation of American atomic policy, and communications between Washington and London confirm this role. Almost all information on atomic matters went via the Joint Staff Mission, much of it from Makins albeit nominally from Halifax or Wilson. He was the leading member of the very small group of Washington diplomats, including his successor, Donald Maclean, who knew anything of atomic matters.[21] Though stressing when advice given was personal, his inititative was likely to be accepted. Certainly there would be less need of the technique he and 'Jumbo' Wilson had adopted in 1944 of polishing prime ministerial telegrams.[22]

Post-war Anglo-American collaboration remained tied to the wartime agreement though the legitimacy of Quebec and Hyde Park were increasingly questioned by the United States military. Article 4 of the Quebec Agreement ruled out British commercial post-war exploitation without United States consent, but this was balanced by Article 2 giving either side veto on use of the bomb, which particularly galled the Americans. Clause 5 had authorized the establishment of the CPC which it suited both to keep since it provided a forum for joint discussions. Both wanted Quebec amended or replaced by something similar, with Article 4 eliminated and the Hyde Park endorsement of continued post-war cooperation acknowledged.

At first the majority of Truman's Cabinet hoped to maintain mutual trust in atomic affairs between the three wartime allies, a view reflected in Truman's statement to Congress on 3 October 1945. However, more powerful dissident voices prevailed and although publicly committed in November 1945 to support for United Nations control, United States policy became increasingly complex. The President, the military, and sections of the State Department all opposed further cooperation with the British whose wartime participation was described by the Secretary of War, Robert P. Patterson, as 'a curse we had to carry', though conceding that the agreements themselves had 'some residual advantages'.[23] Congress, however, was as yet unaware of any such commitment. Especially secret was the bilateral Declaration of Trust of 13 June 1944 which provided for the creation of the Combined Development

Trust, a body administered by the CPC. It was mainly through the Trust that the British retained any authority in atomic energy negotiations since the Trust administered the supply of raw materials — mostly uranium obtained from the Belgian Congo — through secret agreements between Belgium, the United States and Great Britain running well into the post-war period. If the Trust were dissolved the Belgians would not necessarily conclude similar agreements with either country, and therefore both sides were obliged to retain the Trust and the CPC from which it derived.[24]

On 15 September 1945, at the height of the furore created by the revelations of the spy Gousenko, Makins, now well versed in atomic energy negotiations, had arrived back in London for consultation. Knowing the United States Secretary of State James Byrnes was undecided on the issue, he pointed out that little progress would be made unless the British could come up with concrete proposals for the Americans 'to bite on'. He warned colleagues that United States opinion regarded the bomb as an American possession, and that congressional opinion would 'certainly incline to the view that it ought to remain one'. Prompt action was needed if Britain wanted to retain her wartime position as America's partner in atomic energy development.[25] Yet the complexity of the issues — military and domestic nuclear needs, allocation of uranium, uncertainty of Russian attitudes following the Soviet take-over of the Czechoslavakian uranium mines, international control, Commonwealth interest, public ignorance of the secret agreements, the need to log new agreements with the United Nations — all meant that policy formulation was slow and tentative. Unsurprisingly, the ensuing November meeting between Truman, Attlee and Mackenzie King was, Makins later wrote, 'hastily and ill prepared' and 'something of a shambles'.[26] He was a constant adviser at that tripartite conference and with a team of British, American and Canadian colleagues drafted a memorandum expressing the intention to continue cooperation under the auspices of the CPC and to produce a new agreement to replace those of Quebec and Hyde Park. The resulting document signed on 16 November by Sir John Anderson (Chairman of the new British Advisory Committee on Atomic Energy), and General Leslie R. Groves, chief of United States atomic energy development, became known as the Groves–Anderson memorandum, and eventually formed the basis of the 1948 Modus Vivendi.

Unfortunately Attlee's efforts to maintain the atomic partnership according to brief tripartite statement of intent, signed during the same conference, came to grief. Truman misconstrued the document and disputed Attlee's interpretation of its first clause on 'full and effective cooperation', later dismissing Attlee's call for continued exchange of information on the grounds it contradicted the conference's Washington Declaration of 15 November 1945 committing the three governments to support a United Nations commission on nuclear control.[27]

Over the next months Groves, Makins and Lester B. 'Mike' Pearson, the Canadian representative, continued their efforts in line with the intention of the Groves-Anderson memorandum to produce a workable replacement for the Quebec Agreement. Groves nevertheless made it plain that there could be no exchange of information which would cut corners for the British — 'technical know-how' as opposed to pure scientific knowledge — until a new agreement to replace the existing arrangement of sharing raw materials (mainly uranium) for one pooling them according to need was reached. The British were therefore in an anomalous position and in April 1946 began their own atomic energy development construction at Harwell. In fact, obligation to register any new agreement with the United Nations implied disclosures of the kind both sides still preferred to avoid.

During the 1945 negotiations it had been suggested that existing uranium agreements were Britain's trump card and 'principal bargaining counter'. This confidence reflected Britain's leading role in the secret wartime agreements with Belgium, but also the recent discovery of impressive deposits of uranium in South Africa. When Lord Halifax suggested placing South African uranium before the CDT 'in the interests of Anglo-American relations', it had been argued that this was 'much too valuable a card for the British Commonwealth to throw away'. At that time, however, it is doubtful whether any single ace could have extricated the British negotiators from the twin liabilities of Britain's loan negotiations, and the Gouzenko spy scandal.[28]

After 1945 the British predicament continued to find some sympathy in the State Department, but it was with the more 'hardboiled' War Department and General Groves in particular that negotiations were conducted. Others noted Groves's 'ruthless determination to see the project succeed at whatever cost' and his 'lack of sympathy . . . with all efforts to develop atomic energy outside North America', but Makins, who bore the brunt of these exchanges, liked and admired Groves with whom he had 'very good personal relations'. Even so, after months of work the proposals put to the CPC in April 1946 foundered. Two letters from Attlee to the President in 1946 made no impact. To the first of April Truman replied brusquely; to the second of June he did not reply at all. The question of atomic relations remained unresolved, and with the passage of the McMahon Act in August 1946 setting up the United States Atomic Energy Commission (USAEC) under joint Congressional supervision, all hope of exchange of information seemed precluded.

Suddenly, in the more hawkish atmosphere preceding the pronouncement of the Truman Doctrine in March 1947, atomic energy negotiations received something of a jolt. Unsatisfactory progress of discussions on international atomic control at the United Nations revitalized State Department interest in existing arrangements: a limited alliance with Britain as the junior partner in order to keep the Belgian agreements. At the same time, prodding from the British seems to have reminded the American military of their junior ally's embarrassing atomic potential. Moreover, the constitution of the USAEC at the end of 1946 led to the initiation of members into wartime secret agreements which had come 'as a great shock to them'. On the eve of his return to the Foreign Office in February 1947, Makins called on Lilienthal, Chairman of the USAEC, only to be confronted by the entire Commission who made it clear they believed an official statement to Congress or at least to senior congressmen would have to be made, if only to protect themselves.[29]

The British Embassy was hurriedly instructed to approach the American Chiefs of Staff (previously opposed to development of a British bomb on security grounds) and enlist their help in pleading with the State Department the strategic case for British atomic weapons. The American Chiefs of Staff were to be persuaded to revise their views and inform the State department they saw 'positive advantage in the U.K. strengthening their defence in this way'.

The moment seemed ripe since the new Secretary of State George Marshall had expressed interest in hemispheric defence and had already made it clear he regarded the British Commonwealth as 'outposts with Canada forming a link in the main defensive area'. Moreover, General Eisenhower, who sympathized with the British, agreed to support the British proposal for a joint informal meeting in February. Instructions from the British Chiefs of Staff who wanted to include the Commonwealth in atomic policy, contained an element of pressure to be used if necessary. If challenged on the security of the British weapon by the Americans, Field Marshal Wilson could reply that only 'provided a satisfactory system of co-operation' could be established would Britain continue to respect the Quebec veto on communicating atomic information to a third party. In contrast, Makins, now back in London, and acting chairman of the Official Committee on Atomic Energy, advised a generous approach on the matter of uranium ore. Acknowledging that the Americans had made 'a muddle of their early explorations', he continued: 'But we are talking about our partnership with the Americans and relying on it in various ways, and a true partnership involves, I suppose, paying a share of the other fellow's mistakes and not being too hard about it.'[30] In the event, the proposed military meeting was pre-empted by a report from the United States Chiefs of Staff reiterating much of their previous opposition to British development largely on grounds of 'the risk of locating any plant on the periphery of the Anglo-American zone of Defence'; their own need to produce 'fissile material ready to put into bombs as fast as possible so as to create a large stockpile for defense purposes'; and the inadvisability of placing 'plants so close to a potential enemy'.[31] The British approach had proved abortive, partly because Pentagon planning was found to be way ahead of actual bomb production. The most recent plan, PINCHER, already a year old, assumed an availability of fifty atomic bombs. However, by mid-1947, there were still only thirteen, though Truman was not informed of this discrepancy until April. By then members of the joint Congressional Committee on atomic energy were hot on the trail of the secret agreements, and Donald Maclean who succeeded Makins on the CPC was warned that these could be contained no longer. Acheson's revelations to the Senate Joint Committee on 12 May were humiliating: not only did the British know how to make the bomb, but half the supplies of uranium essential for production were legally going to Britain under arrangements hitherto concealed from Congress. Worse, the British had the reciprocal right under the wartime agreement to veto American use of the bomb.[32]

The reaction of powerful senators, Hickenlooper, Vandenberg and Connally, was immediate and predictable: in return for financial assistance Britain must renounce her 50 per cent share of Congo ore. The pressure was on, but official opinion on both sides of the Atlantic was divided. In the State Department, for example, George Kennan, who feared that if a barter deal for uranium became public the effect would be counter-productive, argued that 'aid to Europe must stand on its own merits'. This was to remain policy until September.[33]

The British therefore still held the uranium trump, such as it was, and at the United Nations were moving away from the Americans on the nuclear issue. On 16 June, Makins chaired the first meeting of an Anglo-US committee on international control, but positions were hardening among the Americans who now believed the international problem 'insoluble — except by withholding dangerous materials or facilities from nations altogether'. Two days later Makins called on Lewis Douglas, the American Ambassador, who expressed muted sympathy for the

British on the question of exchange of information, blaming the MacMahon Act of 1946 for 'fettering' the United States administration. He suspected the recent unhelpful attitude of the British at the United Nations on control was due to failure of the United States to agree on cooperation. Echoing hints from Washington, Douglas therefore suggested to Makins that once the proceedings of the Atomic Energy Commission ended in the autumn, 'the position of the U.S. Government in regard to co-operation might change very radically.'[34]

In this uncertain atmosphere, changes in the British atomic energy project were considered. Abandoning American designs, piles would be built to improved British specification — less reliant on American 'know-how'. The Chiefs of Staff, as Makins briefed Bevin, had already approved a Cumberland site, and the Cabinet would review the issue early in July. On 20 June, Douglas repeated the charge that the British attitude on international control at the United Nations arose from dissatisfaction with American attitudes on atomic cooperation. This Makins denied, adding that the British were aiming at minimum measures of ensuring adequate security. If the Russians rejected these at least 'it would appear to the world at large that we had made a reasonable attempt to find common ground'. However, he confessed that although the British scheme was well advanced it did not yet have ministerial approval.[35]

On 10 July, Makins enlisted the Foreign Secretary's support and the next day Bevin forwarned Douglas of a ministerial meeting on 23 July to decide international control policy. The Americans would be expected to 'go some way' to meet the British view, though he could promise 'not to appear to diverge from the U.S. representatives in public'. By early August, however, differences between America and Britain seemed 'infinitely smaller' than between Britain and Russia, though Bevin still hoped to stave off a formal break with the Soviet Union until after the autumn Foreign Ministers' Conference. Six weeks later, Makins told Bevin that while the attitude of the Soviet delegate had become 'completely uncompromising', there were signs that the United States would shortly propose tripartite talks, with Belgium.[36]

By now, the departure on overseas appointments of other leading Foreign Office atomic specialists, Sir Ronald Campbell and Sir Nevile Butler, and rationalization of the atomic energy administration reinforced Makins at the pinnacle of policy planning as chairman of the Official Committee on Atomic Energy (composed of representatives from relevant departments). Decisions were formally taken by the Ministerial Committee on Atomic Energy which was chaired by the Prime Minister, but in any case, Makins briefed both Ernest Bevin and Attlee. However, from here on atomic and economic policy were increasingly set on a collision course, and it is necessary to break off and bring up to date Makins's role in Britain's economic policy.

Economic policy

Separate issues or not, within the Foreign Office aid and atomic energy policy, noted by Truman to be the dual basis of American power, were both supervised by Roger Makins during this critical period. 'This place is a regular madhouse', he wrote to a colleague on returning to the Foreign Office in February 1947, 'and I do not believe that I shall be able to function here effectively unless I go mad myself'. Atomic energy though complex was nevertheless still a relatively narrow field. By contrast, the Economic Intelligence, and Economic relations Departments of which Makins was Supervising Under-Secretary, embraced a wide range of economic policy including: the International Trade Organization, the International Bank and Monetary Fund, the Food and Agriculture Organization, the United Nations Relief and Rehabilitation Administration (UNRRA), and later the European Recovery Programme. Moreover, in August 1947, following withdrawal of convertibility, an inter-departmental Overseas Negotiations Committee was set up. Chaired by Leslie Rowan of the Treasury, it met daily, often on Sundays, and no decisions relating to bilateral treaties were taken without reference to it. Roger Makins represented the Foreign Office on this vital but time-consuming committee. The same duo represented the Treasury and Foreign Office on the transatlantic London Committee with American representatives such as Tom Finletter, and later W. John Kenny who recalled it as a forum where 'we would generally describe what projects were needed in order to strengthen the British economy'.[37]

Not only did questions of economic aid claim much of his attention in Washington and later in London, but these formed the basis of debate about the very nature of British post-war survival. Until 1947, matters of aid were largely dealt with by UNRRA which had been established in 1943. When Makins (then in Washington) took over the British seat on UNRRA in 1945, the equivocal attitude of the United States to that body had been made plain in reservations adopted by Congress the previous autumn. Equally, the stonewalling tactics of the Soviet Union ('a typical example of negotiating with the Russians'), presaged later difficulties.[38]

With UNRRA to be wound up in 1947, both Britain and America

began in 1946 to consider other routes for aid. There had been accusations concerning UNRRA's infiltration by communists but these were partly symptomatic of the underlying problem of funding which relied heavily on the United States. Consequently, there was wide American support for a separate organization under United States control and Congress tended to oppose expenditure of American money 'by an organization we did not create, an organization in which we have but only one vote'.[39] Large appropriations voted by Congress in December 1945 and further appropriation in July 1946 pushed Congressional patience to its limits. From the British side the view expressed by one British official was that American fiscal isolation would see him 'as an old Moscow lag ... plant myself down on my Kremlin hams and have a jolly good laugh at the spectacle of the capitalist Gadarene swine careering towards the economic abyss'.[40] But more prevalent in the Foreign Office was the Keynesian belief that a general post-war settlement through North American action would enable Britain 'to be their partners and co-adjudicators in setting up a postwar international economy of the character on which they have set their hearts'.[41] By 1945 this was simply unrealistic but the Foreign Office continued to maintain the myth of its mediatory role.

In 1946, under the threat of a return to American isolationism, the prospective end of UNRRA, concentrated Foreign Office minds on the possibility of re-engaging American interest in Europe. The moment seemed favourable as the United States had enlisted British support both in setting up the International Trade Organization, and, in August, buttressing United States opposition to UNRRA Resolution 100, which called for international aid to be discussed at the next General Assembly. Outvoted, at the United Nations both had reluctantly reaffirmed support for an international solution. By mid-October 1946, the basis of a new British approach to '*Anglo-US Economic Policy towards Europe*' had been hammered out. Objectives were presented as political as much as economic. 'I have been considering', Attlee instructed the British Ambassador, Lord Inverchapel,

how the United States and ourselves, with the means at our disposal, can further our common aim of arresting or reducing Soviet influence in the countries of eastern and southern Europe. There are certain possibilities of action in (the) economic sphere, but the scope of any measures we ourselves can take is severely limited by our financial position.

Although both countries were overtly committed to supporting the United Nations in seeking an international solution to aid, it was felt that Assembly action should ideally not be allowed to go further than 'agreement to make international appraisal of the problem'. Indeed, on the instructions of Secretary of State James Byrnes, Under-Secretary Dean Acheson told Inverchapel the 'United States Government would resist any effort to find an international successor for UNRRA ... If any specific country genuinely needed help, it should address itself to the government or governments best able to give it'. He agreed the United States Government were 'thinking on the same lines' as the British, but one striking difference was evident. Where the British were most concerned about Eastern and South Eastern Europe, Acheson made it clear that the United States Government were already thinking in terms mainly of Western Europe: Italy, Austria and Greece.[42]

After the Ambassador's formal approach, negotiations were conducted by Makins who delegated the allied question of aid to Greece and Turkey to Donald Maclean, his pre-war colleague from the Western and League Department and now First Secretary at the Embassy. Byrnes at the instigation of the JCS asked for British appraisal of the military situation of both Greek and Turkish armies. He suggested that although it would be better if military assistance continued under British charge, the United States would be prepared to examine the possibility of helping and would 'warmly welcome' any suggestions about economic assistance to Greece and Turkey. Since the UNRRA resolution made secrecy imperative, Makins instructed that 'a judicious report of this conversation will be sufficient'. Retrospectively the futility of this caution and the implications of Maclean's access to the very heart of Anglo-American post-war planning have been made plain.[43]

Under-Secretary of State for Economic Affairs Will Clayton[44] was less convinced that Greece needed extra help. But a more practical problem was the difficulty of circumventing clauses of the World Bank's founding charter prohibiting financial deals with political overtones. To ride both national and supranational horses, therefore, skill and discretion would be necessary. Some days before talks began Acheson told Makins his government still believed aid should at this stage be confined to Italy, Austria and Greece. The British Government, therefore reluctantly followed the United States lead in suspending a deal currently being negotiated with Czechoslovakia until US policy was clarified. Makins led the conversations on the British side on 6 November, and emphasized the British 'desire for harmony' of policy with the United States. The American team was led, in the absence of Acheson, by Clayton, whom, having failed to 'formulate his thoughts', was held by Makins responsible for the 'rather disjointed nature of the discussions'.

Little was achieved. Makins's reminder to his American colleagues that *vis-à-vis* countries like Czechoslavakia and Poland they shared common objectives drew only negative response. As to the World Bank's prohibition on loans with political strings, Clayton, US alternate governor with Fred Vinson of the World Bank and the International Monetary Fund, believed that a country trading in one direction while borrowing in another 'would obviously be a bad risk because it would never repay the loan'. This, as Makins later suggested, came 'pretty close to introducing political considerations'. He put the case for Eastern European loans where either country 'might wish to find reasons for giving assistance in order to further their political objectives', but this, too, fell on unreceptive ears. Clayton remained adamant that 'no, repeat no loans or credits from the Import Bank or other' official U.S. sources were contemplated by the United States for Poland, Czechoslovakia, Roumania, Bulgaria or Albania', precisely those countries which ultimately remained outside Marshall aid.[45]

Having drawn a blank, an interdepartmental committee in London re-examined the position from a different angle, particularly *vis-à-vis* trade with Eastern Europe, this time dwelling more on the bleak facts of British requirements and practical rather than political aspects of economic penetration. At the same time Bevin revised proposals on European economic union, last considered in October 1946. His proposals, still stressing the need to avoid the division of Europe into blocs were reconsidered indecisively by the Cabinet at the end of January. Attlee's first approach to Washington had stressed political advantage, the second stressed Britain's need as a trading nation to rebuild and extend her own markets for economic reasons as well as political.[46]

This fresh angle was put by Makins at joint discussions on 'Economic Policy in countries of Eastern and South Eastern Europe' held in the State Department on 21 January 1947. The meeting was chaired by Clayton and his team of seven headed by Willard Thorp, Assistant Secretary of State for Economic Affairs. Makins led the British team. Having failed in November to enlist American Support for aid to Eastern Europe in general, he now suggested individual countries such as Hungary and Finland where joint policy might be effective.[47] Some success was achieved here since it could be argued they provided either a market or a source of essential commodities. Hungary, for example, could be an additional market for, among other things, American cotton, Clayton — in private life a cotton magnate who had successfully refuted numerous charges of manipulating the cotton market[48] — felt a small sum for Hungary could be sliced off the $450 million grant to Austria, Italy and Greece which was about to go before Congress. Finland might be put 'under strong pressure' to increase its paper exports. By contrast, the recent elections in Poland had so 'disgusted' the State Department that nothing could be done there. Indeed, although relief funds were not ruled out, pressure would be put on the International Bank to block any immediate loans to Poland. Utterly thwarted, and about to take up his new appointment in London, Makins sent Clayton his briefing notes and urged the State Department to come up with some ideas of their own.[49]

Two more months passed before the State Department produced its own memorandum, though 'from a somewhat different point of departure' from the Foreign Office. During this time a series of events forced the hitherto sluggish pace of US economic reappraisal. The British call for support in Greece, and a bitter winter which brought back havoc and misery to Europe, had been preceded by an exceptionally vituperative outburst in *Pravda*, in response to a speech by Bevin in December. Coinciding with negotiations for a revision of the Anglo-Soviet Treaty of 1942, it led to a sharp deterioration in relations.

Offence had been taken at a reference taken out of context to the Anglo-Soviet treaty being 'suspended in air'. Perplexed at Stalin's response and not ready for an open break, Bevin tried to explain. 'In fact', he told Stalin, 'I said what all the other major Allies have said, namely that they based their policy on the UNO. I cannot understand what is behind this line of reasoning.'[50] Doubtless all would have been clear to Bevin had he known that secret policy discussions between the United States and Britain concerning the United Nations, Russia and Europe were being leaked. That Makins's assistant Maclean himself handled some of the negotiations, was privy to much else, and was able to keep Moscow informed is now clear.[51] That the extent of United States determination to limit aid to Western and Southern Europe and to circumvent, if possible, United Nations agencies was known in Moscow helps explain Stalin's frustration. Whether it was also known that State Department post-war policy assumed that by giving 'a strong lead in dealing with Russia Britain will follow', is less certain.[52]

At any rate, Bevin assured the new Secretary of State, George Marshall, that negotiations for the review of the Anglo-Soviet Treaty did not indicate any weakening of British desire for the 'closest Anglo-American collaboration'. Acheson was glad to have his misgivings about the possibility of an Anglo-Soviet military alliance allayed, but nevertheless dispatched Marshall's representative, 'Doc' Matthews, to London to discuss the Treaty with Bevin before the Foreign Secretary left for Moscow.[53]

American response to the worsening European scene, and in particular the news that Britain could hold out no longer in Greece, came in the enunciation of the Truman Doctrine on 12 March. The same month saw the setting up of the United Nations' own Economic Commission for Europe (ECE), a body worryingly weighted in votes towards Eastern Europe. Encouraging hints now began to come from the State Department regarding 'a common policy', and in April the British were offered informal discussions 'covering all subjects of common interest in the political and economic fields in the countries which the State Department have in mind'. Apart from some hint at military discussions which Attlee spurned, the core list of countries involved remained much the same: Hungary was the object of special aid; Austria, Italy, Greece, Turkey together with Persia, and now China were in; Poland, Czechoslovakia and Bulgaria were still out. Germany, already a joint concern, was as yet a separate problem. As to the Soviet Union, it had long been believed that even with the best will in the world, economic integration with the West was technically virtually impossible.[54]

With the first meeting of the ECE due in May, it was essential, to come up with an alternative scheme pretty quickly. By late April hastily prepared, pessimistic reports on the plight of Europe from all branches of the executive led to the revamping of Acheson's 8 May Cleveland speech, generally regarded as a test run for Marshall's June speech.[55] Makins, who now supervised the Foreign Office Departments of Economic Relations and Economic Research and Development, was with Bevin on the morning that the Secretary of State heard the first radio news of the speech. As he later discreetly observed, the Washington Embassy had already had 'one or two hints' that Acheson's speech 'represented a new trend in American policy'. In fact two days earlier, Acheson had briefed British journalists on the importance of a European initiative,[56] and Marshall's speech was circulated in advance to the press and the embassy. Indeed, the day before Bevin heard the news, Makins had discussed with two colleagues the probable Soviet attitude towards offers of American aid on the kind of terms anticipated. They concluded that since the Soviets would not cooperate sincerely it would be unwise to use the machinery of the United Nations ECE for aid. The timing of the speech was thought to have been brought forward by Marshall to give Europe the chance to organize an alternative policy in the event of failure of the next Foreign Ministers' meeting in November. Bevin's public reaction, for example, in his speech to the Press Association on 13 June, was one of the fulsome praise for the Marshall initiative. His private undated reservations, however, as recorded on a note directed to him from his Minister of State, Hector McNeil, on 11 June seem to indicate a degree of exasperation: 'Marshall statement might well have to be studied it has upset what I was going to propose EB [sic].'[57] However, whatever his reservations they were evidently soon swept away. Bevin had been a forceful labour leader, and was now an excellent parliamentary orator, a good negotiator and a Cabinet heavyweight. Nevertheless, after an exhausting war and equally pressured two years of reconstruction he was in some respects ill-equipped to match an official of the calibre of Makins, the trained lawyer, seasoned diplomat and forceful Atlanticist who replaced the Europeanist, Sir Edmund Hall Patch, as the senior Foreign Office official in charge of the economic departments, and who at this stage carried the Marshall Plan negotiations forward.

Nine months had passed since Attlee had approached the United States for help in planning a joint policy towards Europe. That the Marshall Plan, or European Recovery Programme (ERP), as it was more properly named, launched at the beginning of June was never intended by the United States for Eastern Europe can scarcely be doubted in the light of preceding negotiations and subsequent pressure from the State Department on the British at the Paris talks to 'confront the Soviets at the outset with "rock-bottom, copper-rivetted positions" from which you would not recede'. That the Labour Government, having 'picked up the ball'[58] was shocked to be regarded as team leader is a matter of record. '... he would be lacking in frankness', said Clayton at a meeting chaired by Attlee late in June, 'if he did not make it clear that the United Kingdom could only receive assistance as part of a general European Plan'. Brushing aside the protests of Dalton and Cripps that Britain 'could not be considered just as one European country among many', Clayton concluded with 'some messages from Mr Marshall of a rather unpleasant character' of which the most crushing was criticism of the inefficiency of the government's socialization of the Ruhr industries. British obstructiveness on Japanese waters were also matters of complaint. On the same day pressure was brought to bear in Washington when Charles 'Chip' Bohlen of the State Department tackled Sir John Balfour about the current British negotiations for substantial grain supplies from Russia, and insisted on assurances that developments in Moscow would not make the British 'unduly dependent on the Soviet Union' for essential imports.[59]

In line with the angry reaction of many others at Britain's downgrading from senior partner, Makins, as Foreign Office representative on the London Committee (set up to coordinate policy on ERP), was determined that Britain's special relationship should be upheld untrammelled by the ECE or relegation to mere European status. Learning that Bevin and Oliver Franks, who led the British delegation in Paris, had discussed the key question of whether negotiations with the United States after the Paris conference should be bilateral (in line with the French and Italian position) or multilateral, Makins reminded Bevin crisply that Franks's existing instructions were to aim at bilateral negotiations since these were regarded as more likely to safeguard the special position of the United Kingdom. 'These instructions', he added magisterially, 'will be maintained'. 'I agree', wrote Bevin, and in reply to the incoming query from Paris, dutifully minuted, 'This is covered by instructions to Franks'.[60]

British scrutiny of all aspects of the Marshall Plan now continued in the London Committee. Of urgent interest was the report of the Harriman Committee drafted by isolationist and anti-Lend Lease senator, Robert M. La Follette Jr. In early November, Makins briefed the committee on a forthcoming press release the introductory tone of which was reassuring: 'The whole spirit on which the U.S. Administration has approached this problem is extremely encouraging'; and 'the attitude of the Harriman Committee on the subject of conditions is very satisfactory to us.' The fourth point, however, was less euphoric:

4. The main criticism at first glance relates to some of the Harriman proposals which would have the effect of reducing European productive capacity and ability to earn dollars and pay its way, e.g. the comments on building up of European agriculture, the question of scrap and steel exports from the U.S. and European shipbuilding.

Referring to overlapping interests of the United Nations ECE schemes for cooperation and those schemes to be embodied in the Marshall Plan, Makins argued that Britain 'must be firm in insisting that the Marshall Plan came first'. Suggestions from the Board of Trade — doubtless mindful of the United States mercurial behaviour after the First World War — that the United Nations ECE might be needed as insurance 'in case Marshall aid failed to materialise or was inadequate', and that for the same reasons Britain also needed 'to foster trade with Eastern European countries', appear not to have found sympathy.[61]

A week later he chaired the London Committee meeting called to discuss Oliver Franks's report from Washington on the Marshall Plan. Still hopeful of securing a special role for Britain, Makins opposed a proposal to unify the European plan by convening a meeting of European states in mid-December to prevent unilateral approaches to the United States. He argued that Britain might be outvoted, for example, on purchases of Argentine grain, and maintained Britain stood more chance in bilateral negotiations rather than 'trying to maintain our leadership at a meeting where we might have to forego some of our own objectives in order to obtain agreement'. She would do better 'lobbying the principal countries in private rather than by having a public meeting involving differences with Congress.'[62] It is in Makins's insistence on unilateralism within ERP that British attitudes to European union can be seen to have crystallized into policy in the period before the Marshall Plan provisions were put to Congress. During that time pressure to accommodate the United States which might have been avoided under a multilateral approach would grow, and not least in the field of atomic energy.

The *Modus Vivendi* and the Marshall Plan

In November Makins, as chairman of the Official Committee on Atomic Energy, guided the renegotiation of uranium allocation which the Americans were now eager to begin. He also studied the American reports on United States requirements for the Marshall Plan, contributed to the Paris Plan, chaired departmental discussions on the European Recovery Plan and, among other duties, handled press briefing. As to nuclear policy the British had four options. First: to pursue Anglo-American cooperation and to build on those areas where progress had been made such as declassification of information. This policy assumed the sincerity of State Department allies, and their ability to prevail over the military. It also assumed congressional opposition could be overcome or circumvented. Second: to buttress the British project and enhance independence by including Commonwealth countries. To do this in conjunction with continued United States cooperation would require the Americans to relax the Quebec Agreement provisions on disclosure of information with third parties. Third: to conclude separate agreements with South Africa on new uranium finds, whether independently or in conjunction with either of the first two options. The fourth, and least attractive, option was to consider some form of European co-operation with France as a leading partner. A possible fifth — submission to United Nations control — was never really a contender, and after August 1947 effectively ruled out.

For political reasons the French option was equally a non-starter. Makins learned in September that the supposedly 'secret' wartime raw materials agreements had been leaked by the Belgian Communist Party to the press. The Party believed the agreements contrary to national interests and called for construction of Belgium's own atomic pile. The embarrassed premier, Spaak, admitted that though very few ministers were privy to the uranium contracts, traditionally Belgium was opposed to secret agreements. The danger was underlined by the proximity and vigour of the French Communist Party with its link into the atomic energy world through Joliot Curie, who had consistently campaigned for French participation. At this critical point M. Sengier, head of Union Minière and negotiator of the Belgium uranium agreements, disclosed to Makins his company's pre-war contract with Joliot whose primary aim was thought to be non-military Western European atomic collaboration. However, as one colleague pointed out, problems with such arrangements would arise 'if relations between the USA and Russia got very much worse and France plunged in on the Russian side'.[63] Fear of association was now paramount. Even before his appointment in June as Secretary of the newly created Department of Defence, James Forrestal asked Truman what America should do if faced 'during this summer with a Russian *démarche* accompanied by simultaneous coups in France and Italy?' Six weeks on his concern shifted to Britain: should the United States 'underwrite the stability of a government whose objectives seem to be moving farther to the Left as they lose the support of even moderate Liberals'.[64] In such a fraught atmosphere an Anglo-French atomic alliance could scarcely be contemplated.

The more tempting option of Commonwealth atomic collaboration was therefore now discussed in an Official Committee paper. Makins's authority can be gauged by the brevity of the synopsis he made for Bevin of this paper and the assumption of its acceptance. The thesis outlined for the benefit of the Foreign Secretary was 'that we should lay the foundations of a Commonwealth programme as soon as possible, but that the first step must be to consult the Canadians, in view of their special relationship in this matter both with us and the United States'. In an atmosphere of deteriorating Anglo-American trust Makins told Bevin, 'it will be sufficient if the Prime Minister and yourself approve the action proposed', and to this Bevin agreed. The paper itself considered only the Dominions. It argued that the Americans were less likely to oppose Commonwealth collaboration since they were increasingly aware of Britain's past role in Belgium uranium procurement and the part she might play in South Africa in the future.[65]

Indeed, South African uranium was beginning to look a stronger trump than the Belgian agreement. At the Prime Ministers' Conference of May 1946, Field Marshal Smuts had assured colleagues that South African uranium would stay 'in our group'. He was next in London for the royal wedding in November 1947 and an Official Committee brief for his visit argued the need for a speedy agreement as the Americans were after a separate deal with South Africa. The British did not intend to exclude them only to strengthen their hand in any future Anglo-US atomic energy negotiations. Although this was a major policy decision, Makins, having consulted Sir Edward Bridges, told Bevin it need not go to the Ministerial Committee. In the event Attlee and Smuts came to an agreement which was to be formalized the following year. Smuts was not 'disposed towards the participation of U.S. capital', but there would be plenty of uranium for both the British and the Americans.[66]

For a while therefore, despite renewed threats from Senator Hickenlooper to use Marshall aid to force the pace in uranium talks, the signs were promising. From Washington Maclean assured Makins that Congress 'probably realize that any Congressional discussion of uranium stock is likely to lead to the whole story coming out, with attendant disadvantages in the UN, Belgium and elsewhere'. In retrospect that seems misleadingly optimistic. On the same day as Maclean's letter of 5 November, Marshall, Forrestal and David Lilienthal, the chairman of the United States Atomic Energy Commission, met to discuss requirements for the forthcoming talks. Their objectives, leaving no room for negotiation and in the event obtained, were first to dissolve clause 2 of the Quebec Agreement on consent for use of the bomb; to continue the CPC and CDT; then to obtain a greater share of raw materials to the United States; finally, the British and Canadians were to give up accumulated stocks in excess of what was needed for current projects.[67]

Yet at the same time, encouraging reports from the USAEC were taken as 'evidence that the Commission are reaching for closer cooperation with us'. Momentarily, therefore, so far as the British were concerned, all seemed set for negotiation on relatively promising terms, and Makins himself seemed reassured by 'the first concrete evidence that the U.S. authorities may shortly relax their prohibition on the release to us of secret information which will be of assistance to us in developing our programme'.

However, within days, a strong warning came from Sir Gordon Monro, Makins's recent colleague at the British Embassy in Washington, against 'too hard-hearted a line with the Americans'[68]. But the main explanation for the sudden abandonment of any attempt at bravado lay in the rising crescendo of 'hints' from the Americans that unless the British concluded an agreement quickly, atomic energy negotiations would be 'caught up' in Congress in the ERP debate. The administration would then be unable to prevent Congress demanding heavy uranium penalties as a quid pro quo for aid. At a meeting on 26 November, Acheson's successor, Robert Lovett, tried to play up the strength of the British hand, but Hickenlooper and Vandenberg remained adamant that they would brook no dependence on Britain's approval for use of the bomb.[69] Although there had been no meeting of the CPC for eighteen months a meeting was abruptly called and the British, heavily involved in hectic ERP planning, were summoned to attend.

Yet to Washington Embassy staff State Department intentions were still not altogether clear. Indeed, Maclean briefed Makins on the strategic element believed to be on the agenda and the inclusion in the talks of George Kennan, principal State Department planner and regarded as well disposed to Britain. Nevertheless, the next day, 5 December, Makins presented Bevin with a paper outlining recent events and the possibility of a new American initiative. The salient point was that: 'The Americans now regard this question as urgent as they are being pressed against their will on the question of supply of atomic raw materials in connexion with Marshall aid and wish to get a fresh working basis established between the three countries in order that they can resist this pressure.' No formal agreement was possible under Article 102 of the United Nations Charter requiring international agreements between members to be registered. Instead, Makins proposed 'identic recommendations by the representatives of the three Governments which could then be approved by the Governments as the basis of their policy.' These would be based on the tripartite agreement worked out at the end of 1945 but vetoed at the time by Byrnes. The Foreign Secretary, rightly surmising that he was being used to rubber-stamp policy he had had no part in formulating minuted: 'has this been discussed with the PM I never have his views [sic]'. Assured by Makins that the Prime Minister had seen the relevant telegrams and a separate note 'on the lines of paragraph 6' (which simply advised no action until it was clearer what Washington really wanted), Bevin minuted 'I approve'.[70]

So far as Anglo-US atomic energy cooperation was concerned therefore, it seemed unlikely that uranium could be kept separate from the Marshall Plan which was expected to provide for the stockpiling of strategic raw materials in the United States. With only two days' notice for the CPC meeting on Monday 8 December, proper preparation was impossible. The two most tricky questions would be the location of the British stockpile, and the allocation of uranium to the United States for bomb production. On the eve of the meeting Kennan was still hinting at a return to the tripartite cooperation of wartime, although he was in no position to offer something neither Congress nor the military would deliver. Even if there remained ambivalence in the State Department, it had never been reflected among the military. At the meeting of the heads of the State, War and Navy Departments in the Committee of Three on 11 September, despite strong opposition from Kennan that atomic energy and economic aid should not be connected, Forrestal had challenged the 'alleged Churchill-Roosevelt agreement', and been firmly backed by General Marshall, on the uranium question.

Meanwhile, no matter to what extent British atomic policy was normally something of a one-man band, the existing uranium agreements could not be sloughed off without ministerial approval. Concerted pressure was therefore applied to Bevin. On 10 September, the American Ambassador, at first ignoring formal instructions to see Bevin, called on Makins. Douglas said things might get 'pretty bad' if the raw materials debate 'got mixed up with the debates on the Marshall Plan', and warned that the British would be asked to transfer part of their stockpile of uranium to the United States. Makins stoutly rejected 'Any suggestion that valuables were not safe in this island', but agreed there might be room for discussion on current Congo uranium imports. Advising Douglas to see Bevin as soon as possible, he set off for Washington.[71]

Within a week broad agreement was reached — except on allocation of stocks in Britain. Having discussed the deadlock over the British stockpile with Makins in Washington before he left for the Foreign Ministers' meeting in London, Marshall wrote a last-minute note to Bevin as he prepared to return to the States.

> I am referring to 'stock piles' in the British Isles of critical ores. What we need urgently *in the near future* is more of such, which you have. Probably a basis of arrangement could be worked out on future replacements from elsewhere — if you understand me. The issue is of vital importance to us in our present situation. Hastily, . . .

At the airport farewell ceremonies Douglas seized the opportunity to renew this enigmatic message which Frank Roberts relayed to Bevin: 'there would be serious trouble in Congress and more particularly in the Senate if we were not cooperative on this point'. Under repeated pressure, therefore, the British team, with authority only to give way on the 1948 allocation of uranium, was recalled for consultation. Marshall's note went to the Defence Committee, but it was all too clear the Authorization Bill on which Marshall Aid depended meant British acquiescence on uranium. On this basis Makins returned to Washington two days before Christmas for negotiations which concluded in the Modus Vivendi of the new year. As the senior responsible official on the British side, be believed it would 'wipe out the misunderstanding and bitterness of the past and put our relationship on a solid basis'.[72]

What then did these unflagging efforts achieve for Britain? The chief loss in the Modus Vivendi was right of veto on use of the bomb, which, as Gowing indicates, was of immediate importance in 1948 with the stationing of American bombers in England. On the other hand, the British programme did not lack raw materials by relinquishing its lawful share, and reclassification, though not an 'Open Sesame', may have eased tension.[73] But there was little real progress for at least a decade. Indeed, by ensuring Britain kept a toe-hold in the US atomic programme, the Modus Vivendi — given the presence of Donald Maclean and the leaky nature of the Washington Embassy — may well have proved more fruitful for the Soviets than for the British.

Makins's own attitude to Anglo-US negotiations changed: in 1949 he warned defence chiefs that 'whatever the proposals were the Americans would attempt to attach strings to them'.[74] In January 1952, the Americans themselves tacitly acknowledged the one-way nature of the Modus Vivendi. Anticipating that Churchill would complain the agreement had 'been interpreted in a far more limited fashion by the United States than by the United Kingdom', a list of *desiderata* was drawn up for the forthcoming Truman-Churchill conversations. The first was 'to maintain the *modus vivendi*'; the second, 'to ascertain if there were areas where cooperation with the British might be beneficial to the United States'.[75] Little had changed.

It is not surprising to learn that Roger Makins was highly regarded by the American administration for his part in smoothing the path of Anglo-US relations during a Labour administration regarded in some United States quarters as more malleable than a Conservative one. Makins was admired for his ability, and from his long association with atomic energy was dubbed 'Mr Atom'. Indeed, this close identification eventually became something of a handicap in making it difficult to conceal the purpose of his visits to the United States. The Americans thought his marriage to an American advantageous in making him 'thoroughly familiar with American attitudes', and ranked him 'a good talker', who always showed 'friendliness and cooperation in dealing with U.S. officials' while lacking 'the aloofness so common among British officials'.[76] American acceptance (as well as respect) was an unusual distinction at that time, and undoubtedly stood him well in his career. The unique combination of economic experience and a formidable overview of atomic affairs gave him Bevin's ear, and placed him in an exceptionally powerful position at a time when ministerial strength at the Foreign Office was markedly lacking.[77]

Whether it was ultimately to Britain's advantage that one official should dominate two such vital areas of policy may be questioned. Certainly the conflict of departmental interests during the Modus Vivendi and Marshall Aid negotiations did nothing to diminish British vulnerability, and placed an almost impossible burden of judgement on one official. Equally, even setting aside problems surrounding the later Maclean defection,[78] it is necessary in the light of Macmillan's and Halifax's fulsome praise to ponder whether gullibility as to American intentions and eagerness to preserve the 'special relationship' will suffice to explain Makins's determination to seal the Modus Vivendi at any cost. Was the secrecy surrounding the deal a buffer which isolated the overworked official in charge too successfully from the broader advice of colleagues or cabinet members other than the compliant Bevin, or the distant Attlee?

Such questions do not, of course, reflect on the abilities of Roger Makins himself, who was rapidly promoted to Deputy Under-Secretary. So highly was Makins regarded that it was arguably only a quirk of fate which kept him from the very highest office since the outgoing Permanant Under-Secretary, Orme Sargent, considered him then 'far too young', though his wartime clash with Attlee may also have influenced the issue.[79] His ambassadorship to the United States, and appointment as joint head of the Treasury were doubtless compensation enough. However, notwithstanding these great prizes, it was in the earlier, formative years of 1945-48 that Roger Makins's influence in atomic energy and economic policy helped set the direction of Anglo-American relations, and hence Britain's position in the post-war world.

Notes

1. Roger Makins was knighted in 1953 and raised to the peerage in 1964 as Lord Sherfield. I should like to thank Lord Sherfield for allowing me to interview him, and wish to express my gratitude to colleagues and archivists here, and in the United States who have helped me in preparing this essay. Errors are my own. The nickname 'Mr Atom' comes from an undated memorandum (?1952) on Roger Makins in the National Archives, Harry S. Truman Library, Independence, Missouri (hereafter HSTL), President's Secretary's Files (hereafter PSF).
2. HSTL, Oral History Transcript of interview with W. John Kenny, 43.
3. Harold Macmillan, *War diaries: the Mediterranean 1943-1945*, Macmillan, 1984, 29 September 1944, 537.
4. Public Record Office, London (hereafter PRO), Foreign Office General Correspondence files (hereafter FO371), FO371/50912 U5471/5471/70,

Sir Orme Sargent, 11 July 1945.
5. PRO Private Papers of Foreign Office Officials (hereafter FO 800), F0800/551, Ronald Campbell to Sir Orme Sargent, 30 July 1945.
6. The term 'atomic' as opposed to 'nuclear' has been adopted throughout in accordance with contemporary usage. It is impossible to approach the complexities of economic or atomic issues without drawing heavily on work done by British and American scholars, and notably the official atomic energy historians. However, in the main these texts have been cited only where it has seemed especially helpful to the reader, who for the full account should consult the works of Margaret Gowing, *Britain and atomic energy, 1939-1945*, Macmillan, 1965 (hereafter cited as *Atomic Energy*), and *Independence and Deterrence, Britain and Atomic Energy, 1945-1952*, I, Macmillan, 1974 (hereafter cited as *Independence*); Richard Hewlett and Oscar E. Anderson, *A History of the USAEC: The New World, 1939-1946*, Pennsylvania, 1962; and Richard Hewlett and Francis Duncan, *Atomic shield, 1947-1952*, 1969; and Richard Hewlett and Francis Duncan, *Atomic shield, 1947-1952*, 1969. Private Papers of Roger Makins, F0800/42; 614-26 of which are still retained by the Department. For the Marshall Plan see, for example, Michael J. Hogan, *The Marshall Plan, America, Britain, and the reconstruction of Western Europe, 1947-1952*, Cambridge University, Cambridge, 1987; Alan S. Milward, *The reconstruction of Western Europe, 1945-1951*, Methuen, 1984.
7. Daniel Yergin, *Shattered Peace*, Houghton Mifflin, Boston, 1977, 137.
8. Ferdinand Kuhn, Jr., *Washington Post*, 3 August 1947; Roger Bullen and M.E. Pelly (eds), *Documents on British policy overseas*, Series I, II, 529-31 (hereafter DBPO).
9. Interview with Lord Sherfield July 1986 (hereafter Sherfield-Edwards interview).
10. The Dalton Papers, Part IIB 7/2, 61, London School of Economics.
11. F0800/432, Makins to William Strang, 24 September 1942.
12. Harold Macmillan, op. cit., 27 April 1943; 29 September 1944. Sir (later Lord) Henry Maitland Wilson was Commander-in-Chief, Middle East, 1943-4.
13. Private Papers of Sir Ronald Campbell, who preceded Makins at the Washington Embassy and Mr Nevile Butler of the North American Department, F0800/524 45/20, 17 February 1945, Halifax to Anderson; 45/54, Dixon to Campbell, 17 March 1945; 45/64, Anderson to Halifax, 21 March 1945.
14. The Combined Policy Committee of British and United States representatives was set up under the Quebec Agreement of August 1943. See Gowing, *Britain and atomic energy*, 170-1. Sherfield-Edwards interview; F0371/44614, 1 April 1945.
15. PRO, British Washington Embassy Papers (hereafter F0115), F0115/4233, CPC mtg, 22 January 1945; F0800/529 14/17, Cherwell to Churchill, 27 March 1945; F0800/523, 14/17, Churchill to Eden, sent 8 April 1945; 14/20, 12 April 1945.
16. Gowing, *Atomic energy*, Quebec Agreement, 439; Hyde Park Aide Mémoire, 447.

17. F0800/524, 45/22 minute by Campbell, 21 February 1945; F0800/523, 14/22A, Wilson to Anderson, 30 April 1945, reporting Makins-Bundy conversation, 28 April 1945.
18. F0800/523, 14/26, May 1945, Campbell to Sargent, minute on meeting of Cadogan, Strang, Ronald, Harvey, Butler and Cavendish-Bentinck.
19. F0800/523 CANAM 310, Anderson to Wilson, 14 May 1945. F0800/529, Anderson to Makins, 18 May 1945; Robert Rhodes James, *Anthony Eden*, 1986, 294.
20. F0800/529, 14/28, Dixon to Eden; F0800/529, 10 May 1945, ANCAM 266; F0800/523, 14/24, CANAM 310, 14 May 1945; 14/34, 2 June 1945; 14/36, 1 June 1945; CANAM 327, 9 June 1945; F0800/530, CANAM 334, 22 June 194; F0115/4231, 42/2, War Cabinet, 2 July 194; F0800/530, CANAM 327, 9 June 1945; F0115/4231, FO mins., 27 June 1945.
21. Sherfield-Edwards interview.
22. Macmillan, op. cit., 524, 17 September 1944; F0800/531, 14/96.
23. HSTL, The Matthew Connally Papers, Cabinet mtg., 21 September 1945; National Archives Washington (hereafter N.A.), Diplomatic Branch, RG59 Committee of Three Papers, 10 October 1945.
24. Gowing, *Atomic energy*, 297-319; F0115/4231, 14/46, ANCAM 305, 26 June 1945.
25. F0800/555, Butler to Cadogan, 12 September 1945; Peter Wright, *Spycatcher*, Viking, New York, 1987, 182. James Gormley, The Washington Declaration and the 'Poor relation': Anglo-American atomic diplomacy, 1945-1946, *Diplomatic History*, **VIII**, (2), Spring 1984, 126-9; 56. F0800/551, 30 July 1945; F0800/512, US/45/19; DBPO enclosure to No. 197, Note to Cadogan, Butler and Dixon, 19 September 1945; 543-4, No. 195, 24 September 1945; F0800/555, Prague to FO, 17 September 1945.
26. Lord Sherfield, On the diplomatic trail with LBP: some episodes, 1930-1972, *International Journal* **XXIX** (1), 1973-4.
27. Gowing, *Independence*, 85-6, 76; DBPO, Washington Declaration, 618-20, No. 233; Tripartite Minute, 627, No. 239.
28. DBPO, No. 212, 4 November 1945; 607-8, 14 November 1945; No. 226, 19 October 1945, 560, No. 200, Butler to Bevin, 12 October 1945; F0800/554, GEN 75/8th Mtg, 16 December 1945.
29. PRO Atomic Energy Papers, AB16/285, May 1946,; Sherfield-Edwards interview.
30. F0800/597, JSM for P.M., 23 January 1947; AB166/285 E17, JSM to Cabinet Office, 25 January 1947; F0800/597, Top Secret, PM to Ambassador and Field Marshal Wilson, 7 February 1947; F0371/61043, AN119/28/45, Bevin to Attlee, 9 January 1947; AN 539/28/45G, Bevin to Attlee, 5 February 1947; F0800/597, JSM for PM, 23 January 1947; F0800/597, 20 February 1947. F0800/615, Makins to D.E.H. Peirson, Ministry of Supply, 24 February 1947.
31. F0800/597, T.S. J.S.M. to Cabinet Office, 5 March 1947.
32. Michio Kaku and Daniel Axelrod, *To Win a Nuclear War: The Pentagon's Secret War Plans*, South End Press, Boston, 1987, 43.
33. AB16/285, JSM to Cabinet Office, 6 May 1947; Richard G. Hewlett and Francis Duncan, USAEC, II, *Atomic shield*, 1947-1952, 274-5; AB16/

285, E34, JSM to Cabinet Office, 14 May 1947.
34. CAB 133/2, AE(US) (47), 1st Meeting; F0800/617, Miles to Makins, 20 June 1947; F0800/618, Makins to Bevin, 19 June 1947.
35. F0800/618, Makins record of conversation, 20 June 1947.
36. F0800/618, Makins to Bevin, 10 July 1947; minutes 11 July 1947; memo of conversation, 6 August 1947; Makins to Bevin, 17 September 1947; F0371/66371, N9549/271/38, Russia Committee mtg., 14 August 1947.
37. The Economic Intelligence Department had been created in mid-1945 from certain sections of the Ministry of Economic Warfare. Roger Makins also supervised the General Department which controlled telecommunications, postal and censorship questions. F0800/614, Makins to R. Gordon Munro, 3 March 1947; F0371/62782, UE12315/53, FO circular, 24 December 1947; HSTL OHI, W. John Kenny, 31; CAB21/2476 CP(48)45, 10 February 1948.
38. PRO Treasury Papers, T232/47, UK Attitudes towards the Economic Commission for Europe; F0371/51333 UR288/18/850, Law to Killearn, 6 February 1945; F0371/51365 UR1586/114/850, Halifax to Sargent, 30 May 1945. For Congress and UNRRA, *Documents on American foreign relations*, VII, 1944-5, Princeton, 1947; HSTL OHI Lord Sherfield-Theodore A. Wilson, 1970, 4.
39. FO 371/38555, A957/34/45, 1 March 1945, American Opinions on International Issues.
40. F0115/4206, 3168/9/45, GB-US Financial Agreements, Balfour, 26 December, 45, 39.
41. Alec Cairncross (ed.), Sir Richard Clarke, *Anglo-American economic collaboration in war and peace, 1942-1949*, Clarendon, Oxford, 198, 54; see also Michael Hogan, The search for a creative peace: the United States, European unity and the origins of the Marshall Plan, *Diplomatic History*, Winter 1982, 269.
42. FO115/4259, G275/1/46, 18 October 1946; G275/3/46, Jackling, 21 October 1946; G275/4/46, Inverchapel, conversation with Acheson.
43. ibid., D.D. Maclean, 24 October 1946; G275/8A/46, Maclean, Assistance for Greece and Turkey, 28 and 29 October 1946. For Maclean's role see, Andrew Boyle, *The climate of treason*, 1979, 295-304.
44. Clayton was nominated Assistant Secretary of State for Economic Affairs on 20 December 1943. The new post of Under-Secretary was created in June 1946 and Clayton's appointment announced 1 August 1946.
45. FO115/4259, G275/35/46, 5 November 1946, G275/46/46, Inverchapel to FO. 11 November 1946.
46. F0371/62388 UE112/227/53, FO to Duff Cooper, 7 January 1947; UE416/1658/53, C.P. (47) 35, 18 January 1947; UE592/168/63, Cabinet Conclusion, 28 January 1947 and CAB28/9, CP(47)35, Proposal for study of possibility for closer economic cooperation between this country and Western Europe.
47. FO115/4319, G62/5/47, January 1947, Note on Private Trade with Eastern Europe.
48. Ellen Clayton Garwood, *Will Clayton: a short biography*, University of Texas Press, Texas, 1958, 134.

49. FO115/4319, G62/5/47, 21 January 1947; and Makins to Clayton, 30 January 1947.
50. ibid., Bevin to Stalin, 17 January 1947.
51. Numerous accounts. Recently, Peter Wright, *Spycatcher*, Viking, New York., 1987, 182-4; Robert Cecil, *A divided life: a biography of Donald Maclean*, Bodley Head, 1988, 84-5. On the difficult question of how much information Stalin may have received, see forthcoming thesis by Sheila Kerr, London School of Economics.
52. N.A. RG 59 711.61/12-1045, *Capabilities and intentions of the Soviet Union as affected by American policy*, Interim Research and Intelligence Service, 10 December 1945.
53. FO115/4315, G45/37/47, 6 February 1947; FO371/66379, N394/343/38, Gore-Booth, 3 January 1947; N1382/343/38, Sir Maurice Peterson, 28 January 1947; F/115/4315, G45/37/47, 7 February 1947.
54. F0115/4316, G49/13/47, 9 April; G49/16/47, 14 April 1947; FO181/1016, 81/1/46, 2 January 1946; Hogan, op. cit., 274.
55. Dean Acheson, *Present at the creation: my years in the State Department*, Norton, New York, 1967, 226-35; John Gimbel, *The origins of the Marshall Plan*, Stanford University Press, 1976, 8-10; T232/47.
56. HSTL, OHI, Lord Sherfield with Philip C. Brooks, 15 June 1964; conversation, May 1989, with Leonard Miall, BBC correspondent in Washington, 1947.
57. FO371/62548, UE4527, FO Minute, Roger Makins, 5 June 1947; F0371/62398, UE4614/168/53, FO Minute, Hector McNeil, 11 June 1947; FO371/62401, UE4991/168/53, Inverchapel to Bevin, 23 June 1947.
58. HSTL OHI, Lord Sherfield-Theodore A. Wilson, 10 August 1970, 19.
59. FO371/62405, UE5388/168/53/G, Meeting 24 June, FO Minute, 27 June 1947, Bullock, op.cit., 413-17; FO371/62420, UE505/168/53, Inverchapel to FO, 25 June 1947.
60. FO371/62563, UE5866/5865/53, Gen 188/14, E.E. Bridges to Makins, 7 July 1947; FO371/62576, UE 7748/6169/53, 22 August 1947; UE7850/6169/53, 23 August 1947.
61. FO371/62804, UE9891/1830/50, Bridges to Makins, 15 October 1947; FO371/62746, UE1109/10857/50; FO371/62567 UE11010/5865/53 GEN188. 10 November 1947.
62. FO371/62567 UE1146/5865/53, GEN 188/35, Cabinet Office Meeting, 20 November 1947.
63. FO371/62804, UE10220/1830/50, Brussels to Makins, 17 October 1947, *Le Drapeau Rouge*, 11 October 1947.
64. *The Forrestal diaries* (ed.) Walter Millis, New York 1951, 281, 23 June 1947; 303, 8 August 194; FO371/62804, UE11331/1830/50, 17 November 1947, Perrin to Makins, 4 November 1947; Gowing, *Independence*, 155-8.
65. FO371-62804 UE10722/1830/50, Makins to Bevin, 5 November 1947; UE11329/1830/50, 17 November 1947.
66. FO371/62804 UE11151/1830/50, JSM to Cabinet Office, 13 November 1947, and Makins to Bevin, 17 November 1947; UE11835/1830/50, 26 November 1947.

67. FO371/62804 UE10955/1830/50, Maclean to Makins, 5 November 1947; Hewlett and Duncan, op. cit., 276.
68. FO371/62804/1630/50, UE11835/1830/50, 26 November 1947, Monro to Makins.
69. Hewlett and Duncan, op. cit., 279.
70. FO371/62804 UE12106/1830/50, Maclean to Makins, 4 December 1947; UE11885/1830/50, 5 December 1947, Makins to Bevin, Bevin minute 7 December; UE12107/1830/50, Makins to Bevin, 7 December 1947.
71. FO371/62804 ANCAM 934, 6 December 1947; UE12186/1830/50, Makins to Bevin, 10 December 1947.
72. ibid. UE12183/1830/G, 13 December 1947. ibid., UE12527; UE12644/1830/50, F.K. Roberts, 18 December 1947; Gowing, *Independence*, 250-7.
73. Gowing, ibid., text of Modus Vivendi, 266-72. Gowing, *Independence*, 252; Sherfield-Edwards interview.
74. DEFE 4/23, COS(49), 17 August 1949.
75. HSTL, PSF Intelligence File, CIA Report, ORE9-50; PSF TCT D-2/8, 3 January 1952.
76. HSTL PSF, undated memorandum; HSTL OHI.
77. Christopher Mayhew, *Time to explain*, 1987, 98.
78. Robert Cecil, op. cit., 142-3.
79. Kenneth Young, *The diaries of Sir Robert Bruce Lockhart 1939-1965*, 1980, 660.

2 Three Letters to Bevin: Frank Roberts at the Moscow Embassy, 1945-46

John Zametica

Born in 1907, Frank Kenyon Roberts was educated at Bedales, Rugby, and Trinity College, Cambridge, where he held a history scholarship. Entering the Foreign Office in 1930, he served at the Paris and Cairo Embassies before returning to London in 1937. His next stay abroad was between 1945 and 1947 as British Minister at the Moscow Embassy. This was followed by a period as Principal Private Secretary to Ernest Bevin, the Foreign Secretary, and two years as United Kingdom Deputy High Commissioner in India. In the 1950s he served as Deputy Under-Secretary at the Foreign Office, Ambassador to Yugoslavia, and United Kingdom Permanent Representative on the North Atlantic Council. He went to Moscow again in 1960, this time as Ambassador. He retired in 1968 following five highly successful years as Ambassador to the Federal Republic of Germany.

This distinguished career was built on a combination of talent and commitment. Seldom has a Foreign Office man commanded such widespread respect among those who knew and worked with him. Lord Strang remembered him as his 'able and indefatigable junior'; Sir Roderick Barclay considered him 'a man of many talents'; Sir John Colville maintained that there were 'few cleverer or more conscientious members of the Foreign Office'; Anthony Eden recalled in his memoirs 'Sir Frank Roberts, whose information was infallible and whose energy was inexhaustible'; and Harold Macmillan described him, simply, as 'our brilliant Ambassador in Moscow.'[1] Similar effusive praise, combined with an undisguised affection for Roberts, also came from his American colleagues. Walter Bedell Smith, the United States Ambassador to Moscow from 1946 to 1949, considered him 'one of the best of the younger British career diplomats in a service the ordinary standards of which are very high'. Roberts and his wife were to

Bedell Smith almost as close 'as members of our family'. And George Kennan, at the time second in command at the United States Moscow Embassy and thus Roberts' counterpart, knew him 'not only as a diplomatist of outstanding experience and ability but as a loyal colleague and valued friend.'[2]

And yet, intellect and devotion to duty were not enough to carry Roberts to the summit of his profession, the post of Permanent Under-Secretary at the Foreign Office. For there always existed reservations of one kind or another about him. It has to be said that not everybody liked him. Sir Maurice Peterson, Britain's Ambassador to the Soviet Union from 1946 to 1949, was one.[3] Bevin himself, according to Barclay, 'had a great regard for Frank's ability and liked him personally', but decided nevertheless at the end of 1948 to dispense with his services as the PPS. Roberts, it seems, 'was possibly too dynamic a character to fit altogether easily into the role of Private Secretary.' His 'over-efficiency', in fact, was disliked by Bevin.[4] Geoffrey Harrison, a wartime Foreign Office colleague, was quite blunt in his assessment of Roberts: 'Frank's trouble was that he wanted to run everybody and made his ambition very apparent.'[5] In 1953 Field Marshal Montgomery declared Roberts 'a menace to the country', a man with 'rigid constipated mentality.'[6] In 1961, moreover, Selwyn Lloyd offered his opinion that 'if Frank ever became Head of the Office, there would be a revolution in the F.O.'[7]

A man so energetic and indeed zealous, Roberts was perhaps always destined to make his mark as a career diplomat rather than as a Foreign Office official. Although his ambassadorship to Bonn is widely regarded as the crowning glory of his career, history will remember Sir Frank Roberts perhaps most of all in connection with his period as Minister at the Moscow Embassy during the formative period of the Cold War. He went there in February 1945, having attended the Big Three conference at Yalta. At a time when Britain's Soviet policy was in the melting pot, Roberts' lucid, penetrating analyses of the forces governing Soviet international behaviour attracted, almost invariably, very considerable attention in London. This time also coincided with several long absences abroad of Sir Archibald Clark Kerr, the British Ambassador to the Soviet Union, making Roberts Chargé d'Affaires and leaving him to provide the Foreign Office with advice.

He could hardly have arrived in Moscow at a more important juncture in the development of Anglo-Soviet relations. The post-Yalta period was always going to be a major test of the direction and scope of Soviet policy in Europe after the war. Against the background of wartime Anglo-Soviet relations characterized so often by friction, misunderstanding, suspicion and acrimony, the apparent success of the Yalta conference offered great hope for postwar co-operation. The desire to continue the Anglo-Soviet Alliance of 1942 was, after all, at the heart of British policy towards the Soviet Union. For the purpose of post-war strategic planning the military establishment in Britain began, in the course of 1944, to point at the Soviet Union as the next major enemy. This assumption, however, was based on purely military considerations in order to provide military advice. And the Foreign Office, while not altogether happy on political grounds, never in fact had a fundamental quarrel with the idea of identifying the Soviet Union as a potential foe. But it was not the job of the Foreign Office, nor could it afford such a luxury, to engage in a permanent exercise of analysing the worst-case scenarios. By the end of 1944 the Red Army was victorious in eastern, central and south-eastern Europe. The practical problem, given this advance of Soviet power, was how to avoid a clash with British interests. Churchill's October 1944 Balkan spheres of influence agreement with Stalin seemed to demonstrate that Soviet policy was pragmatic and that Soviet post-war ambitions were not going to spill across the northern frontiers of Greece. The Yalta agreement on Poland and the Declaration on Liberated Europe, moreover, suggested to many in the West that the Soviet Union retained some of its funds of good will.

There existed, on the other hand, a clear awareness in the ranks of the Foreign Office that the Soviet Union would not hesitate to pursue her security interests in Eastern Europe. Jock Balfour, whom Roberts was shortly to succeed in Moscow, reported in mid January 1945 that those interests concerned the south-eastern European area no less than Poland.[8] Indeed, it did not require much geopolitical insight to arrive at such conclusions. From Poland to Bulgaria, the Soviet Union was in an unassailable position to dictate the terms of post-war political arrangements. When, in late February 1945, Andrei Vyshinski shouted at the Romanian king, pulled out his watch and gave him a few hours to find a new government, he was merely displaying the theatrical impatience of a supremely confident political master.[9]

British diplomats and officials, however, failed to perceive anything particularly sinister in the Soviet behaviour just after Yalta. For it was considered neither surprising, nor in itself very threatening to Britain, that Moscow should be attempting to establish political control over Eastern Europe. To that extent, therefore, there were as yet no fundamental anxieties about the future of Anglo-Soviet relations. From Moscow, Clark Kerr argued towards the end of March that the Russians, in pursuing their policy in south-eastern Europe, were not immediately endangering essential

British interests. However distasteful it was to Britain, this policy had 'the air of remaining a policy of limited objectives'. Britain, in fact, would make little headway with the Kremlin so long as she conducted fruitless arguments over countries such as Romania and Bulgaria. Poland was different according to Clark Kerr, though only in the sense that Britain was in this case 'more concerned with decencies'. The British ambassador to Moscow, in fact, was loath to criticize Soviet behaviour in Poland. He thought that in manipulating the Polish provisional government to their advantage the Russians were mainly bent on getting a comfortable neighbour, and to them this was 'a matter of first importance'. In this analysis, which blended indifference and resignation over Eastern Europe, Clark Kerr kept repeating the phrase 'our vital interests', something which he failed to define, which seemed somehow connected with countries like Greece, Turkey and Persia, but in any case something which he did not see as impinged on by the Soviet Union. The Anglo-Soviet alliance of 1942, he reassured the Foreign Office, was one of those 'flashes of genius' that lit British foreign policy from time to time.[10]

Clark Kerr was not putting forward an eccentric, isolated view. Orme Sargent, the Deputy Under-Secretary at the Foreign Office, warned only a fortnight earlier against the futility of pretending that parliamentary democracy could be achieved in Eastern Europe. He suggested that the Soviet Union was creating on her borders a security belt against Germany: prospects for post-war cooperation would be endangered if Britain chose to attack the security interests of the Soviet Union.[11] But the situation was of course not quite so simple. There were two reasons for this: in the first place there was the question of Poland, a case *sui generis*, a problem that became an issue for British foreign policy because it was an issue for British pride; secondly, there was the attitude of the United States, a country which was not going to engage in any East European *realpolitik*, and a country which seemed to understand British concerns in the post-war world even less than those of the Soviet Union. This created a diplomatic minefield given the existence of the Churchill–Stalin spheres of influence agreement for the Balkans. Churchill was keen to uphold an agreement which had delivered Greece to the West in return for nothing other than a tacit recognition of an existing state of affairs elsewhere in the Balkans. Yet he was also eager to see implemented the Yalta agreement over Poland. The two policies – and they were both pursued in the Spring of 1945 – were manifestly incompatible. To support the idea of a representative government in Poland but not in Romania or Bulgaria was as inconsistent as it was unworkable. And each time Britain complained about the absence of such governments in the Balkans, she was undermining the October 1944 agreement which, however, was most emphatically in her interest to uphold. Roberts, in his first despatch since arriving in Moscow, commented that the Russians were no doubt 'genuinely surprised and irritated to find that we are not prepared to adopt in Rumania the same detached attitude which they have shown in Greece.'[12] Moreover, Britain could not in this situation practice bilateral diplomacy with Moscow without reference to the United States. The Americans were interested in operating the Yalta agreement, and in any case they regarded secret arrangements on spheres of influence with profound distaste.

The confusion in British policy towards the Soviet Union during the weeks after Yalta grew greater still with the changes in the military situation. By the last week of March Montgomery was pushing towards Bremen and Hamburg, while Patton was threatening the Ruhr. The Red Army was no longer the only force achieving striking successes against the Germans. Those in Britain with a keen eye on future relations with the Soviet Union attached major importance to this military breakthrough in the west. A new attitude soon emerged in the Foreign Office, something which can be traced back to a weekend in the country. On 31 March Robert Bruce Lockhart[13] was entertaining his friend and colleague Orme Sargent, who had come on a visit, and told him that the time had come for some plain speaking with the Russians. It was possible, he said, that the Russians believed they were very strong and the West was weak. Quite the reverse was the case: 'I am sure', he went on, 'that the Anglo-American armies in the west could go through the Russian armies quite easily because of their enormous preponderance in armour and air power.' There was thus no need to be afraid of plain speaking, according to Bruce Lockhart. He worked again on Sargent the following day using the same arguments.[14] Clearly impressed, Sargent returned to London and duly produced a long minute on 2 April, in which he made much of the military breakthrough in the West and called for a political 'showdown' with the Russians. Both Sir Alexander Cadogan, the Permanent Under-Secretary, and Anthony Eden, the Foreign Secretary, found themselves in substantial agreement with Sargent.[15]

Almost overnight, the mood among the highest officials of the Foreign Office was becoming bellicose towards the Soviet Union. The ambiguity in British policy towards the Soviet Union could now hardly be greater. It was widely accepted in the Foreign Office that the Russians, in building a *cordon sanitaire* in Eastern Europe, were looking after their future security. It was also accepted that Britain, whether she liked it or not, could do little about it given the Soviet Union's physical control of that area. To the extent that Britain talked about representative governments, particularly in Poland, she was bound to be seen by the Kremlin as threatening Soviet security interests. And this was directly undermining the policy of the spheres of influence which Britain was nevertheless still keen to maintain. Moreover, the recent hardening of attitudes in the Foreign Office expressed through the talk about a showdown with the Russians came, conveniently, only after a shift in the European military position and threatened Anglo-Soviet relations with consequences not too difficult to imagine. The whole approach, or collection of approaches, smacked not only of a lack of professionalism but also of a lack of principle.

What is striking is that the Foreign Office was at this time operating in the absence of any coherent, sustained analysis of the motives and objectives in Soviet policy for the post-war world. It was of course quite obvious what the Russians were doing in Eastern Europe. Beyond that, questions were sometimes asked, but only rarely were any answers given. Sargent remarked at the beginning of March that it was 'no longer we who are creating a cordon sanitaire against Bolshevism in E. Europe, but Stalin who is creating out of these same countries a cordon sanitaire against Germanism.' The question was, 'will he be satisfied that it should remain solely as a line of defence, or will he try to transform it eventually into a forward base from which to operate into Central and Western Europe.'[16] Later developments showed that the main thrust of Soviet ambitions, or at any rate diplomatic manoeuvres, was in fact in the direction of the Eastern Mediterranean and the Middle East. Clark Kerr's conclusion at the end of March that the Soviet policy in Eastern Europe was a policy of limited objectives, and his anxiety over Greece, Turkey and Persia, therefore seemed well founded. The Moscow Embassy, however, had as yet not attempted an overall analytical survey of the forces governing Soviet foreign policy. And there is no evidence that the Joint Intelligence Sub-Committee of the Chiefs of Staff Committee was in the difficult weeks after Yalta preparing a major new paper on Soviet strategic interests and intentions to replace their December 1944 report on the same subject. But it would not be an exaggeration to say that any team of bright schoolboys with some knowledge of history, geography and economics could have produced the substance of that report, such was the poverty of British intelligence on the Soviet Union.[17]

It was the restless Bruce Lockhart who again provided some food for thought in the Foreign Office. He had, so his diary relates, been reading Isaiah Berlin's *Karl Marx* and turning his mind to 'the baffling problem of what Russia's real intentions are'. This curiosity led to a memorandum which he sent, on 11 April, to Eden via Sargent. It would be difficult not to see this document as the first British hard-line, 'Cold War' look at the Soviet Union in the post-Yalta period. Bruce Lockhart was in fact not baffled at all by the question of Soviet intentions in foreign policy, for he had no hesitation in describing it as 'an expansionist policy'. A mixture of forces made it such: the Russian character itself ('At different times in their history the Russians have been inspired by a missionary zeal to save the world'); the idea of Russia's predestined role as a mother-state allied with the historical impulse to expand ('Molotov does not forget that the Russians were at Corfu in 1805, and in Paris in 1815'); and, most important, the Marxist ideology. It had to be borne in mind, Bruce Lockhart insisted, that Stalin regarded himself as an infallible interpreter of Marxism, that Marx was the professed enemy of all small national states, and that his whole belief in the social revolution rested on the theory that the smaller must be merged in the greater. It would therefore be 'foolish' for Britain to ignore the influence of Marx on Russian policy. And it would, moreover, 'be positively dangerous for us to lend a wishful ear to those sentimental pro-Russians who assure us ... that we have nothing to fear because Russia has ceased to be Communist'. Bruce Lockhart also argued that Russia had an exaggerated realization of her own strength, and he repeated what he had already told Sargent, namely that the West no longer had to play from weakness because of the immense array of armour and air power at its disposal. He considered that, in fact, the Anglo-American military strength was at its peak, whereas 'Russia's had long since passed it'. Her 'political malfeasance' had to be checked, and the moment was 'highly favourable for a bolder diplomacy.'[18]

It would be only too easy to dismiss Burce Lockhart as something of an outsider within the Foreign Office who was in any case on his way out (he resigned in August). But both Eden and Sargent were his friends. And Sargent had already shown, in his minute of 2 April, that he could easily be influenced by Bruce Lockhart. It was the same this time and he minuted, as he sent the memorandum to Eden, that it was 'full of truth'.[19] As it happened, Bruce Lockhart was not alone in stressing the importance of ideology in the Soviet Union. On 23 April Ralph Parker, *The Times* Moscow correspondent, wrote to his editor Barrington-Ward about 'the quite extraordinary wave of rigid Marxist thought that broke over Moscow during the past few weeks'. He thought that the Communist Party was making a supreme effort to get its basic ideas re-established. And he commented in connection with the Polish problem that he had yet to meet a Russian who could begin to understand the real reason why Britain was concerned about

Poland: 'Most of them think we want to break the Russian security belt there, or rather, to prevent it being completed and thus having a bridgehead for the eventuality of a military challenge to the Soviet Union.' A copy of this letter was sent to the Foreign Office. Usually very well informed, Parker also pointed out that the difficulties in Anglo-American relations with the Soviet Union were connected with the suspicion that Britain and the United States had conspired with the Germans to be allowed their recent military advance virtually unopposed.[20]

Undoubtedly, Anglo-Soviet relations were going through a very difficult patch in April 1945. By this time Frank Roberts had already spent a few weeks in Moscow which he reached via Baku and Stalingrad. Late in April he also found himself in charge of the embassy because Clark Kerr had gone to the United Nations meeting at San Francisco. To be, at such an important moment, the principal figure in what was arguably Britain's most important embassy abroad must have not only flattered him but also made him determined to rise to the occasion. For Roberts spoke no Russian and he was in no sense a Russian expert. However, while his experience of dealing with the Russians was limited, it was not insignificant. His first encounter with them was in the summer of 1939 when he went to Moscow with William Strang for Anglo-French talks with the Soviet Union. These talks were meant to produce an agreement to deter a German attack on Poland and they collapsed partly because Britain and France were unable to offer Stalin the Baltic republics and eastern Poland. Roberts could ponder the Soviet approach to international diplomacy again in December 1941 when he accompanied Anthony Eden on his mission to Stalin. He recalls being impressed by the fact that the Soviet leader chose to raise the question of his country's post-war borders at a time when the Germans had only just stopped before Moscow. During the war he was in the Central Department of the Foreign Office and dealt largely with Polish affairs, for which reason he later attended the Yalta conference. This experience inevitably deepened his understanding of the Soviet Union and left him, because of episodes such as Katyn, 'without any illusions that we were going to have very nice peacetime relations.'[21] Roberts was therefore anything but surprised by the post-Yalta Soviet behaviour in Eastern Europe: 'Those of us who had to deal with Stalin on the question of Poland had grave doubts whether the agreements would be respected.' It was 'quite clear' to them, since the Red Army was in possession of Eastern Europe, that the Yalta agreement was in fact a paper declaration. Roberts recalls in this connection that 'there was a perfect understanding that we were not suddenly producing a marvellous solution for Eastern Europe

— we were simply doing the best diplomats could ... Churchill shared this understanding although he tended to go up and down a bit.'[22]

Evidently, however, this 'perfect understanding' did not stop the officials at the Foreign Office from developing an attitude increasingly hostile to Soviet action in Eastern Europe. From Moscow, Clark Kerr had argued that Britain should not waste time on developing a feud with the Soviet Union over Eastern Europe where she had no vital interests. This view did not cut much ice at home. Sargent wanted a political showdown and Bruce Lockhart talked of the military superiority of the West over the Soviet Union. Bruce Lockhart, in fact, detested Clark Kerr who had in his opinion 'made rather a cheap reputation for getting on with the Russians by a policy of surrender and of careful avoidance of all difficult problems.' It is not clear what Sargent thought of Clark Kerr, but he told Bruce Lockhart on 18 March that Churchill and Eden were 'down on Archie Clark Kerr (who wanted to sell out to Lublin) for being always ready to surrender to the Russians'.[23] In this situation the work of the Moscow Embassy under the temporary command of Frank Roberts was going to be followed very carefully in London.

Roberts' first major despatch from Moscow was written on 25 April in the form of a letter to Christopher Warner, the head of the Northern Department of the Foreign Office. Like Clark Kerr a month earlier, he was anxious to indicate a fruitful way in which Britain should approach and conduct relations with the Russians in the period after Yalta when she was being 'confronted with example after example of power politics in their crudest form.' He suggested that one would be, given 'our national proclivity for wishful thinking', to dismiss the difficulties experienced since Yalta as a passing phase before Russia settled down to become a normal member of the family of nations. But these hypotheses seemed to Roberts equally far from the truth and equally dangerous. The second would indeed rest on wishful thinking because Kremlin policy was controlled by the 'tough, tricky and untrustworthy' Politbureau members. He also reminded his audience in London that these people were orthodox Marxists, and that Soviet political philosophy and practices differed fundamentally from those of the outside world. It was in looking at the first hypothesis that Roberts saw a reason to avoid extremes of gloom. For he could see 'no essential conflict of interests' between Britain and Russia. Those in charge of Russian policy were 'mainly guided by considerations of national self-interest'. And he though that this was in fact the real difference between Germany's pre-war position and the existing Soviet position.

Having set up arguments only in order to knock them down, Roberts proceeded to recommend a policy which seemed very tough. It was important, he argued, to 'show these hard-headed realists that we are determined and strong enough to defend our own interests and that we are just as capable as they are of conducting a policy designed primarily to secure our own national interests'. But this, of course, was a toughness of a kind very different to that advocated recently by Sargent and Bruce Lockhart. For Roberts was not interested in Eastern Europe. He was not suggesting that Britain should pursue some principles in Eastern Europe, only her national interests elsewhere. Without actually spelling it out, it is clear that he did not see those interests in any way connected with Eastern Europe: 'Russia is organising eastern Europe in her own way', he commented, 'regardless of our wishes or prestige.' For some time to come Britain should expect to be excluded from that region, but the lesson was a clear one: 'Since Europe has been divided by Soviet action into two parts, we had better lose no time in ensuring that ours remains the better and — with the support of the outside world — the stronger half'. These were prophetic words.

Unlike Clark Kerr, Roberts did not maintain that Soviet policy was one of limited objectives. But he did maintain that there was no real parallel between Hitler's Germany and Stalin's Russia. He thus seemed to be pointing to a certain grey area in between, to the factors of unpredictability and opportunism in Soviet foreign policy. His advice to stand firm, when he was clearly not very concerned about the situation in Eastern Europe, would otherwise make little sense. Like Clark Kerr, and presumably like most of the officials in the Foreign Office, he wished to see Britain's long-term strategy 'remain based upon the Anglo-Soviet Alliance and upon the necessity for avoiding conflict between Russia and the West'. Tactically, however, Britain's approach to relations with the Soviet Union should be such 'that there is no possible danger of any misunderstandings regarding our strength, our capacity and determination to use all the cards in our hand in order to protect our own interests and those of our friends'.[24]

Roberts' letter to Warner was considered important enough to be passed along all the way to Anthony Eden. Although he paid him a handsome tribute in his memoirs, during the war Eden considered Roberts, along with his Central Department colleague Roger Makins, a very able man but 'too prejudiced' in his views.[25] It is not clear to what extent he now agreed with Roberts' analysis from Moscow, except that he made no comment which would indicate disagreement. Clark Kerr, on the other hand, expressed reservations when he saw an earlier version of the letter to Warner. In fact he told Roberts to hold it up in the light of what then seemed a favourable development in Soviet policy expressed in the decision to send Molotov to the San Francisco meeting. But Roberts subsequently saw nothing very encouraging in Molotov's behaviour or in general Soviet policy, and so sent the letter regardless. He was evidently not afraid to demonstrate independence of action as well as thought.[26]

At the beginning of May 1945 the Foreign Office and the Moscow Embassy, with the possible, complicated exception of Clark Kerr, were united in the belief that Britain should stand up to the Soviet Union. But there were important, indeed fundamental differences between Roberts and the Foreign Office. Roberts was not making any noises about Russia's inherent or imminent expansionism, and he had no time for a confrontation over Eastern Europe. It has to be said, however, that the new combative attitude of the Foreign Office had its precise limits. When late in May Sir Owen O'Malley, Britain's ambassador to the Polish government in London, suggested that Britain should take the gloves off, criticize the Soviet Union in massive fashion, and risk precipitating a crisis in Anglo-Soviet relations immediately rather than in five or ten years time, the response was little short of incredulous. Sargent thought that such 'desperate remedies' should prove unnecessary. 'In any case', he minuted to Eden's approval, 'how does he [O'Malley] think we could apply these remedies without the support of the United States Government — and of that I should say there would be no prospect whatsoever on present form.'[27]

The Foreign Office was thus blowing hot and cold. Churchill's own thinking on Anglo-Soviet relations appeared during May to be well outside any considerations of tactics. In mid May General Sir Alan Brooke, the Chief of the Imperial General Staff, found it shocking that the Prime Minister was 'already longing for another war! Even if it involved fighting Russia!' What is most interesting is that a report was commissioned from the Joint Planning Staff of the Chiefs of Staff Committee to examine precisely that contingency. 'This evening', Brooke noted in his diary late in May, 'I went carefully through the Planners' report on the possibility of taking on Russia should troubles arise in the future discussions with her. We were instructed to carry out this investigation. The idea is of course fantastic and the chances of success quite impossible!' A few days later the Chiefs of Staff Committee discussed the 'unthinkable war' and became, according to Brooke, convinced more than ever that it was indeed 'unthinkable'.[28] However mystifying and bizarre, there can be little doubt that only Churchill could have ordered this report.[29]

While Churchill was ordering war plans against Russia, the

increasingly active Roberts was from Moscow attempting to explain the riddle of Russia in her communist incarnation. In a long letter to Eden on 24 May he reported that the 'Soviet peoples', following the unconditional surrender of Germany, regarded their country 'as the principal architect of victory and saviour of civilisation and feel immensely proud of their military, economic and moral strength and supremely confident of their ability to heal the wounds of war and grapple successfully with the problems of the future'. In particular, the Communist party had emerged from the war 'stronger, more self-confident and all-persuasive than ever before'. Party leaders regarded their dialectical materialism as an unfailing guide to action, and they believed they had already solved the class problem and the problem of reconciling different nationalities within a single state. While fully conscious of the vast problems of reconstruction, they were 'in no sense overwhelmed' by them, nor did they regard them as a likely source of national weakness in the postwar period.

Roberts drew attention, however, to the fact that, 'somewhat paradoxically', this immense self-confidence and sense of power was accompanied by suspicions and fears about the outside world and about the policies of the Soviet Union's major allies. A continuous propaganda campaign played down and denigrated the Anglo-American victories in the West and hinted that these victories were really the result of some underhand deal with the Germans. All of which, Roberts continued, may well suggest that the prospects of continued co-operation between the Soviet Union and the western capitalist world were somewhat gloomy. In particular, high-handed and unilateral Soviet actions throughout eastern and central Europe were far from reassuring: 'They lend colour to the theory that the Soviet State, by its very character and ideological foundation, can never settle down comfortably to co-operate with States with a different ideological basis. Indeed, it might be argued that the Soviet leaders must always have some outside enemy against whom they can concentrate the energies of the Soviet people and so justify the continued demands made upon them.' It was clear, according to Roberts, that Britain's relations with the Soviet Union could not really be comfortable 'for many years to come'. He thought, however, that it would be 'althogether wrong' to conclude that the elimination of Germany and Japan had to result in the Soviet Union substituting them by the British Commonwealth and the United States as her potential enemies. It did not follow that because Soviet propaganda made outrageous attacks on certain manifestations of British or American policy, these attacks were necessarily directed against Britain or America as a whole. Such attacks were, Roberts argued, often intended as a warning. 'In pursuing their own national interests', moreover, 'the Soviet Government are unlikely to show any consideration for our peculiar difficulties and embarrassments. In particular, they invariably suspect our motives when we speak to them in terms of high principle and of moral obligations.' The rulers of Russia were determined not to throw away the fruits of victory, and they were taking no chances, either with their own people or with their allies. 'In this mood', Roberts emphasized, 'we shall receive scant consideration. We shall meet with hard words and inflexible opposition on all issues regarded as vital to the security of the Soviet Union.' But he concluded with the thought that as long as the West was not suspected of any fundamental hostility to the Soviet Union, her attitude was likely to remain essentially defensive rather than aggressive.[30]

This analysis, with its mixture of deliberate emphasis of difficulty and an underlying streak of optimism, was typical of the approach that Roberts was to employ in the months to come. In the meantime other diplomats had been hard at work with significant results. Truman, the new man in the White House, sent Roosevelt's veteran adviser Harry Hopkins to Moscow in an effort to recapture the spirit of Yalta. Incredibly, Hopkins did rather well. Stalin showed himself conciliatory on many issues, agreed to a new meeting of the Big Three, and broke the Polish impasse by allowing the formation of a new government which would include the London Poles. Sargent thought, privately, that 'Hopkins . . . would receive all the credit for this change, but . . . it had taken place before Hopkins's arrival.' Be that as it may, the Foreign Office was not displeased. Bruce Lockhart talked to Sargent all day on 3 June. Although he was still 'very upset by General Patton's failure to push on to Prague', Bruce Lockhart found him at the same time 'more optimistic than usual . . . He said there were signs that Uncle Joe had come to the conclusion that he had gone too far and was now pulling back.'[31] The Polish affair now claimed much of the attention not only of the Foreign Office but also of the Moscow Embassy. Roberts wrote to Warner at the end of June that the Embassy had become *'in partibus'* to Poland, so that they had little time for their main business, Russia herself. By this time an agreement had been reached on the composition of the Polish government and Roberts could scarcely hide his jubilation. He now wrote about 'the very welcome *détente*' which had taken place. Recent events, he thought, confirmed the view that 'there was no reason for undue despondency over the future of Anglo-Soviet relations.'[32]

Roberts was perhaps over-optimistic in this instance. Having already recognized that the Soviet union was organizing Eastern

Europe in her own way, which was the outstanding bone of contention between her and the West — the latest Polish development notwithstanding — he had excellent reasons to reflect that any East European *'détente'* with the Russians was potentially a fragile affair. Clark Kerr was only marginally more anxious. On 10 July he wrote to Eden, expressing concern over Soviet policy towards Greece and Turkey. As regarded Greece the Soviet press had cast aside its previous restraint, while Turkey was being subjected to increasing pressure with the far-reaching demands for Soviet bases in the Straits. Otherwise, however, Clark Kerr was as encouraged as Roberts by the recent improvement in relations with the Soviet Union. He was in general inclined to take a benign view of her foreign policy: 'Russia of to-day', he suggested, 'is rejoicing in all the emotions and impulsions of very early manhood that spring from a new sense of boundless strength and from the giddiness of success. It is immense fun to her to tell herself that she has become great and that there is little to stop her making her greatness felt. Why resist therefore the temptation to put a finger into every pie?'[33] Perhaps both Clark Kerr and Roberts could be forgiven for taking a rather relaxed view about relations with the Soviet Union. It was not just the Polish question which seemed satisfactorily solved. The Russians had also stopped being difficult about the implementation of the decisions about the zones of occupation in Germany, western contingents were being moved into Berlin, the Reparation Commission had begun its work, and the United Nations Organisation was finally being established with full Soviet support. But it is curious that Roberts, who claims to have been sceptical about Yalta, should now anticipate a bright future for Anglo-Soviet relations.

Certainly, British policy towards the Soviet Union was anything but settled and it is not an exaggeration to say that it was being formulated almost on a weekly basis. By this time Eden had effectively blocked any further pursuit of the policy of the spheres of influence in the Balkans. Towards the end of May he proposed, and Churchill accepted, the idea of concluding peace treaties with Romania, Bulgaria and Hungary in the hope of eventually getting the Red Army out of these countries.[34] United States support would be required for this new course, and indeed it was partly because of the increasing American interest in Eastern Europe that the policy of the spheres of influence was now being abandoned by Britain. Churchill himself, by all accounts obsessed about the forthcoming General Election, wanted to 'stave off as much as possible' until the Potsdam conference, and was now happy to see the Americans take the initiative and responsibility in dealing with the Soviet Union.[35] In fact there was a growing awareness of the importance of the United States as a factor in Britain's policy towards the Soviet Union. Clark Kerr, for example, was much impressed by the recent American readiness to contemplate military operations against Tito over Trieste. He thought there was a lesson to be drawn here, that the successful solution of the crisis emphasized 'the importance of securing full and unquestioned American support on any question likely to involve trouble with the Russians.'[36]

Sargent joined this chorus a few days before the Potsdam conference. In a major memorandum entitled 'Stocktaking After VE-Day' he foresaw an economic crisis in post-war Europe, something which made it very important to obtain the cooperation of the United States, who alone had the material means of coping with such a crisis. What Britain had to do was to start the process of inducing the United States to support a British resistance to Russian penetration in Europe: 'This ought not to be too difficult.' On the question of Britain's policy towards the Soviet Union Sargent was once again in a robust mood. He noted that the Soviet Union was much weakened by the war; that she had either held back or even compromised over Greece, Venezia Giulia and to some extent Poland; and that it could surely be assumed that Stalin 'does not want and could not afford another war in Europe.' Since, however, Britain's military strength in Europe was going to decline from its existing peak, she had to maintain her interest in Finland, Poland, Czechoslovakia, Austria, Yugoslavia and Bulgaria. Now was the time 'to take the offensive by challenging Russia in these six countries, instead of waiting until the Soviet Government threatens us further west and south in Germany, in Italy, in Greece, and in Turkey.' This, of course, was an enormously ambitious plan. Sargent was ready to concede Soviet domination only in Romania and Hungary. In substance, the idea did not really differ from that of O'Malley, who had been so severely criticised by Sargent. One is struck by a further inconsistency in the Deputy Under-Secretary's views on the Soviet Union. For as recently as March he argued that Britain would be endangering prospects for post-war cooperation if she attacked Soviet security interests in Eastern Europe. Clearly, Sargent no longer worried about this point. Again, there is a case to be made for the influence of Bruce Lockhart: Sargent had his April memorandum printed and attached to his own.[37]

'Stocktaking After VE-Day' confirmed the wide differences between the Foreign Office and the Moscow Embassy regarding the policy towards the Soviet Union. The whole sense of Roberts' and Clark Kerr's advice pointed at the need to maintain some kind of spheres of influence agreement. This advice stemmed from the recognition that the Soviet Union, whether Britain liked it or not, was going to have the upper hand in Eastern Europe. It was futile to antagonise her in that area and in any case Britain had no vital interests there. Britain should, according to this view, preserve her strength and her arguments for situations in which those interests were under threat, and in any event she was not dealing with a Soviet programme of deliberate, systematic expansion abroad. This advice, however, seemed to have made no impression at all in the Foreign Office.

Sargent at least believed that the Soviet Union, weakened as she was by war, did not wish to fight another war in Europe. But he also maintained that is was 'particularly dangerous to assume that the foreign policies of totalitarian governments are opportunist and fluctuating ... All totalitarian governments — and Russia is certainly no exception — are able to conduct a consistent and persistent foreign policy over long periods because the government is not dependent on public opinion and changes of government.'[38] This was something of a doctrinaire position. Gladwyn Jebb, the head of the Reconstruction Department, commented that he was in favour of a tough line with the Russians because they only understood and appreciated 'pretty crude bargains' (in itself a rather crude view). On the other hand, Jebb could see no point in resisting them in countries such as Finland and Bulgaria, which they regarded as within their orbit and because were likely to retaliate in Western Europe. 'It would be simpler', he suggested, 'for us to say that we do not wish to meddle in Soviet preserves provided they for their part definitely renounce any meddling in what we consider to be our sphere.' Evidently, the attraction of the concept of the spheres of influence, at least in some quarters in the Foreign Office, continued to be irresistible. Sargent, however rejected it emphatically, 'Mr. Jebb's argument', he replied, 'lands us, I fear, with the conclusion that the only thing to do is to reach an agreement with Russia for dividing Europe into spheres of influence. This is a policy of despair which runs counter to the principles underlying the whole of my memorandum'. Significantly, Cadogan found little to quarrel with in Sargent's memorandum, while Eden remarked that he was tempted to show it to the Cabinet.[39]

The Foreign Secretary went to Potsdam rather unhappy. He still had, in the first place, misgivings about the Polish government which Britain had recently recognized.[40] But he was even more concerned about the demands on Turkey and the situation in Persia where the Russians appeared determined to establish political control. During the conference they also expressed an interest in Tangier and the Levant. It was all too much for Eden. He sent

Churchill this famous minute: 'The truth is that on any and every point, Russia tries to seize all that she can and she uses these meetings to grab as much as she can get... I am deeply concerned at the pattern of Russian policy, which becomes clearer as they become more brazen every day.'[41] In the event Eden and Churchill became bystanders in these events because of the extraordinary outcome of the British General election. It was of some importance, therefore, that the new Prime Minister Clement Attlee had only recently argued for a sympathetic consideration of the Soviet point of view in international affairs and urged, rather idiosyncratically, that Britain 'ought to confront the Russians with the requirements of a world organisation for peace, not with the needs of the defence of the British Empire'.[42]

Roberts had stayed in Moscow while Clark Kerr attended the Potsdam conference. During July and August he dealt with routine matters as the Chargé d'Affaires. (Towards the end of August he shrewdly anticipated the problems which the Soviet Union would have with Tito.)[43] In September, with the first meeting of the newly-established Council of Foreign Ministers in London, he was again far from the focus of international diplomatic action. By this time a new calm prevailed in relations with the Soviet Union. At the beginning of the month Clark Kerr noted a shift of Soviet attention to the Far East, accompanied by a relaxation in Eastern and Central Europe. This was, he thought, perhaps a new mood of compromise and a new respect for the West on the part of the Russians brought about by the atomic bomb. But he also noted that the danger-spots in Anglo-Soviet relations remained in the Near and the Middle East: the Soviet Union had not renounced the claims on Turkey and the Straits, she was 'embarrassingly active in Persia', while Greece was a stick with which to beat whatever British government was in office.[44] Leaving Roberts yet again in charge at Moscow, Clark Kerr went to London for the first Council of Foreign Ministers (11 September – 2 October 1945) and saw at first hand that, in claiming a trusteeship for Tripolitania, the Soviet Union indeed seemed ambitious to make inroads in the Eastern Mediterranean. Roberts himself does not, in retrospect, believe that the Soviet Union was really determined to replace Italy as a Mediterranean power in Libya: 'This was, in my view, a bit of a great-power swagger. It sounded impressive, especially to Stalin himself, but I think he knew that he was not in a position to do it.'[45]

In the middle of the Council's proceedings in London, Roberts reported on the 'deep seated' Soviet suspicions of the West, particularly in connection with what the Russians took to be attempts at forming western groupings hostile to the Soviet Union. 'We are in effect accused', he observed, 'of constantly meddling in countries where we have no real interests, refusing to recognise other peoples vital interests and working for the formation of hostile coalitions. The most effective reply seems to be to proceed with our plans in those parts of Europe where our primary responsibilities lie... and leaving it to events to show that they are not in fact hostile to the Soviet Union.' Commenting on this, however, Sargent wondered hawkishly whether Soviet fears and suspicions were indeed real and not merely the tactics with which to disguise what was 'in fact an offensive foreign policy'.[46]

Roberts, it must be said, was addressing an audience in the Foreign Office which seemed to have little time for interpretations of Soviet policy from a Soviet perspective. The Moscow Embassy, which after all was meant to provide such interpretations as part of its work, was being in effect ignored. There was of course nothing unusual in the existence of a difference of views between the Foreign Office and a British embassy abroad, but in this particular case it was a difference of views which was persistent and increasingly sharper. It was not surprising, in this situation, that Roberts was becoming more than just concerned about British policy towards the Soviet Union. He had of course followed from Moscow the progress, or rather the lack of it, of the Council of Foreign Ministers in London. Towards the end of September he sent a lengthy telegram to the Foreign Office. He noted that 'out of a relatively clear sky' came a storm in Anglo-Soviet relations, a difficult phase comparable with the post-Yalta period. Disquieting signs included the decision to maintain large Soviet forces in Czechoslovakia, the renewed pressure on Turkey, and press criticism of Britain over India, the colonies and Egypt. 'Before the atomic bomb', Roberts pointed out, 'the Russians had immense self-confidence. This has been shaken, although by no means shattered, and they fear that foreign machinations may yet deprive them of the place in the post-war world to which they consider their war effort entitles them.' And he stressed, again, that 'genuine suspicions' existed behind Soviet policy. For example, the Russians were quite alarmed by what they saw as the threatening possibility of a Western European bloc utilizing the industrial strength of the Ruhr and supported by the United States. They had a renewed obsession with their security, they were touchy about the Balkans, they were putting forward extravagant requests such as the one over Tripolitania (although there was also an element of blackmail there), and in general they exhibited the urge to safeguard their vital interests 'and incidentally to pocket whatever may be going before the general world situation crystallises'.

The result of this seemed to Roberts to be a dangerous mixture of Soviet suspicion with a temporarily uncertain sense of power. He had not, however, abandoned his previous ideas about how the West should deal with the Soviet Union. He believed, in the first place, that she needed world peace to enable her to recover from the exhaustion of war. It followed, therefore, that 'we should state our policy and our vital interests as clearly as the Soviet Government claim to have stated theirs. They will then know, as they do not seem to know now, the point beyond which they cannot safely go.' Roberts seemed anxious to highlight the pointlessness of talking to the Russians in terms of general principles rather than of vital interests. And he was at pains to stress in this connection that they, despite their great strength, feared the unknown, readily attributing the most sinister motives to the West. He was very much aware, moreover, that the success of his scheme depended crucially on the inclusion of the United States. The Soviet Union should accordingly be presented with proposals in which British requirements would constitute elements of a global pattern. 'This would remove the very real risks of the Russians endeavouring to isolate us from the Americans and of the latter slipping into the tempting position of mediating, probably at our expense.' It was perhaps a little optimistic of Roberts to expect the United States acquiescence in a policy of spheres of influence. For the latter was precisely what he was suggesting, 'frankly to reach agreement with the Russians upon our respective interests'. He believed, however, that it was as much in the interests of the United States as it was in Britain's to make the British position quite clear to the Soviet Union. He did not wish to leave the impression that there should be approval or condoning of 'undemocratic procedures' in Eastern Europe, though the logic of his proposals could in the last analysis point to little else. There was a chance, he thought, that the West could satisfy the Russians as to its motives and thus improve its position in Eastern Europe. Failing this, it would still be better to reach an agreement with them rather than let matters continue to drift. 'This would', he concluded, 'at least dispel the present misunderstandings which would endanger the whole organisation as much as the future of the Anglo-Soviet alliance.'[47]

Roberts' telegram was duly passed on to Ernest Bevin. The new Foreign Secretary merely put down his initials in his characteristically tortured handwriting. According to a minute by Christopher Warner, however, Bevin' tactics were at this juncture 'to leave the Russians alone and not as Mr. Roberts suggests to take the initiative in discussing with them our essential and vital interests'. Warner, in fact, must have been quite pleased by the Foreign Secretary's approach. He was quite critical of the ideas in Roberts' telegram and suggested, 'with some diffidence', that there was a good deal less suspicion behind the Russian attitude than Roberts indicated. He considered, regarding the large proposals in the telegram, that 'it would be very hard to prevent a discussion with the Russians on the basis of respecting each others vital interests not to result in an agreement on spheres of interest'. The unmistakeable implication of Roberts' ideas was of course exactly such an agreement. It is exceedingly difficult to see what else could have been hoped for from Anglo-Soviet discussions about respecting the vital interests of each side.[48]

Admittedly, Soviet behaviour at the Council of Foreign Ministers hardly encouraged the officials at the Foreign Office to think that the Soviet Union could not wait to conclude agreements with the West. Aggressive from the outset, Molotov refused any compromise on the Balkan peace treaties, demanded a trusteeship in Tripolitania, and proved implacably hostile to French and Chinese participation in the important decision-making of the Council. This last problem was the formal reason for the collapse of the meeting at the beginning of October. What alarmed the British most of all was the Tripolitanian affair — the Soviet Union was meddling in *their* sphere of influence, the Mediterranean.[49] Yet the Foreign Office was now aghast that Roberts should be proposing a policy of mutual respect for vital interests. There was more than just a touch of hypocrisy here. The hypocrisy was massive. From October 1944 to May 1945 Britain was keen, despite the inevitable difficulties, to base her Soviet policy on the Moscow agreement. And this was not just Churchill's obsession, for the Foreign Office frequently echoed his reasoning if not his enthusiasm. Nothing which the Soviet Union did between June and September 1945 could have fundamentally invalidated the concept of the spheres of influence from the British point of view. There existed, of course, the Yalta declaration. An official in the Foreign Office argued in July 1945 that 'we were before Yalta perfectly prepared to allow the Russians the predominance in the ex-satellite Balkan countries to which we agreed in Moscow last October, but it has unfortunately been quite impossible to persuade them to realise that the Yalta Declaration on Liberated Territories altered this and not only entitled us, but even obliged us, to interest ourselves in what the Russians were doing.'[50] This view is interesting because it suggests that Britain's international behaviour was really a matter of signatures over documents rather than beliefs in certain large principles. But such attitudes were rare even in the chameleon-like Foreign Office. Far more characteristic was the Foreign Office advice to the newly arrived Bevin on Britain's policy towards the Balkan ex-satellites of Germany: 'Whether or not we make peace treaties with any of these governments will in the last resort depend upon whether it is in our interest to do so and not upon the character of the government in question.'⁵¹ Bevin, in any case, had robust views of his own on the Balkans. Just before the break up of the Council of Foreign Ministers he argued with the Americans that 'in these countries we must be prepared to exchange one set of crooks for another'.⁵²

For their part, the Russians made little attempt at disguising their profound dislike of the new Labour government in Britain. Thus Roberts reported to Warner: 'In the toasting which, as you know, is so prominent a feature of Russian dinners, the N.K.V.D. guests always coupled the toasts of Churchill and Eden with those of Stalin, and never toasted or even mentioned the names of Attlee and Bevin.' Roberts thought that this was indicative of a trend of thought in Moscow.⁵³ Warner, in fact, claimed to welcome such guess-work. In a rare letter to Roberts, he expressed his admiration for his telegrams: 'One of the advantages of having at a post abroad someone who has worked long in the Office is that his reports have the Foreign Office approach, and one feels one understands the processes of mind which lie behind.' And he felt that this was particularly useful and important in dealing with the Russians where there was necessarily a large element of speculation. 'Everybody who comes back', he added, 'gives you and your wife full marks.'⁵⁴ Instead of receiving such meaningless gestures of approval, Roberts might well have preferred some reaction from the Foreign Office to his substantive proposals in relation to Britain's Soviet policy. In fact, there is no evidence that he even knew his views had been brushed aside. As for the point about the Office man abroad, Warner was merely arguing with the prejudice of someone whose own career had been characterized by a distinct lack of enthusiasm to serve broad. Similarly, it was rumoured in the Foreign Office that Sargent, soon to become the Permanent Under-Secretary, had once crossed the Channel — but only for a few hours.⁵⁵

There was, of course, a sense in which British policy towards the Soviet Union now amounted to nothing, for no British initiatives were contemplated. Following the breakdown of the Council of Foreign Ministers Bevin stipulated that the Russians were to be left alone. Already by the middle of October, however, he was toying with the idea of embarking on a policy of spheres of influence. He suggested as a possible course of action a tacit abandonment of Eastern and Central Europe, but leaving the Russians in no doubt that 'we intend to resist to the utmost with our vital interests elsewhere.'⁵⁶ This line of thinking may well have been influenced by Roberts whose recent telegram Bevin had read

— no-one else in the Foreign Office, with the possible exception of Gladwyn Jebb (and Clark Kerr who still had not returned to his post in Moscow), was likely to have offered such advice to the Foreign Secretary. Indeed, only a few days earlier Thomas Brimelow, of the Northern Department, argued that Britain's policy was to avoid spheres of influence as far as possible and that, even if there existed an agreement with the Russians they would still be able to exercise influence on left-wing movements outside their sphere. Moreover, it was 'highly doubtful whether the Russians would respond to a frank approach on our part with equal frankness on theirs'.[57]

In addition to such rather contradictory suggestions about the desired substance of Britain's policy towards the Soviet Union, there now also existed a confusion on the tactical level. Towards the end of October the officials at the Foreign Office, having with some difficulty got hold of 'the elusive Sir A. Clark Kerr to be present too',[58] held a meeting to consider Bevin's idea that Clark Kerr should on his return to Moscow talk to Stalin himself about the entire range of Anglo-Soviet differences. Of course, this would have entailed the reversal of Bevin's own policy to leave the Russians alone. Indeed, Cadogan was anxious that Britain should avoid the appearance of 'running after' the Russians. But the Permanent Under-Secretary was actually puzzled as to the exact object of the whole exercise. If Clark Kerr were to seek a special interview with Stalin, what was the primary purpose? Was it, he wondered, to table all the main difficulties impairing Anglo-Soviet relations, or was it to discuss the means of reviving the Council of Foreign Ministers? Or was it both?[59] In the end nothing came of the proposed approach to Stalin.

Roberts would have been appalled to learn just what a sorry mess Britain's Soviet policy presented at this time. And he would have been intrigued to know that the Prime Minister had in the meantime enthusiastically advocated a radically new approach to Britain's foreign and defence policy. 'The British Empire', Attlee argued in a memorandum on 1 September, 'can only be defended by its membership of the United Nations Organisation.'[60] The Russians might have felt less nostalgic about the days of Churchill and Eden had they known of this prime ministerial heresy in Britain. As it happened, however, Roberts was at the end of October reporting a further deterioration in Anglo-Soviet relations, pointing out that the July victory by Labour was regarded by the Kremlin 'as likely to hamper Soviet policies in Europe'. Britain had now come, much more than the United States, under attack in the Soviet press. In fact, the Americans were being handled with some care, while Britain was in the light of her domestic economic problems regarded by Stalin as having for the moment 'nothing to give Russia'. Britain was thus being treated as of less account than America. Soviet policy in countries such as Turkey, Greece and Persia showed attempts to detach them from Britain in favour of 'an exclusively Soviet connexion'. In some respects, Roberts argued, Anglo-Soviet relations were passing through a critical phase. 'The feeling is growing here that we are meddling in the affairs of South-Eastern Europe, where we have no major interests, refusing to recognise vital Soviet interests and working for a creation of coalition which would inevitably become hostile to the Soviet Union.' What worried the Russians above all, according to Roberts, was the emergence of a western *bloc*, particularly a close Anglo-French alliance. And he warned that there was a 'danger that the Russians' attitude towards us may become increasingly embarrassing in India, the Middle East and in our colonies, quite apart from Soviet attempts to prevent British influence consolidating itself in Western Europe and elsewhere'.

But Roberts was far from disheartened by these developments. It would be a mistake, he insisted, to look only for sinister motives behind Soviet policy. Soviet suspicions of British and American motives were genuine enought, their thought processes as Russian nationalists and orthodox Marxists alike driving them to look for the worst interpretations. But security was probably still the mainspring of Soviet policy and 'however dangerous to our interests are many of their apparent objectives, these objectives ... are likely to remain limited'. For example, Roberts saw no reason to doubt the sincerity of Stalin's recent statement that the Soviet Union needed fifty years of peace to recover from the war and to catch up with the West in the economic sphere. In addition to this need for peace there was also the Soviet conviction, born of Russian national traditions and Marxist historical teaching, that in the long term the Soviet Union would inevitably become 'the most powerful, the richest, and the best ordered country in the world'. Roberts thus thought it unlikely that the Soviet Union would either embark on adventurous foreign policies in the near future or relapse into isolation: 'Her desire to get back to the Big Three procedure which worked so well from her point of view at Tehran, Yalta and Berlin, is genuine enough, and if we can find some means to satisfy this desire without abandoning any of our basic principles, we may hope to survive the present crisis in our relations with the Soviet Union as we have survived other awkward crises in the past.' Britain, Roberts concluded, had to demonstrate clearly the limits of her forbearance where her principles and vital interests were involved, and in doing this she may create a more solid foundation for the future of Anglo-Soviet relations.[61]

It was by now abundantly clear what Roberts' recommendations amounted to: a policy of containment which incorporated, critically, an understanding that spheres of influence would have to be respected. In this scheme of things coexistence with the Soviet Union, even collaboration, was possible. It cannot be said that the Foreign Office ignored Roberts' despatches. This latest one was circulated in the different departments and also landed on Bevin's desk. Once again, however, the Foreign Secretary managed to record only his initials. The main comment was provided by Thomas Brimelow.[62] There was probably a good reason for this. True, Brimelow was a junior official and he had only recently joined the Northern Department from the consular section of the Moscow embassy where he had worked since June 1942. But he was perhaps the only person in the entire Foreign Office who could plausibly be described as a Russian expert. Unlike the State Department, the Foreign Office did not produce regional specialists — with the significant exception of its Arabists. As a Russian speaker Brimelow was something of a rarity in the Foreign Office, and this was coupled by his profound knowledge of the Soviet Union and her ideology. 'Brimelow', a former colleague of his has recalled, 'really knew his Lenin. He knew his Soviet scriptures.'[63] The only official able at this time to rival these credentials was Isaiah Berlin, who, however, was hardly a career official.[64]

Brimelow was a good deal less sanguine than Roberts about the future of Anglo-Soviet relations. And he used Roberts' own arguments to make his point. If, he suggested, the Soviet attitude was becoming increasingly embarrassing to Britain, and if Britain was in any case increasingly dropping out of the Soviet picture, this was 'hardly compatible with Big-3 collaboration'. Brimelow, moreover, could not find anything in the general course of Roberts' despatch which would suggest that there existed conditions for the creation of 'the solid foundations' in Anglo-Soviet relations. 'Mr Roberts thinks however that we might achieve this aim by showing clearly where we stand and that there are limits to our forbearance. We have done this, but the result was the breakdown of the Council of Foreign Ministers, and the mutual recriminations which have since taken place.' Brimelow was of course exaggerating here — the Council of Foreign Ministers in London was probably doomed to collapse even before it started. But then he had a general view of the nature of Soviet international behaviour: 'I think we must reconcile ourselves to the fact that the Russians look upon international co-operation of any kind simply as a means to the achievement of the ends of the Soviet Government, and are willing to give up the idea of such collaboration when it would involve any sacrifice of their immediate objectives.' Not surprisingly, Christopher Warner found himself in agreement with Brimelow's criticisms of Roberts' despatch.[65]

The question of spheres of influence, however, kept exercising the minds of British officials in the Autumn of 1945. Thus the idea originated in the India Office that Britain and the Soviet Union should, to improve their relations, frankly state to each other their minimum interests in Persia and Afghanistan. This was precisely the kind of thinking favoured by Roberts and he naturally welcomed it. But he was not necessarily keen that Britain should be seen to be conducting an insensitive, old-fashioned diplomacy: 'It is . . . rather difficult to start talks of this kind somewhat on the 1907 model without laying ourselves open to the charge of embarking upon a policy of spheres of interest. Presumably we wish to avoid this, at all events until such talks could be conducted within the framework of an already functioning United Nations Organisation and with the sympathy of the American Government and of American public opinion.' Which, of course, would still amount to a policy of spheres of influence. Roberts, moreover, did not want this to be a piecemeal policy with, say, Persia and Afghanistan isolated from contries such as Greece and Turkey. His was a global, and once and for all approach. The 'tentative' view of the Moscow Embassy, he explained, was that Britain and the Soviet Union might find it useful to discuss 'the whole general tour round the world, pointing out to the the Russians exactly what we regarded as our essential interests and our general plans in each main area of mutual interest and asking them to do the same.'[66]

Brimelow agreed with Roberts in this instance, which was strange. He had already expressed strong doubts about the desirability of a spheres of influence agreement with the Russians, and indeed he had poured scorn on Roberts' cautious optimism about the future of Anglo-Soviet relations. But he now took the view that there was 'much to be said for negotiating or trying to negotiate a general understanding with the U.S.S.R. . . . What is called for is a comprehensive brief on our minimum interests in the areas where we are likely to run foul of the Russians.'[67] He did not elaborate. Sargent's thinking was only marginally less inconsistent. He told Bruce Lockhart on 17 December that he was 'quite eager for us to keep out of the Romanian commitments, and to recognise Romania frankly as a Russian sphere of influence. We had been pushed into this by the Americans.'[68] Admittedly, in his memorandum 'Stocktaking After VE-Day', Sargent had already argued that Britain might have to acquiesce in Soviet domination in Romania and Hungary. But he had thereafter severely criticised Gladwyn

Jebb's proposal for a spheres of influence policy. It is hardly nit-picking to point out this contradiction. For Sargent's position does not bear a moment's examination. To condemn the spheres of influence policy in general and then to be 'quite eager' for its implementation in, say Romania, was as hypocritical as it was impractical.

In the course of November and December 1945 Roberts receded somewhat into the background at the Embassy owing to Clark Kerr's return to Moscow. The Ambassador, however, would not be there for long. Already at the beginning of October he had asked Bevin to be released from his post. He argued that four years of Molotov was enough for any man.[69] The request was granted, but Clark Kerr would in the meantime stay in Moscow to assist and be present for the meeting of Molotov, Bevin and Byrnes, the United States Secretary of State. Bevin went reluctantly to the Moscow meeting (16-26 December) which was instigated by the impulsive Byrnes who had not even consulted with the British. He was persuaded to attend at least partly by Clark Kerr who presented this as an opportunity of dissipating with Molotov and the Russians in general 'the absurd notion that you are a big, bad wolf'. There was, Clark Kerr emphasized, 'a marked and growing tendency to pick upon His Majesty's Government and upon you in particular as the villains of the peace who are hostile to the Soviet Union at every turn'.[70] Roberts had of course already noted the anti-British concentration in Soviet propaganda. But Bevin went to Moscow also because, as his private secretary recorded in his diary, in the contrary event 'we fear the Russians will gain, we shall gain nothing, and the Americans will give away our interests to the Russians for the sake of a settlement'.[71]

This was hardly the basis on which Roberts had hoped to persuade Bevin to start talking to the Russians. British policy towards the Soviet Union consisted, it seemed, of nothing more than short-term manoeuvres. The American initiative, on the other hand, emphasized most forcefully the need for Britain keep the United States as a permanent factor in her own dealings with the Soviet Union. This need had never been far removed from the thoughts of officials at the Foreign Office. Roberts himself had already urged the adoption and presentation of a joint Anglo-American Soviet policy. There were two aims here. The first, indeed, was to prevent any damage to Britain resulting from bilateral American-Soviet diplomacy. But the second aim was the more ambitious one of enlisting the support of the American diplomatic effort in defence of British interests. This meant, clearly, that Britain could not so easily embark on bilateral diplomacy with the Soviet Union. The Americans were in any case eternally suspicious. Isaiah Berlin, seconded to the Moscow Embassy from Washington, thus reported during the Moscow meeting of foreign ministers: 'The thing which rankled most in American memories was the arrangement made by Mr.Churchill in 1944 in Moscow concerning spheres of influence, which Mr. Byrnes still occasionally referred to as typical of what we did when we were not watched.'[72]

The Americans need not have worried. The negative reception accorded to Roberts' steady stream of advice from Moscow indicated that, irrespective of the American position (and regardless of the occasional contradictory noises being made by Brimelow and Sargent), there was little desire in the Foreign Office to engage in any direct, far-reaching talks with the Russians. But the Moscow meeting must have convinced many in the British delegation that the support of the United States was of rather dubious value. Byrnes failed spectacularly to back Bevin over the inclusion of India in the peace conference, and went ahead with proposals on atomic energy without clearing them with the British. Anglo-American cooperation was a shambles. What is interesting is that the Foreign Office, for all the hard-line attitudes expressed in reactions to Roberts, had by now completely abandoned any idea of getting representative governments in the Balkans. The brief which Bevin took to Moscow concentrated on proposals for Anglo-American acquiescence in recent Bulgarian elections and a minimal reorganisation of Romanian and Bulgarian governments. The hope was that, if these proposals were explained to the Americans as a change of tactics rather than a change of policy, they might prove acceptable.[73] This resembled in some ways a spheres of influence approach, even though the rationale was to speed up the movement towards the conclusion of peace treaties, leading possibly to an early withdrawal of the Red Army from the Balkans. It was the kind of realism which Roberts, and indeed Clark Kerr, had advocated for some time. Byrnes, anxious to achieve success, eventually went along. In the course of the discussions in Moscow Molotov told the British that a Balkan settlement would have to be reached 'which did not ignore the facts of life'.[74] The Moscow agreement on Romania and Bulgaria, which paved the way for Western diplomatic recognition, followed this precisely.

From the British point of view, the most problematic area in Anglo-Soviet relations just before and during the Moscow meeting for foreign ministers was the Eastern Mediterranean and the Middle East. Soviet pressure on Turkey was maintained, there were renewed attacks against the regime in Greece, and the Russians still sat and plotted in northern Persia. These were the three points, an anxious Bevin commented, 'where the USSR rubbed with the British Empire.'[75] In Moscow he tried without any success to put Persia on the agenda. Whether all this was indicative of a general, deliberate hardening of Soviet attitudes is a matter of conjecture. One Foreign Office official thinks in retrospect that Stalin, who had returned to Moscow for the meeting of the foreign ministers after spending three months in a Black Sea resort, had used his holiday to formulate with members of the Politbureau a new, uncompromising policy towards the West.[76] In March 1946 Roberts already reported to the Foreign Office the same conclusion: 'It would now appear that Stalin, in fact, passed his vacation at Sochi last autumn in planning the Soviet foreign ... policy which is causing us anxiety to-day.'[77] But Soviet relations with the West had been uneven for some time — there were ups and downs throughout 1945. And there was certainly nothing new about the exertion of Soviet pressure in the Eastern Mediterranean and the Middle East. For example, while the war of nerves against Turkey was quite intense in November, it was as intense in June.

Roberts, however, began in January 1946 to perceive a definite trend in the policy of the Soviet Union along her southern borders. His despatch at the end of October had already alerted the Foreign Office about the likelihood of a growing Soviet interest in Greece, Turkey and the Middle East. Clark Kerr was by now in the process of leaving Moscow for good and his successor Sir Maurice Peterson would not arrive until May 1946. In charge again, Roberts wasted no time in letting the Foreign Office have his views on the developments in Soviet foreign policy. This he did on 16 January in a long letter to Bevin. He felt that his warning in October about Soviet aims in the Middle East becoming embarrassing to British interests was justified, particularly as regards Persia. And he believed that the Russians, in this traditional area for their expansion, were bound to assert themselves with increasing vigour: 'The Soviet Union sees before her, barring her own way to the Mediterranean and to the Indian Ocean, a world empire whose main lines of communication run through the Mediterranean and the Middle East to India and Australasia, and an empire which can be accused in Soviet propaganda of all the crimes of imperialist and colonial exploitation.' Although she had emerged from the war with an immense sense of power and purpose, the Soviet Union was 'probably as yet' not intending to press forward with her plans to the point of provoking a major clash. The southern frontiers, however, provided 'the line of least resistance along which the Soviet Union is inevitably tempted to expand, using for this purpose political, economic, strategic and ideological weapons'.

According to Roberts, the foundations of this urge to expand were historical, while the motive was to gain access to the open sea — a motive undiminished by the advent of atomic energy and advances in air power. But he repeated that Soviet aims did not 'at present' include a willingness to risk a head-on collision with Britain. Throughout this area Soviet policy was 'likely to be one of gradual penetration with control of North Persia and the Straits as immediate objectives and with long-term aims including the domination of Turkey and Persia, access to the Persian Gulf and, if all goes well for them, an extension of Soviet strategic, economic and even ideological influence throughout the Arab world'. Roberts thought that the Soviet rulers may show little regard for Britain's interests unless these were very firmly stated to them. This line of thinking, the idea of drawing the line and standing firm, must have by now become familiar to those in the Foreign Office who had been reading his Moscow despatches. Roberts, in any case, did not see much cause for alarm in the Eastern Mediterranean and the Middle East. He considered, for example, that in this region Soviet vital interests were not at stake to the extent that they were in Europe or even in the Far East, and that the Soviet government 'must realise that there is a limit beyond which we cannot allow what are clearly our own vital interests to be endangered in the Middle East'. The Russians also knew, he believed, that the United States, being closely interested in the Middle East, had an increasing stake in maintaining British influence there. In general, there was 'no reason for undue despondency, but only for constant vigilance in that area.'[78]

Within days some aspects of this analysis began to be confirmed by diplomatic developments. On 19 January the Persian government lodged a formal complaint at the United Nations Security Council against the continued Soviet military presence in the north of their country. Two days later the Soviet Union requested that the Security Council should address itself to the Greek situation, while the Ukrainian delegation brought up the question of British troops in Indonesia. Suddenly there was a new crisis in Anglo-Soviet relations. Bevin thought, as did many others, that the Russians were retaliating in consequence of the Persian appeal.[79] Not so, argued Roberts. He thought this was more than mere counter attack: 'One of the most disturbing features of this crisis in Anglo-Soviet relations', he informed the Foreign Office on 12 February, 'has been the way in which Vyshinski, in connexion with Greece and later with Indonesia, has played up our differences instead of attempting to dismiss . . . charges against the Soviet Government and Communist Parties as unfounded.' Roberts noted at the same time Soviet criticisms of British troops not just in Indonesia, but also in the Levant states and Egypt, claims against Turkish Armenia, allegations against Britain's protection of 'Fascists' in her zones in Germany and Austria, and the revival of the theme of the inadequacies of social democrats compared with communists. But he was equally concerned not to exaggerate the sum total of these matters. Thus he quoted rumours of further demobilization in the Soviet Armed Forces. And he did not think that there would be any fundamental departure from previous policy since 'Stalin and Molotov both attached primary importance to building up the economic strength of the Soviet Union, for which a long period of peace is needed, and ... Molotov again pledged the Soviet Union to full co-operation with the U.N.O.' He emphasized here, however, that Soviet conception of peace and international cooperation within the United Nations remained widely removed from Britain's: 'They seem all the time to be testing the Organisation to see whether it will work in conformity with Soviet interests'.[80]

Roberts' calm and sense of perspective contrasted sharply with the reactions of the Foreign Secretary. In March, for example, Bevin took quite seriously some unconfirmed American reports that Soviet troops were moving towards Tehran. 'This means war', he privately told the Chancellor of the Exchequer.[81] Perhaps it is not surprising that Sargent thought Bevin at this time 'slightly hysterical'.[82] Admittedly, the Foreign Secretary was now under much pressure and not least from his own Prime Minister. This should not have been altogether surprising to those who knew Attlee. It has to be said that Attlee's views on foreign and defence policy were nothing less than revolutionary. He regarded the continuation of Britain's great power role and the defence of her traditional interests as little short of absurd in the post-war circumstances of changed conditions of warfare, the country's economic weakness and the emergence of the United Nations Organisation. Attlee's radicalism found its most obvious targets in the Chiefs of Staff Committee, but the Foreign Office was clearly affected in the ensuing clash. When, on 2 March, Attlee challenged the assumption that it was necessary to safeguard the lines of communication through the Mediterranean and the Red Sea ('We must not, for sentimental reasons based on the past, give hostages to fortune.'),[83] Bevin had to step in to defend the entire basis of British policy, and indeed presence, in the Mediterranean area.[84]

It is remarkable that such arguments were taking place at a time when Anglo-Soviet relations were reaching their nadir in the post-war period. At the beginning of February Soviet leaders used the elections to the Supreme Soviet to make tough ideological speeches warning of capitalist encirclement. What was increasingly disturbing to Roberts, however, was the fact that Soviet attacks were being concentrated on Britain. In a telegram which was given Cabinet distribution, he reported on 23 February that it was 'hard to avoid the conclusion that the Soviet Government are deliberately stoking up an anti-British campaign'. The United States, he added, were at the same time being handled with great care. And he confessed to an 'uneasy feeling' that the Russians were perhaps preparing the ground for serious trials of strength with Britain.[85] Roberts was of course hardly in a position to predict that, in fact, the next crisis in Anglo-Soviet relations was going to be provoked by Winston Churchill. The ex-Prime Minister's 'Iron Curtain' speech on 5 March in Fulton, Missouri, led to bitter reactions in the Soviet Union. Roberts' own impression was that the Soviet authorities were 'much taken aback' by Churchill's frankness. He suggested that they were genuinely alarmed by the prospect of closer Anglo-American cooperation and that they feared, 'however illogically', the establishment of an Anglo-Saxon atomic bloc. Their natural reaction was to try to frighten British and American governments, and public opinion in both countries, with the bogey of their withdrawal from international cooperation. Referring to an outburst in *Pravda* following Churchill's speech, Roberts argued that it should not be seen as exclusively directed at American fear of pulling British chestnuts out of the fire. For it was perhaps also part of a campaign of intimidation covering Britain's global interests, intended to teach Britain that she must expect trouble is she failed to acquiesce in Soviet policy or to support Big Three collaboration on Soviet terms. 'On this assumption', Roberts speculated, 'the Soviet Union are not out to break the Anglo-Soviet alliance but to browbeat us into compliance with their requirements in return for a quiet life, for however short a period.'[86]

Once again, Roberts refused to see Soviet behaviour in apocalyptic terms. And once again the reaction in London was to disagree with him. This was particularly true in the case of Thomas Brimelow. He had by now established himself in the Northern Department as the chief commentator and critic of Roberts' despatches and telegrams. His long, mostly typewritten, minutes invariably display an attitude of keen interest rather than a routine approach to the subject. In this instance another long minute concluded with the suggestion that Roberts was wrong if he had implied that the Soviet government was holding out a hope of reconciliation. Brimelow thought it doubtful that the Russians would do so even on their own terms. He opined that so long as the Soviet Union was consolidating positions outside her own frontiers, she needed a potential enemy country of 'reactionary' tendencies. The British Empire fitted the bill perfectly. Churchill's speech was merely a windfall to the Russians who, for the time being, would depict the British as rogues and villains, 'and will continue to do so whether or not we give them provocation'.[87]

'I am afraid', Christopher Warner minuted after this, 'Mr. Brimelow's last para. is right.'[88] Warner had recently been promoted to the rank of Superintending Under-Secretary of the Northern and Southern departments. And Sargent had stepped into Cadogan's shoes, much to the delight of his friend Bruce Lockhart: 'He has a high sense of duty and, apart from having a keener mind, takes a far deeper interest in foreign affairs than Alec Cadogan.'[89] Sargent, Warner and Brimelow, together with Robin Hankey, the new head of the Northern Department, now formed a group of officials who were most closely involved with comment and analysis of reports from the Moscow Embassy. Such was the importance of the times, however, that by this stage almost every telegram and despatch from Roberts was also being seen by Bevin. The evidence of this is constituted by his initials on minute sheets and on Roberts' despatches themselves. Occasionally he would make some minimum comment, as he did when he wrote 'Very good' on a letter from Roberts to Warner of 2 March. The letter in question informed Warner that George Kennan, Roberts' opposite number in the United States Moscow Embassy, had recently communicated to Washington his ideas about the future of American-Soviet relations, with recommendations on the policy line.[90] Roberts had been authorized by Kennan to let the Foreign Office know of this development. And he gave the gist of Kennan's submission to Washington, which was 'that the Soviet Union is, and must be, fundamentally hostile to the outside capitalist world and, in particular, to America and to a social democratic Britain'. This had to be faced squarely and the western policy had to be framed realistically. However, 'although the Soviet union would neglect no opportunity to weaken us, she was not, like Hitler, out to destroy us, and provided we put our own house in order and maintained our strength there was no reason why we should not live in peace in the same world with the Soviet Union'. Roberts commented with evident satisfaction that while American policy under Byrnes was 'of course quite incalculable', at least for the time being the state Department seemed inclined to follow the realistic line advised by the American embassy in Moscow.[91]

Kennan sent his report on 22 February. It has become known, indeed famous, as 'The Long Telegram'. Even Roberts' very brief summary already suggests that in some respects the two men held strikingly similar views on the Soviet Union. In fact, Kennan privately joked to Roberts in this connection that there was no need to have in Moscow both the United States and British Embassies when just one would suffice.[92] Roberts, it so happened, was at this time preparing his own major assessment of the Soviet Union. Unlike Kennan, who had been specifically asked for his views and who eagerly seized a rare opportunity, Roberts was acting on his own initiative, as he had done so often in the past, addressing an audience in the Foreign Office which, on past record, was not waiting to be educated or persuaded.

He organized his thoughts in a series of three letters to Bevin, dated 14, 17 and 18 March, and numbered 181, 189 and 190 respectively. The first was received in the Foreign Office on 27 March and the last two a day later. All three subsequently received the K.C.D. printing (King, Cabinet and Dominions), representing the widest possible distribution, reserved for documents which were 'frightfully important, but not terribly secret.'[93] Letter 181 carries the 'Confidential' classification, while nos. 189 and 190 are classified 'Secret'.[94] Like Kennan's Long Telegram, they make compelling reading.

Certainly Roberts required little excuse for a fresh review of Soviet policy and the state of Anglo-Soviet relations. For, as he pointed out in his opening letter, this was 'a time when there is more anxious questioning concerning the present behaviour and ultimate intentions of the Soviet Union than at any period since the collapse of foreign intervention.' Casting his glance at the recent past, he began with the 'shadow of the atom bomb' and what the Soviet leaders, until then militarily confident, saw as the menace of an Anglo-American *bloc*, in the possession of this decisive weapon and thus capable of depriving the Soviet Union of the fruits of victory and even endangering her hard-won security. 'The Soviet Government seemed to feel that in such an atmosphere they could make no concessions, and, indeed, they soon began to counter-attack against Britain as the weaker member of what they regarded as an Anglo-American combination.' Existing difficulties in Greece, Persia, the Middle East in general and over the 'Western *bloc*' and the administration in Germany were intensified, while Soviet propaganda also turned its attention, for the first time, to questions such as India, Egypt and South-East Asian colonies. 'Above all', Roberts continued, 'increasing attention was devoted to the renewed Marxist-Leninist ideological campaign. Britain, as the home of capitalism, imperialism and now of social democracy, is a main target and is shown up as the centre of opposition to the progressive and forces of which the Soviet Union claims to be the chief patron.'

Constructing 'a sombre picture', Roberts was determined to leave out nothing from the catalogue of Soviet misbehaviour towards the West and Britain in particular. He drew attention to the Soviet attacks on British policy in Greece, and the brazen proposal of the Soviet ambassador in Greece for a Soviet base in the Dodecanese; there were also the Soviet attacks on British policy in Indonesia and the Levant; there was no agreement on Persia and a constant press campaign against alleged British actions in that country; there was already the semblance of an autonomous state in Persian Azerbaijan, set up by Soviet agents; there was the continued pressure on Turkey, concurrently with publicity for Armenian and Georgian territorial claims; there was the encouragement of 'national liberation movements' against Britain; there was, in Europe, the continued criticism of Allied military administration in Trieste; Western influence was being weakened in Poland, Yugoslavia, Hungary and Austria; there was a renewed Soviet interest in Spain, and encouragement of communist parties in Italy and, particularly, France; and most serious of all, Anglo-Soviet differences were also coming to a head in Germany where communists were being urged to advocate a united 'democratic' state in full control of the Ruhr.

What exactly, Roberts asked, stood behind the almost hysterical manner in which Britain was presently being attacked. His own impression was that 'the present Soviet push ... is partly an attempt to profit from the present fluid state of post-war Europe and the world, and from immediate post-war difficulties, but partly also an almost desperate effort to seize advanced positions and to dig in before the inevitable reaction against high-handed Soviet actions sets in with a return to more normal and peaceful conditions.' But it was not clear, Roberts conceded, to what extent Soviet actions and statements were purely tactical and to what extent they were the first steps in a carefully considered, long-term offensive strategy.

Accordingly, Roberts proposed to consider the essential factors in Soviet thinking and in the Russian national traditions. This he did in the second and the longest of the three letters. And he came to the point at the outset: 'There is one fundamental factor affecting Soviet policy dating back to the beginnings of Muscovite State. This is the constant striving for security of a State with no natural frontiers and surrounded be enemies.' Roberts considered this factor to be all-important. National security was at the bottom of Soviet policy, as it was in that of Imperial Russia, something which explained much of the high-handed Soviet behaviour and many genuinely held suspicions of the outside world. Western democracies, though shown in Soviet propaganda as weak and disunited, were presented to the Soviet people as the main dangers in a continued capitalist encirclement which before the war included Germany and Japan. There existed the danger, according to this party line, of capitalist countries uniting in an attack on the Soviet Union if only to distract attention from internal problems. The Soviet Union therefore had to be on her guard, she had to build up her industrial potential, maintain, even in peacetime, a strong military establishment, improve the air force and the navy and, above all, catch up with the West in the atomic energy sphere. It was perhaps safe to assume, Roberts suggested, that the rulers of Russia — Stalin, Molotov, Malenkov and Beriya — actually shared this view of the external world so sedulously propagated by the party. For they were brought up in the pure Marxist doctrine and they were for the most part ignorant of the outside world. This being so, they were in fact 'incapable' of believing in the same things which Western democracies believed in.

It is perhaps curious that Roberts should in his letter also take the view of the Kremlin as 'certainly incapable, in conducting international relations, of the give-and-take which is normal and, indeed, essential as between other States'. After all, the whole thrust of his previous advice had been that the West should state clearly to the Russians its vital interests, stand firm in defending them, but at the same time agree with them to observe each other's spheres of interest. The Soviet approach to international relations, Roberts now maintained, lacked even the minimum of good will and good faith. 'The Soviet Union . . . approaches a partner, whom she regards as potentially hostile, endeavours to exact the maximum advantage for the Soviet Union, if possible without any return, and having obtained what she wants, reopens this issue or raises another at the earliest possible moment in order to achieve the next item on her programme. There is, therefore, no degree of finality about any agreement reached with the Soviet Union, depite her much vaunted fidelity to international obligations.' Apparently anxious to ensure that this point was not lost, Roberts emphasized again that in the view of Soviet leaders 'relations with the outside world, and even alliances, are short-term arrangements for definite objectives, and can be modified or rejected as soon as they no longer suit the purpose of the Soviet Union.' However, he then introduced a new context: 'Although Soviet Russia intends to spread her influence by all possible means, world revolution is no longer part of her programme and there is nothing in internal conditions within the Union which might encourage a return to the old revolutionary traditions.' Clearly, by 'world revolution' Roberts meant to describe a political method, not the ultimate aim of Soviet leaders. This argument of course fitted in with his often expressed view that the West could, essentially, coexist with the Soviet

Union. And he thought in this connection that any comparison between the pre-war German menace and an existing Soviet menace had to allow for some fundamental differences. These included the fact that the Soviet Union, possessing a vast territory and all the primary products, lacked the motive force of pre-war Germany. Moreover, however much they were wedded to Marxist doctrine, the latter in fact allowed the rulers of Russia considerable flexibility in the areas of tactics and timing. The Russians 'do not charge into brick walls even when they have the necessary strength to break them down, but prefer to wait and find some means of either getting round or climbing over the wall'. There was thus hardly any danger of sudden catastrophe with the Russians, unlike with the Germans. And despite a certain Messianic strain in the Russian outlook, there was in Soviet Russia an absence, largely, of any sense of racial superiority or of a mission to dominate the world. 'Her methods are much more subtle and they aim at the ultimate creation of a Communist or Socialist society throughout the world in close communication of spirit with the Soviet Union. They do not call for open conquest and least of all for the launching of a war of aggression, except possibly for limited aims.'

In fact, despite his best efforts, Roberts found it impossible to see the Soviet Union as an immediately dangerous state. What clinched this belief was his perception of Soviet internal weakness, particularly in the economic structure: the Soviet Union, 'although confident in its ultimate strength, is nothing like so strong at present as the western democratic world, and knows it'. The Soviet leadership, on the morrow of the greatest Russian victories in history, had seen the opportunity to achieve their ambitions unless the capitalist world united against them and trumped the Red Army ace with the card of the atomic bomb. 'Basically,' Roberts continued, 'the Kremlin is now pursuing a Russian national policy, which does not differ except in degree from that pursued in the past by Ivan the Terrible, Peter the Great or Catherine the Great. But what would, in other lands, be naked imperialism or power politics, is covered by the more attractive garb of Marxist-Leninist ideology, which, in its turn, moulds the approach to world problems of statesmen whose belief in their own ideology is as profound as that of the Jesuits in their own faith during the Counter-Reformation.'

Roberts now proceeded to identify six main elements in the long-term policy of the Soviet Union:

(a) In the first place the Soviet Union would make every effort to turn herself into the most powerful state in the world, during which time she would also provide for her security. The search for security, however, was 'a constantly expanding process'.

Thus the domination of Persian Azerbaijan to protect the Baku oil would lead on naturally to the domination of Persia as a whole, to encouragement of a Kurdish republic, to the isolation of Turkey, and eventually to infiltration of the whole Arab world. 'In fact, Soviet security has become hard to distinguish from Soviet imperialism and it is becoming uncertain whether there is ... any limit to Soviet expansion.'

(b) A connected objective was to weaken capitalist or social-democratic countries in every way, which in Britain's case meant the encouragement of 'national liberation movements' in her colonies and in the Middle East. And any tendency by Western European countries to draw closer together would be bitterly opposed.

(c) Everything possible would be done to keep the United States and Britain apart.

(d) Communist parties everywhere would be supported and used to promote Soviet interests and ultimately to take power, while organizations such as the World Federation of Trade Unions would also be used for Soviet political ends.

(e) Social democracy, together with all moderate progressive forces, would be attacked as the main dangers to communism and so to the Soviet Union. 'These forces are regarded not so much as an ultimate alternative to communism but rather as an opiate for the workers, who, after they have received certain limited benefits which social democracy can offer, will no longer have the necessary incentive to carry through the revolution within their own countries.'

(f) Finally, the full weight of Soviet propaganda, and where possible active support, would be brought to bear in favour of the so-called oppressed colonial peoples. This was in line with orthodox Marxist teaching as well as Soviet national interests. From Stalin downwards the Soviet peoples were embarking on this campaign with the zeal of crusaders, believing sincerely that they were contributing to the progress of the world.

Although he had already described these Soviet policies as being of long-term character, Roberts did allow for a different interpretation. For it was difficult to decide, he admitted, how exactly to interpret them. Perhaps they represented mainly a 'tactical short-term campaign' to get the maximum advantages for the Soviet Union in the existing fluid state of international society, and to intimidate the West into renewed co-operation, but on the Soviet Union's own terms. However, there was a sense in which such analyses were not helpful: 'With a regime whose ultimate ambitions, although not its immediate aims, are unlimited and which views the world as a whole *sub specie aeternitatis*, much as the

Catholic Church might do, policy is probably not so clear-cut and the contrast between short-term tactics and long-term strategy may be unreal'.

Roberts concluded this letter by emphasizing that security was the first consideration with the Soviet Union and that, except as the result of a miscalculation of forces, she would not endanger the realization of her long-term projects by pressing immediate issues to the point of serious conflict. It was 'therefore possible, though difficult, to reconcile British and Soviet interests in any problem with which we are likely to be faced, granted the right mixture of strength and patience and the avoidance of sabre-rattling or the raising of prestige issues.'

There was of course nothing new in this last piece of advice from Roberts, for he had given it repeatedly over the previous year. As might have been expected in such an elaborate analysis, he had now devoted considerable attention to the ideological aspect of Soviet foreign policy. Evidently, however, this made not the slightest difference to his conclusion about the aims, tactics and methods comprised in that policy and what could be expected from it. In his third and last letter from the series, which considered 'the most important question of all, what British policy should be towards the Soviet Union', Roberts also offered some practical advice. He suggested that the first essential was to treat the problem of Anglo-Soviet relations in the same way as major military problems were treated during the war. Such an approach called for 'the closest co-ordination of political strategy, for a very thorough staff study embracing every aspect of Soviet policy ... This would mean the establishment of a team of experts covering the military, economic, social and political fields and drawing largely upon the knowledge of trade unionists and others who have had close experience of working with and often against Soviet representatives at international gatherings of Communists in Britain. This body, which need not necessarily be a large one, might be a standing sub-committee of the Cabinet offices, and its sole function would be to collate information and study and advise upon the Soviet Union.' Roberts saw the rationale for such a body behind the fact that of 'no other country is it harder to know the true position or to form an unbiased judgement.' All those responsible for formulating policy towards the Soviet Union would be enabled by the creation of the proposed body to face the real facts, however unpleasant at first sight, 'instead of being led astray as so often in the past by wishful thinking on the one hand or by extravagant suspicions and fears on the other'.

Roberts urged at the same time that there should be a campaign in Britain to educate the British public about the Soviet Union, the responsibility for which should be with the government and 'the editors in London'. But the most important factor in Britain's long-term strategy was to ensure that Britain, the Commonwealth, the colonial Empire, and those countries of western Europe and the near and Middle East whose fortunes were bound up with Britain's, 'should be healthy political and economic organisms, pursuing progressive policies, raising the standard of living of their peoples, and removing the causes of social strife . . . In fact, we should act as the champions of a dynamic and progressive faith and way of life with an appeal to the world at least as great as that of the Communist system of the Kremlin.'

This, of course, brought Roberts dangerously close to becoming a self-appointed political adviser on domestic British concerns. It is difficult to imagine that Sargent, who resided in the Conservative Club, could have welcomed such advice. At any rate Roberts quickly returned to the subject of Anglo-Soviet relations. Britain, in dealing with the Soviet Union, should base herself 'firmly on the principle of reciprocity, and give nothing unless we receive a counter-advantage in return'. Britain also had to be strong, and look strong, because of the 'absolute need' to earn and maintain Soviet respect. This strength, however, should not be paraded unnecessarily, Britain should never 'rattle the sabre', for there was the factor of Soviet susceptibility and prestige, and Britain should not make it difficult for the Russians to climb down without loss of face. But in order to be strong, Britain should cherish her special relationship with the Dominions, foster the 'natural community of interests' between herself and the democracies of western Europe, and support and strengthen her friends and allies in the Middle East. There existed for Roberts in this connection a further, paramount need: 'I cannot lay too much emphasis upon maintaining our special relationship with America in a form consistent with friendship with the Soviet Union. Whatever private differences may arise between us, America and the British Commonwealth must remain firm friends in the eyes of the Soviet Union, otherwise she may succumb to dangerous temptations.'

What, then, had happened to the idea of spheres of influence? It was still there, perhaps more explicitly so than ever before in Roberts' despatches. He brought it up again in the context of his argument for maintaining the Anglo-American special relationship, something which he thought the Soviet Union could not legitimately object to, although she would use her influence to retard it. 'Indeed', Roberts continued, 'if we were thinking simply in terms of Anglo-Soviet relations, these could probably be most solidly established on the basis of zones of influence in which we each left the other party free from interference or criticism within specified areas.' He did not elaborate and there was really no need to. In concluding this letter to Bevin, Roberts suggested that his advice 'may not seem a very inspiring policy and will indeed be a sad disappointment to those who had set their hopes of post-war Anglo-Soviet relations very high'. He ended, however, on an optimistic note: 'The many important interests we have in common, and most of all our joint determination that no other one Power shall ever become a menace to us both, should remain a solid bond, despite the deep gulf between our social systems.'

These three letters to Bevin constituted the most sustained presentation by Roberts, or for that matter by anyone else in the Foreign Office, of Soviet foreign policy and the ways to deal with it. They have been seen as the British version of Kennan's Long Telegram.[95] Roberts himself, indeed, has since stated that their preparation began partly because the embassy in Moscow knew the Americans were engaged in the same exercise.[96] What little scholarly comment Roberts' three letters have attracted, however, has been merely to note, almost in surprise, the similarities with the Long Telegram.[97] In fact, such comment understates the case. For Kennan's Long Telegram and Roberts' three letters to Bevin are in many ways virtually indistinguishable in terms of their premises and conclusions. Kennan argued in the Long Telegram, much as Roberts did, that 'Soviet power, unlike that of Hitlerite Germany, is neither schematic nor adventuristic. It does not work by fixed plans. It does not take unnecessary risks . . . Thus, if the adversary has sufficient force and makes clear his readiness to use it he rarely has to do so'. He recalled later that he was 'convinced' at the time 'that only when we had proven to the Russians that they could not get what they wanted without dealing with us, would they consent to deal with us.[98]' This, it is plain, was not a recipe for confrontation, but rather a method of avoiding it. And he suggested, as Roberts had already done several times, that the Soviets were still by far the weaker force, something which made their success 'depend on degree of cohesion, firmness and vigor which the Western World can muster'. Moreover, his idea of what motivated Soviet policy was identical to that held by Roberts: 'At bottom of Kremlin's neurotic view of world affairs is traditional and instinctive Russian sense of insecurity.' Like Roberts in this connection, Kennan saw the existing Soviet policy as 'only the steady advance of uneasy Russian nationalism, a centuries old movement in which conceptions of offense and defense are inextricably confused.'

Kennan did not actually propose in the Long Telegram a policy of the spheres of influence, but this was inherent in his analysis, though by no means as clearly so as with Roberts. He had in fact pleaded as early as February 1945 for a 'decent and definitive compromise', namely 'divide Europe frankly into spheres of influence – keep ourselves out of the Russian sphere and keep the Russians out of ours', rather than refusing to name the limit for Russian expansionism and Russian responsibilities, which only served to confuse the Russians and made them wonder whether they were asking too little or whether it was a trap.[99] In later years he also explained that he had seen 'an immense and tragic misunderstanding growing and being cultivated day by day; and I wished that we would begin to face up to the realities of the situation, so that the eventual shock of adjustment would not be too severe. This, incidentally, was why I favoured a complete sphere of influence policy.'[100]

Roberts, too, considered that a major analysis of Soviet policy was required because 'there were too many illusions about what kind of man Stalin was and what his policies were.'[101] Much more than Kennan, however, he attempted to give a picture of the Soviet Union as a country which, while definitely dangerous and implacably hostile, could nevertheless be dealt with, and lived with, given a rational response and sufficient strength on the part of the West. That is why he drew his important distinction between the ultimate objectives and immediate aims of the Soviet Union. Clearly, also, he was fascinated by the way in which Marxism-Leninism had blended with Russian nationalism. 'I was rather interested,' he has recalled, 'in this very interesting interweaving of the national policies with the ideological ones.'[102] Perhaps it was, to some extent at least, this particular interest which enabled him to offer such a measured analysis in his three letters to Bevin. There was another difference between Roberts and Kennan. 'Frank Roberts', Isaiah Berlin has commented, 'took a deep interest in the minutiae of what was likely to be relevant in foreign policy. George Kennan was not somebody who was particularly minutely observant of the turns and twists of Russian foreign policy ... Roberts had a much sharper eye, and was much more glued to the relevant facts than George Kennan was.'[103]

When compared with these letters, Kennan's Long Telegram is in every important respect similar or identical, but paradoxically it leaves a very different impression. It conveys a sense of urgency, almost alarm, which is lacking in Roberts' submission. Thus Kennan argued that the Soviet party line was 'not based on any objective analysis of situation beyond Russia's borders'; that the Russians had 'learned to seek security only in patient but deadly struggle for total destruction of rival power, never in compact and compromises with it'; that the Russian rulers had sacrificed, in the name of Marxism, 'every single ethical value in their methods and tactics'; that 'no one should underrate importance of dogma in Soviet affairs'; and that 'we have here a political force committed fanatically to the belief that with US there can be no permanent *modus vivendi*, that it is desirable and necessary that the internal harmony of our society be disrupted, our traditional way of life be destroyed, the international authority of our state be broken, if Soviet power is to be secure.' Such language has given rise to the interpretation that 'Kennan had placed so much emphasis on ideology, theology even, as to virtually ignore the role of realpolitik in shaping Soviet policy.'[104] But there is a sense in which this is quite misleading. Kennan, no less than Roberts, insisted that the monster of Soviet foreign policy should be viewed in its proper perspective. 'I would like to record my conviction', he wrote in the Long Telegram, 'that problem is within our power to solve – and that without recourse to any general military conflict.' And he went on to argue that the Soviet Union was not a country in the mould of Hitler's Germany, and that she was by far the weaker force gauged against the Western world as a whole. It is clear that, from this point of view, it did not really matter what the men in the Kremlin thought or believed in, or whether they had heard of *realpolitik*. What mattered was that, in the face of western strength and firmness, they would be forced to adjust their behaviour. Kennan, incidentally, proposed the same practical method of coping with the problem of Soviet policy as did Roberts in his third letter to Bevin: 'It should be approached', he suggested, 'with the same thoroughness and care as solution of major strategic problem in war, and if necessary, with no smaller outlay in planning effort.'

The question of who influenced whom in the Kennan–Roberts relationship is as unimportant as it is naively postulated.[105] With such highly intelligent men, their relationship can only be likened to two blades sharpening each other. Roberts has freely said that he was influenced by Kennan.[106] And Kennan has had no hesitation in admitting that he had derived instruction from his relationship with Roberts.[107] The real question concerns the extent to which they succeeded in influencing the policies of their respective countries. In the case of Kennan the answer is well known. The Long Telegram, whatever the original intentions of its author, provided the intellectual cement for the subsequent Cold War policy of the Truman administration, known as 'containment'. It is one of the most celebrated documents in twentieth-century diplomatic history. Roberts' three letters to Bevin are by comparison obscure. Certainly, there was no possibility that they would have the kind of sensational impact created in Washington by Kennan's Long Telegram.

The truth was that it hardly mattered to the Foreign Office what

Roberts was reporting from Moscow. In the first place, no one had asked him to put forward a large view on the nature and aims of Soviet foreign policy. The three letters to Bevin, moreover, contained nothing that was substantially new or different from his previous analyses of the subject. Finally, Sargent, Warner and Brimelow had in any case already taken different lines from Roberts on this question. Perhaps it was not altogether surprising, accordingly, that Soviet policy was now being discussed in London without any reference to the views of the Moscow Embassy. On 18 March, as the last of Roberts' letters began to travel slowly by bag, a meeting was held in Sargent's room at the Foreign Office, ostensibly to brief Sir Maurice Peterson, Clark Kerr's successor as Ambassador to Moscow. This was a meeting of some importance. Apart from Sargent, Warner, Hankey, Brimelow and Peterson himself, high-ranking officials from eight departments of the Foreign Office were present, as was Harold Caccia, the chairman of the Joint Intelligence Sub-Committee (JIC) of the Chiefs of Staff Committee.[108] There were excellent reasons for holding a major meeting at this time to discuss policy. The state of Anglo-Soviet relations was worse than at any stage since the war. And there had in fact been no clear-cut British policy towards the Soviet Union ever since Yalta. Even in the area of British strategic planning there existed no coherent conception whatsoever about a military strategy for the post-war world.

This was the background against which the meeting in Sargent's room proceeded to hold its 'general discussion of Russian policy and the British attitude towards it.' What it revealed was extraordinary confusion. A point that was made at the outset was that the extent to which Britain should counter Soviet policy in various areas depended on how vital the Chiefs of Staff considered those areas for the security of the British Commonwealth. It transpired, however, that the Chiefs of Staff had not yet considered this rather important question. There followed, according to the report of the meeting, a long discussion of the aims behind Soviet 'expansion' in the Middle East: 'Were they only after oil, or were the hoping to establish a defensive *glacis*, or were they pursuing an offensive and expansionist policy?' There is no reference in the report of the meeting to Roberts' long despatch on the Middle East from January. Amid this speculation Warner added his own: 'It was not just a question of Turkey or Persia. They [the Russians] were pushing much further afield. The probability was that their aim was not either economic or defensive or ideological, but all three combined.' The meeting discussed the possibility of establishing spheres of influence in Persia and politically neutral buffer states in the Middle East, but it was considered that the Soviet Union would not respect or be interested in such arrangements. Exactly why this would be the case is not stated in the report of the meeting. Pessimism was much in evidence. Thus it was agreed that Britain would have great difficulties in finding effective means to counter Soviet propaganda, especially in the Middle East, and that she could not count on steady support from the United States in any policy designed to oppose communism. Sargent, furthermore, raised the possibility of France becoming governed by communists after the next election. And, as it emerged that the Chiefs of Staff had never been asked to prepare a paper on Central Europe, 'it was contended that it would be unrealistic for us to try to hold Western Europe if the whole of Germany were under Communist control'.

There was also discussion whether the Russians were playing from strength or from weakness. 'Whatever their motives', Warner told the meeting, 'the Russians were completely unconstructive in their approach to international relations.' Warner's voice, in fact, was the loudest in this meeting. When Sargent suggested that a paper be put up on the subject of countering communist propaganda, Warner seized on this immediately and said that 'we should think out how to minimise, both by measures of defence and counter-offensive, the Russian attack which might be expected against this country.' By 'attack' he no doubt meant propaganda rather than physical assault. But the fear was also expressed that there existed the danger of an actual military development. At the end of the meeting Harold Caccia, in a grim mood, warned of a 'situation in which the Russians had to depend on their unaided judgement in deciding whether or not to carry through some act of foreign policy which might lead at once to a major war'.[109]

Roberts, of course, had in the past been at pains to stress that the Soviet Union required a period of peace in order to rebuild the economy. This was also the conclusion reached by the British intelligence. The JIC produced on 22 February a report entitled 'Russia's strategic interests and intentions' in which they took the view that the Soviet Union would not engage in a major war within the next five years![110] The purpose of the paper was 'to give the Chiefs of Staff, as a basis for planning, an expression of the J.I.C.'s estimate of what Soviet intentions and policy are!'[111] The reason why the Chiefs of Staff required at this time a major intelligence assessment of Soviet policy may well have been due to the fact that Attlee had on 21 January proposed dramatic cuts in manpower ceilings for the armed forces. He argued that there was 'no-one to fight'![112] Be that as it may, following the policy meeting on 18 March the Foreign Office sent four telegrams to Roberts, giving the gist of the JIC report and asking him to comment on its conclusions. He was also asked about the nature and aims of Soviet foreign policy, about Soviet policy in the Middle East and the Eastern Mediterranean, and about Soviet Policy in the Far East.[113] He replied with his customary speed and thoroughness in a series of four telegrams of his own.[114]

Roberts worked on these telegrams between 20 and 21 March. His three letters to Bevin had of course not been received yet in the Foreign Office, and there was little of substance that he could add to them. But now he was actually being asked for his views, as Kennan was a month earlier. It was a good opportunity to restate them, and he was not going to waste it. In the first telegram he agreed generally with the conclusion of the JIC paper, his main criticism being that it was perhaps misleading to distinguish between offensive and defensive Soviet moves and between long-term and short-term aims: 'The Soviet State whose policy is determined by a mixture of Marxist-Leninist ideology (the importance of this is perhaps underestimated in the paper) and Russian national traditions, does not plan its political moves step by step as Germany did. She has interests everywhere and plans for most eventualities, but her policies are entirely flexible . . . In the long run she thinks she is bound to win out and can afford to be patient.' This, of course, summed up Roberts' understanding of Soviet world outlook and policy. He agreed with the JIC conclusion that the Soviet Union would try to avoid a major war until the completion of her five-year plan at the end of 1950. He stipulated, however, that this estimate should be on the assumptions that Britain and the United States retained sufficient strength to discourage any Soviet adventures, and that the Soviet Union did not act now in the belief that she would later have to defend herself against a stronger and aggressive coalition. Roberts thought this second assumption unlikely, since Stalin himself had stated that three or more five-year plans would be needed to overtake the United States, and that the existing plan aimed to reach in 1950 only 150 per cent of the 1940 production, which was not particularly high.

Some of these thoughts were repeated by Roberts in his following telegram. He pointed out that, while the Soviet Union was in a hurry to achieve as much as she could in the fluid post-war situation, she would not consciously provoke a major clash on any single issue. And he emphasized that especially if only Britain seemed to stand in the way, a 'red light' would not be enough to 'realists in Kremlin', influenced as they were only by their assessment of the balance of forces. But provided the Soviet Union knew that there was strength and the determination to use it behind the red light she would stop in time. Present crises, Roberts thought, would no doubt abate provided the Soviet Union did not get too far involved in the Middle East through some miscalculation, and to that extent the crises were short-term. In the next telegram Roberts in fact concentrated on the Middle East (in the last of these telegrams, where the Far East was the subject matter, Roberts restricted himself to speculative comments, pointing out that the Moscow Embassy had few direct sources of information on Soviet policy in that area). He was convinced, 'and so is my American colleague', that the Soviet Union was attempting to secure an outlet on the Persian Gulf and to control South Persian oil. But these were not immediate objectives, the attainment of which at this stage would entail war with Britain and probably also with the United States. This risk, Roberts insisted, the Russians would not take. And he continued to entertain the idea of spheres of influence. The Soviet Union, he argued, would from Northern Persia try to extend her domination over whole Persia 'unless there is some prior Anglo-Soviet agreement on zones of influence.'

These four telegrams are often confused with Roberts' three letters to Bevin. The time factor separating the two sets of despatches is neglegible, however, and in any case they carried the same message. But it was not really the message that the Foreign Office wanted to hear. Commenting on the view of the Director of Intelligence, South East Asia, that the Soviet Union would seek to continually broaden the security belt around her frontiers, Hankey concluded that 'the moral of all this seems to be that appeasement won't pay. The more Russia gets the more she will want.'[115] Brimelow, moreover, inferred from Roberts' telegrams that 'Russian expansionism is likely to lead quickly to a serious clash of interests', and that 'in such circumstances the only safeguard of peace is the reluctance of both sides to go to war with one another and the shrewdness of the side which happens to be on the offensive in judging how far it can go without provoking hostilities'.[116] This, of course, was a complete misrepresentation of Roberts' position, since he had at no point suggested or even hinted that there existed an imminent and persistent danger of open clash with the Russians. But the mood in the Foreign Office was both bellicose as well as alarmist. Hankey wondered 'whether we can afford to allow a Power with so much ambition and such lack of scruple to control such colossal manpower and industrial potential.'[117] In a further minute Brimelow referred to the 'red light' sections in the third telegram by Roberts, and thought that the moral to be drawn from them seemed to be 'that so long as we allow the Soviet Union to keep the offensive, we stand to lose one position after another.'[118] This was another misleading comment in that the whole sense of Roberts's advice was precisely that the Soviet Union should not be allowed to keep the offensive.

Clearly, the Soviet Union was being likened to Nazi Germany, however much Roberts had tried to negate this view. By the time the Northern Department finished commenting on his recent telegrams, his three letters had also arrived. And for the first time there was something of a positive response to Roberts' proposals. This response did not, predictably, concern any of his analyses of Soviet international behaviour, but rather the suggestion he made in his third letter, that a team of experts be established to collate information and study and advise on the Soviet Union. Brimelow minuted that the proposal required and deserved 'the most serious consideration'. He complained that the arrangements for studying Soviet strategy and tactics were inadequate, with two people on the Russian desk spending their time doing current work. There was 'rarely any hard thinking on what the Russians are up to and what we ought to do.'[119] Indeed. Had Brimelow been even more observant he might have added that the only hard, sustained thinking of that kind had over the past twelve months been done by Frank Roberts. Hankey, too, liked the third letter to Bevin: 'I agree generally with Mr Roberts' conclusions and if they are approved will submit proposals regarding their implementation.'[120] There can be no doubt that he was referring to the proposal for the establishment of a team of experts. Warner, however, had different ideas. He disagreed with Brimelow and Hankey. Roberts had advocated, tentatively, a standing sub-committee of the Cabinet Offices to study and advise on the Soviet Union, and this was what Warner did not like: 'I doubt if there is a great deal to be gained by collecting information from outside sources other than service sources etc. For the purpose of collating and studying this information, and advice on policy, the J.I.C. and the Foreign Office and Chiefs of Staff are in my view the proper people.'[121]

In fact, by the time Warner had registered his protest on 5 April, a group of Foreign Office officials, including himself and Hankey, had on 2 April already formed what became known as the 'Committee on Policy Towards Russia' or the 'Russia Committee' for short.[122] It is not inconceivable that the establishment of this body was speeded up by Warner in order to make superfluous any serious consideration of Roberts' rival proposal. The idea behind the Russia Committee was undoubtedly his.[123] Roberts, on the other hand, has stated that 'the Russia Committee was partly my child'.[124] This is a fair comment given the circumstances of the Committee's creation.

But it is extremely doubtful that Roberts would wish his name associated with the initial premise of the Russia Committee. At the inaugural meeting on 2 April Warner 'recalled that the outcome of a recent meeting in Sir O. Sargent's room had been that a general paper should be put up to the Cabinet on policy towards the Soviet

Union, which it was clear had returned to pure Marx-Leninism'.[125] Such a dogmatic analysis would have been anathema to Roberts. All his efforts to explain the Soviet Union and her foreign policy had been in vain. In this complete and extraordinary refusal to accept the interpretations by the Moscow Embassy, Warner produced a memorandum entitled 'The Soviet campaign against this country and our response to it'. Here he identified and emphasized three points in the policy of the Soviet government: the return to the pure doctrine of Marx-Leninism; the intense concentration on building up the industrial and military strength of the Soviet Union; and the revival of the bogey of external danger. The Soviet Union had 'announced to the world that it proposes to play an aggressive political role, while making an intensive drive to increase its own military and industrial strength. We should be very unwise not to take the Russians at their word, just as we should have been wise to take Mein Kampf at its face value.' Warner conceded that the Soviet Union was war-weary, wanting a prolonged peace to build up her strength. But she was practising 'the most vicious power politics', and seemed 'determined to stick at nothing, short of war, to obtain her objectives'. In fact Warner went even further. In their use of military power, the Russians would 'have to rely on their own appreciation to judge how far they can go without making war inevitable. As in the case of Hitler and Poland, they could miscalculate.'[126]

There was clearly no room for compromise in this analysis. Warner emphasized that Russian aggressiveness threatened British interests all over the world. Britain had to defend herself, for 'concessions and appeasement will merely serve to weaken our position while the Soviet Union builds up her industrial and economic strength'. He proposed a 'defensive-offensive', a propaganda campaign not so much against the Soviet government as against international communism in order to expose it as totalitarianism. And he advocated that Britain should be prepared, as in the case of France, to consider 'exceptional measures' to strengthen the hands of her friends. The Soviet government, he concluded, 'have made it clear that they have decided upon an aggressive policy based upon militant Communism and Russian chauvinism'. In his view 'it would be in the highest degree rash to suppose that they will drop their policy of challenging this country, which they must regard as leader of Social Democracy and the more vulnerable of the two great Western powers.'[127]

It would be difficult to imagine an interpretation of Soviet foreign policy more hostile or pessimistic than Warner's. His memorandum constituted an implicit yet spectacular rejection of the views and recommendations from the Moscow embassy. It contained not a word about Soviet security considerations, Soviet fears and suspicions, the possibility of contolling and limiting the Anglo-Soviet conflict, and indeed about the chances of living peacefully together in the postwar world. Of all the Cold War, hardline British documents the Warner memorandum must rank as perhaps the most one-sided. And this despite the fact that a persistent flow of balanced analyses of the highest quality had been arriving from Roberts in Moscow over the past twelve months. The Foreign Office, clearly, had decided on a course of confrontation. If a precise date is sought to determine the birth of Britain's Cold War policy towards the Soviet Union, then 2 April 1946 is without any doubt the most appropriate.

It so happened that the date of Warner's memorandum coincided with a Chiefs of Staff report entitled 'Strategic Position of the British Commonwealth', their most important paper yet since the end of the war.[128] Although the two were unconnected, there is a sense in which the Chiefs of Staff submission was the military equivalent of Warner's memorandum. For it argued the need for an early strategic air offensive against the Soviet Union in the event of war and a 'forward' policy in such areas as the Middle East. This was something which would shortly be opposed by Attlee.[129] The Prime Minister was therefore highly unlikely to endorse Warner's hard-hitting memorandum. Only days earlier he had argued, in connection with the Greek situation, that there was a need for 'an agreement with Russia'.[130] This was more in tune with Roberts' ideas.

In fact Roberts may well have played a role in strengthening Attlee's stand at this time for a flexible, less ideological approach to the Soviet Union. On 9 April he wrote a letter to Sargent, reporting a conversation between Stalin and Bedell Smith, the new American ambassador to Moscow. Stalin had apparently thought it essential for the great powers to reach agreement between themselves on potentially controversial issues before they were placed before the United Nations Organisation. Bedell Smith's impression, according to Roberts, was that Stalin realised that the Soviet Union had gone rather too far recently, and that Churchill's speech was seen as the red light.[131] Now, this was a somewhat calmer view of the Russians and to his credit Sargent suggested that Roberts' letter should be passed on to Attlee 'with reference to the recent memo on Russian policy which we sent him the other day'.[132] Attlee must have been pleased to read this letter, while he merely approved that Warner's memorandum could be circulated to the Cabinet ministers who would be involved in discussions at a forthcoming conference of Dominions prime ministers. He stipulated that the memorandum could not be communicated to the

Dominions prime ministers themselves.[133] There is really no evidence whatsoever of any support by Attlee of the Warner memorandum.

But Warner was not going to be impressed by reports that Stalin was making conciliatory noises. 'We have foreseen', he wrote to Roberts on 1 May, 'that the Russians would pretty soon realise how clumsy they have been in the last few months, and would attempt to pull a velvet glove over their iron hand; and that public opinion and many important people both here and in America might well be misled into thinking quite erroneously that the iron hand had been discarded, or even that it had been a figment of the imagination of wicked Foreign Office and Foreign Service officials'.[134] Roberts of course hardly required lectures on this subject. Already on 21 March he reported that the Soviet government had recently made certain moves, such as the withdrawal from Manchuria and further demobilisation, which could be regarded as indicative of its desire to reduce international tension. He thought, however, that this was perhaps mere tactical preparation for the Security Council meeting. He emphasized that if, alternatively, these moves represented a more conciliatory Soviet attitude, this would have been the result of recent frank statements in Britain and America. But he warned that their effect would be completely undone if a special attempt were now made 'to show understanding for the Soviet case' as he gathered had recently been suggested by Henry Wallace in the United States.[135]

Such advice reflected yet again Roberts' view that firmness in dealing with the Russians was an indispensable prerequisite of conducting successful relations with them. The Northern Department now enthusiastically embraced this latest exposition of that view from the Moscow embassy.[136] But this was an approval entirely outside any context of the larger view held by Roberts. Certainly, the officials at the Foreign Office were not so imbecilic as to believe that he shared their view of the Soviet Union. When Roberts left Moscow briefly to be with Bevin for the Paris Council of Foreign Ministers he was 'begged' not to criticise to the Secretary of State the proposals for a defensive-offensive campaign against the Russians. Warner explained in this connection that 'what we have wanted is covering authority to go as far as may be necessary'.[137] No doubt he had in mind authority for clandestine actions against communism as well as propaganda. But his memorandum was not an overnight development. It represented the culmination of his and some of his colleagues' thinking about the Soviet Union over a period of many months. If deliberate exaggerations existed in the memorandum then deliberate exaggerations existed all along. And that was not the case.

Bevin was initially far from happy about the concrete proposals for anti-communist action which followed Warner's memorandum.[138] In May he could still maintain that 'he did not know what conclusion to draw as to the ultimate aim of Russian policy. It was dictated, he thought, partly by fear, partly by expansionism and partly by communist philosophy'.[139] Roberts would not have disagreed with this assessment. Increasingly, however, Bevin was to side with his officials on the question of what they saw as the Soviet threat and the methods to deal with it. Exactly how and why he did so is largely a matter of conjecture given that so few of his thoughts were ever committed to paper. This, in any case, eventually led him into a confrontation with Attlee following the latter's radical proposal for far-reaching negotiations with Stalin on all the problem areas in Anglo-Soviet relations. Breathing fire and fury he accused Attlee at the beginning of 1947 of 'surrender', of appeasement, of 'Munich . . . on a world scale'.[140] Bevin could not silence Attlee, but the Chiefs of Staff led by Montgomery did precisely that a few days later when they threatened a collective resignation if their military strategy, based on the assumptions of a hostile Soviet Union, continued to be rejected by the Prime Minister. Attlee then endorsed their strategy.[141]

The January 1947 clash between Bevin and the Chiefs of Staff on the one hand and Attlee on the other was merely the delayed outcome of the process of political and military thinking which was given separate expressions on 2 April 1946 and which was to set Britain on a Cold War policy towards the Soviet Union well before the same policy emerged in the United States. Roberts, who could not have been aware of the January *denouement*, was at this time still at his post. Sir Maurice Peterson, Clark Kerr's successor, had however finally arrived in Moscow on 17 May 1946 and was now the principal voice of the embassy. The new ambassador's view of Soviet foreign policy bore, in fact, important similarities to that of Roberts. In mid July, commenting on the apparent success of the Paris conference of foreign ministers, Peterson wrote to Bevin that the meeting had 'revealed once more how quickly and easily Soviet foreign policy, when met with firmness and when conscious of having over-reached itself, can be put into reverse'.[142] It was utterly predictable, in the light of this opinion, that Brimelow would find Peterson's analysis of Soviet policy 'perhaps over-optimistic'.[143] Roberts himself, it should be pointed out, had by early September apparently abandoned one of his previous recommendations, namely the pursuit of the policy of spheres of influence. He explained in a letter to Bevin that, quite apart from Britain's obligations to the United Nations Organisation and her relations with the United States, 'any attempt to reach an agreement on spheres of influence, for instance in Persia or in the Balkans, is dangerous in so far as our experience over previous agreements - e.g. Yalta, Potsdam, Poland, the Declaration on Liberated Europe, the Balkan Allied Control Commissions etc. - suggests that the Russians will take up to the limit of their share and will then advance further to whittle away our own'.[144]

This change was not really significant, since Roberts continued at the same time to see the future in terms of an East-West coexistence. Characteristically, he was not starry-eyed about this: 'We ... have no option but to accustom ourselves to a constant atmosphere of tension.' Any hope of achieving a 'general settlement' seemed 'illusory' to him. He was still convinced, however, that the Soviet Union would not take any risks which might lead to war. And he stressed again: 'Although the two worlds cannot, I fear, become friends, they can live side by side, and we can continue to work through practical agreements for definite and limited objectives in order to prevent this absence of friendship turning into active enmity'.[145] In a tediously long minute Brimelow pontificated, much as he had already done in connection with Peterson's views, that this talk of coexistence without active enmity was 'too optimistic'. Even Warner was forced to admonish Brimelow: 'I think an uneasy balance of power with ad hoc arrangements is attainable. I think this is what Mr Roberts means'.[146]

Unquestionably, Roberts meant precisely that. He has lived to see the East European revolutions of 1989 which have swept away that 'uneasy balance of power' to usher in a new era in European and world history. This has been achieved, as he advocated as early as April 1945, through the maintenance of Western Europe supported by the United States as the stronger and better half of the continent. There did not exist, in this sense, a fundamental difference between Roberts and the Foreign Office. Both were in favour of firm, tough policy towards the Soviet Union in the post-war period. Roberts, in fact, made his recommendation to that effect much earlier than the Foreign Office and at the same time provided an analytical background which the Northern Department was simply unable to match. 'We were not', he has emphasized, 'on different wavelengths. We in Moscow were advocating a realistic assessment which said "these people were hostile but if you handle them the right way you can live with them." The Northern Department was more hard-line'.[147] But the difference was not simply that Roberts was pragmatic while the Foreign Office was inflexible in the interpretation of Soviet foreign policy. The difference, in essence, was that Roberts refused to declare that meaningful diplomacy was dead in the face of a hostile Soviet Union, while the Foreign Office hardly saw anything beyond the Marxist-Leninist ideology of that country. Roberts' analyses of Soviet foreign policy were not, as Isaiah Berlin confirmed, 'animated by any obvious hostile bias. He did not attribute horrible motives to the Russians when the facts didn't support it'.[148] Perhaps it *was* too late in the spring of 1946 for the pursuit of spheres of influence and traditional *realpolitik* towards the Russians. But the fact remains that Roberts proposed such policies twelve months earlier when the situation was different. In July 1945, moreover, the premiership went to Attlee, a man much inclined to be open-minded about the nature of Soviet policy. There might have been a different British attitude in the early stages of the Cold War had Roberts held a more senior position in the Foreign Office. After all, there is no evidence at all that Stalin was not prepared, until September 1945 and maybe even January–February 1946, to engage in some kind of Big Three understanding.

This, of course, is not to say that the Cold War could have been altogether avoided. After 1945 the Soviet Union was strong enough to begin seriously contemplating the outside world as her potential prey. And there was the in-built animosity towards the West in the ideology of Marxism-Leninism. Roberts has commented in this connection: 'It is hard to think of any item in the various plans and programmes of Communism as institutionalized in the Soviet Union that does not assume a hostile bourgeois world which has to be defeated. It is, indeed, the ineluctability of that defeat that is at the heart of Communist thinking'.[149] But already in 1945 Roberts saw the present-day ruins of the Marxist-Leninist edifice. And he was one of the few not unduly alarmed by the prospect of the intervening period.

Notes

1. Lord Strang, *Home and Abroad* (1956), 173; Sir Roderick Barclay, *Ernest Bevin and the Foreign Office, 1932-69*, 1975, 30; John Colville, *the Fringes of Power: Downing Street Diaries, 1939-1955*, 1985, 671n.; Sir Anthony Eden, *Full Circle*, 1960, 153; Harold Macmillan, *At the End of the Day*, 1973, 178.
2. Walter Bedell Smith, *My Three Years in Moscow*, Philadelphia and New York, 1950, 239, 106; George F. Kennan, *Memoirs, 1925-1950*, Boston 1967, 289n.
3. Kenneth Young (ed.), *The Diaries of Sir Robert Bruce Lockhart, 1939-1965*, 1980, 707.
4. Barclay, 30; Young, 762.
5. Young, 708.

6. Colville, 674.
7. Young, 763.
8. FO 371/47860: N3013/20/38, letter Balfour to Warner, 16 January 1945. Unless otherwise indicated, all references are to documents in the Public Record Office, Kew.
9. Paul D. Quinlan, *Clash over Romania: British and American Policies towards Romania, 1938-1947* Los Angeles, 1977, 124-5.
10. FO 371/47941:N3934/1545/38, letter Clark Kerr to Eden, no. 211, 27 March 1945. See Richard Deacon, *The British Connection*, 1979, 196-208, for a thinly disguised but unsubstantiated picture of Clark Kerr as a Soviet agent.
11. FO 371/48192: R7333/81/67, memorandum 13 March 1945.
12. FO 371/47934: N3998/981/38, letter to Warner, 14 March 1945.
13. Deputy Under-Secretary at the Foreign Office and Director-General, Political Warfare Executive, 1941-45.
14. Young, 411-12, 415-16.
15. FO 371/47881: N4281/165/38, minutes Sargent, 2 April 1945; Cadogan, 4 April; Eden, 8 April.
16. FO 371/48217: R3459/3168/67, minute 6 March 1945.
17. FO 371/47860: N678/20/38, JIC(44)467(0). (Final.), 'Russia's Strategic Interests and Intentions From the Point of View of Her Security', 18 December 1944. The evidence of post-war intelligence papers, at least with regard to major reports, is normally not difficult to obtain and is constituted by references to them in other official papers, mostly those of the Chiefs of Staff Committee.
18. Young, 420-22.
19. FO 371/47860: N4102/20/38, minute 21 May 1945.
20. FO 371/47853: N5327/18/38. Subsequently Parker revealed himself as a fellow-traveller, publishing in 1949, in Moscow, his *Conspiracy Against Peace* in which he accused Frank Roberts of anti-Soviet activities. Roberts, who knew Parker at Trinity, recalls this in his article Soviet Policies under Stalin and Khrushchev: A Comparison based on Personal Experiences Between 1939 and 1962, *South Atlantic Quarterly*, **LXXII**, 1973.
21. Interview with the author, 31 March 1989.
22. Sir Frank Roberts in unpublished conversation with George Urban, 1988. I am grateful to Mr Urban for permission to use his material.
23. Young, 409. It is perhaps worth recording Sir Isaiah Berlin's views of Clark Kerr and Roberts: 'Clark Kerr was very impressionistic and romantic, and had all kinds of large ideas, some of which did or did not correspond with reality. Frank Roberts was much more cautious, much more suspicious of the intentions of the Soviet Union.' Interview with the author, 10 April 1989.
24. FO 371/47882: N4919/165/38.
25. Young, 179.
26. FO 371/47882: N4919/165/38.
27. FO 371/47882: N6645/165/38, minutes Sargent, 31 May 1945; Eden 1 June.
28. Alanbrooke, Diary, Liddell Hart Centre for Military Archives, King's

College, London, 5/11, entries for 13, 24 and 31 May 1945. The fact that the Joint Planning Staff report in question is not available, and that no record of this episode can be found in the minutes of meetings of the Chiefs of Staff Committee, is hardly surprising.
29. Something which was later confirmed by Brooke in 'Notes on My Life', vol. XIV, Liddell Hart Centre.
30. FO 371/47923: N6582/672/38, no. 358.
31. Young, 442-3.
32. FO 371/47855: N9416/18/38, 30 June 1945.
33. FO 371/47883: N12165/165/38.
34. FO 371/48192: R9256/81/67, minute Eden PM/45/202 to Churchill, 25 May 1945; PREM 3/379/3: M. 532/5, PM's personal minute 28 May 1945. The idea was originally suggested by Pierson Dixon, Eden's private secretary.
35. PREM 3/379/3: M.635/5, minute Churchill to Cadogan, 17 June 1945.
36. FO 371/47883: N12165/165/38, letter Clark Kerr to Eden, no. 468, 10 July 1945.
37. FO 371/50912: U5471/5471/70, memorandum dated 11 July 1945.
38. ibid.
39. FO 371/50912: U5471/70, minutes Jebb, 20 July 1945; Sargent, 31 July; Cadogan, 11 July; Eden, 12 July.
40. David Dilks (ed.) *The Diaries of Sir Alexander Cadogan, 1938-1945*, 1971, 759.
41. The Earl of Avon, *The Reckoning* 1965, minute 17 July 1945, 546-7.
42. Rohan Bulter (ed.), *Documents on British Policy Overseas*, I, series I, 1984, no.179, minute to Eden, 18 July 1945. For Attlee's views on this subject see Raymond Smith and John Zametica, The Cold Warrior: Clement Attlee reconsidered, 1945-7, *International Affairs*, **61**, no.2, Spring 1985.
43. FO 371/47883: N11605/165/38, letter to Warner, 27 August 1945.
44. FO 371/47883: N13784/165/38, letter to Clark Kerr to Bevin, no. 642, 6 September 1945.
45. Roberts in conversation with George Urban.
46. FO 371/47861: N13100/20/38, Moscow no. 4261 to Foreign Office, 22 September 1945; minute 23 September.
47. FO 371/47856: N13432/18/38, Moscow no. 67 Saving to FO, 28 September 1945.
48. FO 371/47856: N13432/18/38, minute 6 October 1945.
49. For the reactions in the Foreign Office to the Soviet demand for access and a base in the Mediterranean see FO 371/47861: N13101/20/38, minutes Dixon, 24 September 1945; Sargent 24 September; Cadogan, 25 September.
50. FO 371/47883: N4909/165/38, minute D.L. Stewart, 12 July.
51. FO 371/48184: R13220/81/67, brief for the new Secretary of State, 7 August 1945.
52. FO 371/50318: U7669/5559/70, minute Dixon, 1 October 1945.
53. FO 371/47857: N13964/18/38, letter 6 October 1945.
54. FO 371/47856: N13432/18/38, 12 October 1946.
55. Sir William Hayter, interview 7 April 1989. According to Sir Isaiah

Berlin, Sargent explained that his attitude served to enable him to preserve perspective and not be influenced unduly by any observations he might make abroad. (Interview with the author.)
56. FO 371/50920: U8353/5559/70, minute Bevin, 16 October 1945.
57. FO 371/47856: N13263/18/38, minute 13 October 1945.
58. FO 371/47857: N15072/18/38, minute Warner, 29 October 1945.
59. FO 371/47857: N15072/18/38, minute Cadogan, 31 October 1945.
60. CAB 129/1: CP(45)144, 'Future of the Italian Colonies'.
61. FO 371/47883: N15702/165/38, letter Roberts to Bevin, no. 799, 31 October 1945.
62. Now Lord Brimelow, he was between 1973 and 1975 Permanent Under-Secretary at the Foreign and Commonwealth Office.
63. Interview with Lord Hankey, 23 May 1989.
64. Otherwise an Oxford don, Berlin was during the war engaged at the Washington embassy's Survey Section in producing weekly political summaries.
65. FO 371/47883: N15702/165/38, minutes Brimelow, 20 November 1945; Warner, 3 January 1946.
66. FO 371/47858: N16807/18/38, letter Roberts to Warner, 27 November 1945.
67. FO 371/47858: N16807/18/38, minute 23 December 1945.
68. Young, 512.
69. FO 800/303: letter Clark Kerr to Bevin, 4 October 1945.
70. FO 800/501: SU/45/40/A, Moscow no. 5151 to FO, 29 November 1945.
71. Piers Dixon (ed.), *Double Diploma: The Life of Sir Pierson Dixon, Don and Diplomat*, 1968, 199.
72. FO 800/501: SU/45/77, minute 21 December 1945.
73. FO 371/48219: R21263/5063/67, memorandum 12 December 1945.
74. CAB 133/82, records of private two-party conversations, minute 2, 18 December 1945.
75. CAB 133/82, record of a conversation at the American Ambassador's residence, 17 December 1945.
76. Lord Hankey, interview 23 May 1989.
77. FO 371/56763: N4156/97/38, letter to Bevin, no. 189, 17 March 1946.
78. FO 371/52327: E797/797/65.
79. CAB 128/5: CM(46)7, 22 January 1946.
80. FO 371/56780: N1965140/38, Moscow no. 606.
81. Hugh Dalton diary, British Library of Political and Economic Science, entry for 22 March 1946.
82. Young, 531. This was an opinion shared by Anthony Eden who was being frequently consulted by Bevin (Young, 526).
83. CAB 131/2: D.O.(46)27, 'Future of the Italian Colonies'.
84. CAB 131/2: D.O.(46)40, memorandum 13 March 1946.
85. FO 371/56780: N2466/140/38.
86. FO 371/56781: N3315/140/38, Moscow no. 987 to FO, 11 March 1946.
87. ibid., minute 13 March 1946.
88. ibid., minute n.d.
89. Young, 520. Bruce Lockhart commented at the same time, however, that in some respects Sargent was 'even more traditional than Alec

[Cadogan] and would sooner have the biggest F.O. "dud" than the best outsider'.
90. Like the British embassy, the United States Moscow embassy was experiencing an interregnum: the last ambassador, Averell Harriman, had departed and the new one, Bedell Smith, had yet to arrive.
91. FO 371/56840: N3369/971/38.
92. Interview with Sir Frank Roberts, 31 May 1989.
93. Interview with Lord Hankey, 22 May 1989.
94. FO 371/56763: N4156/97/38, no. 181; N4065/97/38, no. 189; N4157/9738, no. 190.
95. *Foreign Relations of the United States*, 1946, vol.vi, Washington 1969, 696-709.
96. Interview with the author, 31 March 1989.
97. The following is a list, in chronological order of publication, of some works which have drawn attention to the shared outlook of Roberts and Kennan: Peter G. Boyle, The British Foreign Office View of Soviet-American Relations, 1945-46, *Diplomatic History*, 3, 1979, 310; Terry H. Anderson, *The United States, Great Britain, and the Cold War, 1944-1947*, 1981, 106; Robert M. Hathaway, *Ambiguous Partnership*, New York, 1981, 369-70; Victor Rothwell, *Britain and the Cold War, 1941-1947*, 1982, 247; D. Cameron Watt, *Succeeding John Bull*, 1984, 110n; Ritchie Ovendale, *The English-Speaking Alliance*, 1985, 38; Fraser J. Harbutt, *The Iron Curtain* 1986, 129; Bradford Perkins, Unequal Partners: The Truman Administration and Great Britain in Wm. Roger Louis and Hedley Bull (eds.), *The Special Relationship: Anglo-American Relations since 1945*, 1986, 53; John Lewis Gaddis, *The Long Peace*, 1987, 45n; James L. Gormly, *The Collapse of the Grand Alliance, 1945-1948*, 1987, 144.
98. *Encounters with Kennan*, 1979, 51.
99. Charles E. Bohlen, *Witness to History, 1929-1969*, 1973, 175.
100. George F. Kennan, The View From Russia, in Thomas T. Hammond (ed.), *Witnesses to the Origins of the Cold War* 1982, 30.
101. Interview with the author, 31 March 1989.
102. ibid.
103. Interview with the author.
104. Daniel Yergin, *Shattered Peace*, 1978, 169.
105. Various interpretations, however, have been offered. Lucius Clay, the American general, apparently regarded the Long Telegram as following the 'British Line', and as a success for 'The British technique of needling our people over a period of months'. See Yergin, 212. On the other hand Roberts has recently been described as 'of the same frame of mind as Kennan, by whom he had been influenced', see Hugh Thomas, *Armed Truce*, 1986, 530.
106. Interview, 31 March 1989.
107. Letter to the author, 6 April 1989.
108. A body composed of the three directors of intelligence from the armed forces, heads of M15 and M16, the head the Joint Intelligence Bureau,

and a Foreign Office official as its chairman.
109. FO 371/56832: N5572/605/38, "Report of meeting in Sir Orme Sargent's room on the 18th March, 1946, to brief Sir Maurice Peterson."
110. ibid. The paper in question is J.I.C.(46)1(0) (Final Revise). Although not available for inspection, the conclusion of this JIC analysis can be ascertained from a subsequent JIC report which stated that the Soviet Union had 'resumed the traditional Russian policy of southern expansion ... The Soviet Government will implement this historic policy by every means short of war. Their ultimate goal is clear, but the intermediate moves will be opportunist and their order of priorities flexible.' DO 35/1604: J.I.C.(46)38(0) (Final Revise). 'Russia's Strategic Interests and Intentions in the Middle East', 14 June 1946. It should perhaps be pointed out here that the JIC were in this Middle East report reduced to virtually copying, without acknowledgement, entire paragraphs from Roberts' Moscow despatches. Compare, for example, paragraph 9 of his letter to Bevin of 16 January 1946 (quoted above) with paragraph 13 of the JIC report. They are almost identical. This was a great compliment to Roberts, but a sad comment on the JIC's own intelligence on the Soviet Union.
111. FO 371/56831: N3756/605/38, minute Michael Creswell, n.d., *circa* 26 March 1946.
112. CAB 131/1: DO (46) 3rd Meeting.
113. These telegrams, nos 759, 760, 761 and 762, dated probably 20 March, are not available for inspection.
114. FO 371/56831: N3742/605/38, no. 1090; N3799/605/38, no. 1091; N3812/605/38, no. 1092; N3756/605/38, no. 1093. These are all dated 20 March 1946.
115. FO 371/56831: N4193/605/38, minute 30 March 1946.
116. FO 371/56831: N3742/605/38, minute 23 March 1946.
117. FO 371/56831: N3756/605/39, minute 25 March 1946.
118. FO 371/56831: N3799/605/38, minute 24 March 1946.
119. FO 371/56763: N4157/97/38, 29 March 1946.
120. ibid, minute, n.d.
121. ibid, minute, 5 April 1946. Warner advised in this minute that if his view prevailed the despatch from Moscow should not be given the King and Cabinet distribution. One can only speculate that he did not wish the Cabinet to seize on Roberts' proposal which, if implemented, would entail a dilution of the Foreign Office influence. In a futher minute on 9 April, however, Warner suggested that the passage containing the proposal be omitted from the printed version. This was done.
122. It is curious that Warner failed to mention this development in his minute of 5 April. Nor did Brimelow and Hankey, when they welcomed Roberts' proposal, betray any knowledge that an internal Foreign Office committee on Soviet policy was about to start functioning. There is no clear indication in the record of the policy meeting in Sargent's room on 18 March that any such step was contemplated, although Warner did refer to the need for thinking out

how to minimize Soviet attacks on Britain by measures of defence and counter-offensive. The circumstances surrounding the establishment of Committee remain somewhat obscure while the relevant documents are still closed. Lord Hankey's opinion about the continuing secrecy in this matter should perhaps be recorded here: 'The Foreign Office will never release some of the Russia Committee papers. You can take it from me.' Interview, 23 May 1989.
123. In 1948, writing to Jebb, Warner recalled that the Committee had been set up at his insistance, the idea being that 'the Under-Secretaries should pool recent information regarding Russian doings affecting their various areas in order to get a collated picture *and* consider what action, political, economic or in the publicity sphere should be taken as a result'. FO 371/71687: N12649/765/38, 22 November 1948.
124. Interview with the author.
125. FO 371/56885: N5169/605/38, 'Soviet Policy Co-ordination Meeting'.
126. FO 371/56832: N6344/605/38, 2 April 1946.
127. ibid.
128. CAB 131/2: DO(46)47.
129. CAB 131/1: DO(46)10th Meeting, 5 April 1946.
130. CAB 131/1: DO(46)9th Meeting, 27 March 1945.
131. FO 371/56832: N5502/605/38.
132. ibid., minute n.d.
133. ibid., minute Leslie Rowan to Dixon, 20 April 1946.
134. FO 181/1023: File 2 [504].
135. FO 371/56831: N3888/605/38, Moscow no. 1114 to FO.
136. ibid., minutes Brimelow, 24 march, and Hankey, 25 March 1946.
137. FO 181/1023: File 2 [504].
138. For this see Raymond Smith, A climate of opinion: British officials and the development of British Soviet policy, 1945-7, *International Affairs,* **64**, no. 4, Autumn 1988.
139. FO 371/55587: C5822/131/18, PMM(46)16, confidential annex, 21 May 1946.
140. FO 800/476: ME/47/4, minute Bevin to Attlee, P.M./47/8, 9 January 1947.
141. Smith and Zametica.
142. FO 371/56887: N15843/5169/38, no. 536, 16 July 1946.
143. FO 371/56834: N9460/605/38, minute 26 July 1946.
144. FO 371/56835: N11644/605/38, no. 684, 4 September 1946.
145. FO 371/56835: N11298/605/38, Moscow no. 2875 to FO, 4 September 1946.
146. ibid., minutes Brimelow, 9 September 1946; Warner, n.d.
147. Interview with the author.
148. Interview with the author.
149. Interview with George Urban.

3 Duff Cooper and the Paris Embassy, 1945-47
John W. Young

When Ernest Bevin became Foreign Secretary in July 1945, Alfred Duff Cooper had already been Ambassador to France for over eighteen months. In November 1943 he had been made Britain's representative to Charles de Gaulle's 'Committee of National Liberation' in Algiers, moving to Paris in September 1944, after its liberation from the Germans. Duff Cooper was identified very much by then with the pro-Gaullist position of the Foreign Office regarding policy towards France, which contrasted with the more critical attitude towards de Gaulle taken by the Prime Minister, Winston Churchill. After July 1945, however, even with Churchill gone, the Ambassador remained critical of London's attitude towards France. He became, indeed, the greatest critic of Foreign Office policy in Western Europe in the early post-war years and a leading advocate of an alternative policy of British-led European unity. He was, it may be argued, a visionary whose policies, if pursued with conviction, could have strengthened Britain's role in the world far more than was the case in subsequent decades. An alternative, less kind interpretation is that he was a parochial, narrow-minded thinker, whose proposals were over-influenced by his own desire to make the Paris Embassy the crowning glory of his diplomatic and political career.

Duff Cooper had not been new to the world of diplomacy in 1943. Between 1919 and 1923 he had himself been a Foreign Office official, before setting out on a political career. He entered parliament in 1924 and rose in the Nationalist government of the 1930s to become Secretary for War, in 1935-7, then First Lord of the Admiralty. A popular minister and able Commons speaker, he added to his reputation in 1938 by resigning over the Munich agreement, and was made Minister of Information by Churchill in 1940.[1] It was a vital position in wartime in which, however, Cooper failed to impress, and in 1941 the Prime Minister was forced to move him, to become Chancellor of the Duchy of Lancaster, where his exact responsibilities were never clear. Although Churchill continued to believe that Duff Cooper had a promising future in the Conservative Party, it was partly in order to replace him as Chancellor of the Duchy that the Prime Minister was willing to agree, two years later, to a proposal that Cooper should become Britain's representative to the French Committee of National Liberation. Cooper, exasperated with his position in London, and a convinced francophile (he had written a biography of Talleyrand in 1932), accepted the position with little hesitation.[2] Churchill, in a letter to Cooper in October, made plain his own view that, although there should be 'a strong France friendly to Britain and the U.S.A.', Charles de Gaulle was not the ideal person to lead it, being 'a man Fascist-minded, opportunist, unscrupulous, ambitious to the last degree . . .'[3] (a view shared by the American President, Franklin Roosevelt). But in 1943-4 Duff Cooper remained true to the Foreign Office approach of supporting the nationalist general de Gaulle as the best representative of the French nation, a line which eventually triumphed when de Gaulle was recognized as French President by both Britain and America in October 1944.[4]

Despite the unity between Duff Cooper and the Foreign Office on the support that should be given to de Gaulle, it was already evident by the end of 1944 that differences existed between them on the future development of cooperation with France and Western Europe. These differences revolved around the idea of the so-called 'Western bloc' and remained important long after Bevin became Foreign Secretary. Before the war there had been only a few advocates of greater European 'unity' (though two men who had taken an interest in such ideas in the inter-war years were Churchill and Bevin) but Hitler's victories in the West in 1940 had greatly increased the attraction of, at the very least, a future West European alliance. The exiled leaders of Belgium, Holland and Norway, who had fled to London, all hoped for some form of 'Western bloc', with close British involvement, after the war. Duff Cooper was an early advocate on the British side of such ideas, and on 30 May 1944 had sent a long despatch to the Foreign Secretary, Anthony Eden, arguing that the British should build military, political and economic links to Europe because of the likely Soviet menace after the war. The Ambassador felt it unlikely that the Americans would step forward to face the Russians, pointing to Washington's isolationist tradition and reluctance to become involved in Europe's 'balance of power' politics. Cooper sent copies of his memorandum to various other politicians and officials and won some sympathy for his views, but Eden told him that an overtly anti-Soviet 'Western bloc' had to be rejected and that cooperation with Britain's two major allies, America and Russia, must be preserved if peace was to last in the post-war years. To

Duff Cooper and his biographer this presented a 'cold shoulder'[5], but a full look at the Foreign Office records reveals that the Ambassador 'could claim credit for initiating discussion of the Western group idea, and was wrong to think that the views which he urged on Eden . . . made little impression . . .'.[6] The fact was that the 'Western bloc' *did* win Foreign Office support for a number of reasons: it would strengthen Britain's hand in the world if she was the leader of all the West European nations; a continental alliance would also provide Britain with a 'defence in depth' and prevent a repetition of the events of 1940; and it would be an important element in forestalling any future German militarist revival. Other supporters of the idea included the Chiefs of Staff and the Labour leader, Clement Attlee. The reason that Eden criticized Duff Cooper's arguments was not because of the bloc itself, but because of Cooper's overt anti-Sovietism. The Foreign Office, taking a wider view of events than the Ambassador to France, was keen to preserve cooperation among the 'Big Three' after the war, and build a new international system upon the United Nations, rather than to show a premature lack of faith in their Russian ally. The Western bloc must fit into this wider framework.

As it was, the Office was unable to pursue a Western bloc in any form in 1944–5, for two main reasons. First, the Prime Minister himself was opposed to the proposal, because he feared that Britain's resources would be drained if she became the paymaster of a continental alliance system (as was likely, given the vast reconstruction problems facing Europe). Churchill *was* willing to pursue a French treaty — the necessary basis of any wider bloc — but here the second problem came into play: the reluctance of Charles de Gaulle to make such a treaty until the British had demonstrated a genuine desire to cooperate with France on what he saw as vital issues. In particular the French leader wanted the British to support France's position in the mandates of Syria and Lebanon (where he was convinced that Britain wanted to make use of Arab nationalism to take control of both states) and he wanted an Anglo-French agreement on the fate of post-war Germany (which he wished to see truncated, federalized and forced to pay large reparations). On neither issue was London willing to satisfy him. The British, concerned with their own position in the Middle East, were unwilling to antagonize Arab nations by supporting France: whilst in Germany they feared that a hard-line policy could provoke a nationalist backlash and harm the whole European economy. Discussions on a treaty in December 1944 and April 1945 came to nothing, and in May the prospects for an alliance were dimmed markedly when a clash between French troops and the Arabs in Syria led British forces to intervene in the country to restore order, a move which humiliated and outraged de Gaulle and which sounded the death-knell for French rule.[7] Certainly Duff Cooper had *some* reason to criticize Whitehall for 'lukewarmness' on continental cooperation. In particular, in July 1945, a discussion of possible economic cooperation with Europe revealed that the economic ministries, the Treasury and Board of Trade, had no liking for a West European customs union, because of its practical difficulties, and that their preference was for a global, 'multilateralist' approach to world trade.[8] But in the Foreign Office the Western bloc remained as popular as ever as Labour came to power. The briefs for the Big Three summit at Potsdam, and minutes by leading officials, all revealed support for the bloc as a way to control Germany and strengthen Britain's world role, though there were some fears that it could upset the Americans (with their preference for the United Nations, rather than any division of the world into 'spheres of influence') and the Russians (who might fear that such a system was aimed against them).[9]

Duff Cooper's period as Ambassador to Paris after Churchill's election defeat fall naturally into four phases: first, between July 1945 and February 1946, a period when Anglo-French relations were dogged by continuing problems over the Levant; next, down to December 1946, a phase where differences over Germany remained in the fore; then the three months down to March 1947 which saw the making of an Anglo-French alliance; and, finally, Cooper's last months as an ambassador, down to December 1947.

Bevin reviewed British policy towards Europe soon after the Potsdam conference, on 13 August 1945. With Churchill gone, Foreign Office officials now hoped to press on with the Western bloc at last and Bevin did not disappoint them. Although he was concerned to see, like Eden, that a Western bloc did not antagonize Stalin, the new Foreign Secretary declared that his long-term aim was to build up wide-ranging cooperation — military, political, economic, commercial — with all the states of Western Europe. It seemed that the time for Duff Cooper's vision of continental cooperation had come.[10] The Ambassador himself had actually written to Bevin on 31 July offering to give up the Paris Embassy since, as an ex-Conservative minister, he did not expect to hold office under the new Labour administration. But Bevin had decided to retain Duff Cooper's services: there was no socialist 'scourge' of the foreign service,[11] and in Cooper's case the decision was probably reinforced by his popularity in France, as well as that of his wife, Lady Diana. The couple were certainly well liked by Bevin, and he had made a point of asking Cooper to attend the 13 August meeting — an invitation which delighted the

Ambassador.[12] After the meeting Cooper returned to Paris full of great expectations for the Anglo-French alliance. Bevin had not only given this support to a Western bloc, but had also seen the need to base this 'grand design' upon a sound French alliance; he had declared himself eager to end all personal animosities with de Gaulle, and was ready to seek a settlement to the Syria-Lebanon problem.

On 14 August Duff Cooper visited the French Foreign Minister, Georges Bidault, and told him that Britain wanted to help France's economic recovery, resolve differences with France over the Levant and Germany, and sign a treaty of alliance. Bidault, more keen than de Gaulle to cooperate closely with Britain, was as enthusiastic as the Ambassador, and talked of making such a treaty within a month.[13] This enthusiasm, however, did not last long. It was to be six months before the Levant problem was removed as an obstruction to an Anglo-French alliance; eighteen months before an alliance was actually made. Initially the Foreign Office was somewhat offended by Duff Cooper's approach to Bidault, because Bevin had not yet satisfied himself that Russia would agree to a Western bloc.[14] The Ambassador's action revealed his exasperation at past delays, his determination to pursue his own vision of British foreign policy — with Paris at its centre — and his desire to brush the practical problems with this aside. Having failed to crown his political career with a successful ministerial performance, Cooper was determined to crown his ambassadorial position with a major diplomatic success, in the form of a French alliance, and his behaviour on 14 August was not the last occasion that he was to show such impatience. Even before the war he had told his wife 'I should like to finish up ambassador in Paris', and he was determied to make the post the pinnacle of his career.[15] The advent of the Labour government could only have heightened his desire for swift successes, before he was replaced, but the period 1945–6 was to prove one of exasperations: 'I began . . . to think that work and frustration would kill Duff', his wife later recalled. 'The Anglo-French alliance was making haste very slowly. Generally there was a crisis . . . There was the Ruhr and Syria (Duff's most barbed thorn)'[16] Bevin's early attempts to begin talks on the Levant — the 'most barbed thorn' — were rebuffed by de Gaulle, and it was not until mid-September that real moves towards a settlement of this problem began. Bidault was in London at that time to attend the first Council of Foreign Ministers (CFM) on European peace treaties, and, away from de Gaulle, was able to develop a moderate policy on Syria-Lebanon. The British were willing to accept the first proposal, but the second idea caused some debate in the Foreign Office and brought further delays.[17]

Duff Cooper, as ever, tried to hurry the discussions, suggesting that Bevin might reassure de Gaulle by making a public 'declaration of intent' to pull British troops out of the Levant, but this was felt likely by the Foreign Office to offend Arab opinion.[18] Eventually an agreement was made on the French lines, and signed on 13 December, but hardly had this occurred before de Gaulle broke off talks on its execution, differences over its interpretation having convinced him once more that the British wanted to take control of Syria–Lebanon themselves. As a result the Levant issue was not settled until February 1946, when it was taken by the Arab nations before the United Nations. Here majority support was given to a resolution calling for a complete Anglo-French withdrawal, which Bevin had no hesitation in accepting. The French, too, agreed to leave, thus removing a problem which had succeeded in delaying Bevin's — and Duff Cooper's — hopes in Western Europe for six months. France's surprisingly easy acceptance of the United Nations solution, however, had much to do with an equally important event for Anglo-French relations: the resignation of General de Gaulle, on 20 January 1946.

In mid-1945, at the height of the Levant crisis and with the Anglo-French treaty endlessly delayed, Cooper and the Foreign Office would have welcomed de Gaulle's losing power in Paris, and there were indeed expectations that this might occur.[19] By Janury 1946, however, de Gaulle seemed more secure, the initial Levant crisis was well past, and, though the General's resignation could have been expected to improve Anglo-French relations, Duff Cooper completely failed to predict it. There were certainly good reasons for this failure: the General had apparently established his authority over the political parties, following the first post-war general elections in late 1945; he kept the plans for his resignation from even his closest colleagues, including Bidault; and though there were undoubtedly grave problems facing him — over economic recovery, a new constitution, and the power of the political parties — the moment did not exactly seem opportune to resign. (It was generally felt, later, that he hoped to be recalled to power immediately, by popular outcry.) Duff Cooper had also suffered from influenza for a few days before the resignation and thus was removed from the mainstream of political events in Paris. But his failure to predict such a significant event was doubly embarrassing by the fact that he had earlier dismissed rumours, which had reached Bevin, that the General *would* resign. For a time Cooper feared that he might be removed by Bevin for this error but there is no evidence that the Foreign Secretary even considered this.[20]

Throughout the period from August 1945 to February 1946 (when the Levant problem was effectively removed) Bevin and the

Foreign Office continued to support their long-term vision of West European cooperation, and there were pressures for more visible signs of progress on the 'western bloc' from individuals, like Lord Vansittart (former head of the Foreign Office), from Conservative MPs in the Commons, and from continentals, such as the Belgian Foreign Minister, Paul-Henri Spaak. During the same period Bevin was assured by the Russians that they (despite the attacks in the Soviet press) had no objection to an Anglo-French alliance and wider European cooperation.[21] There seemed every reason in March 1946, therefore, to expect greater progress on Bevin's proposals of August 1945 for European unity, and, indeed, attention was focused once more on an Anglo-French treaty in the Foreign Office. A draft Cabinet paper on the treaty, originally drawn up in November, was circulated around officials,[22] and Duff Cooper contributed to the revived debate with a lengthy despatch from Paris, which revealed the essence of his thinking on British foreign policy and which deserves detailed discussion.

For all its repetition of earlier ideas, Duff Coopers telegram of 19 March 1946 (which was given Cabinet circulation three days later) must be seen as one of the most important despatches he sent to London during Bevin's period as Foreign Secretary — and the main statement of his belief in European cooperation, centring on France. Inevitably Cooper recalled his earlier despatches, particularly that of 30 May 1944 from Algiers, and repeated his arguments from there. The first was that the United Nations was likely to fail as a basis for world peace, because of 'the reluctance of all nations . . . to go to war, unless they are convinced that their own vital . . . interests are at stake', so that Britain must rely on a policy of alliances to defend its interests (the third alternative, that of isolationism, being unthinkable). Secondly, Duff Cooper argued that, once Britain did begin to look for a suitable ally she had to rule out the United States, partly because of its anti-colonialism (it was unlikely to defend Britain's imperial interests), partly because it did not share Britain's interest in Europe, but also because of its historic tradition of isolationism (the Ambassador cited American reaction to Churchill's recent Fulton Speech as further evidence of this). Cooper then went on to argue that, though ideally a policy of cooperation with Russia should be pursued, the Soviet Union was the obvious potential menace to British interests and precautions should be taken against her. Finally he reached the inevitable conclusion that Britain's chief allies must be the European democracies, with whom she shared common interests, common values and a common colonial position. If such a course was pursued, he argued, a European 'federation' could become the most powerful force on Earth. Foreign Office representatives, he knew, were sympathetic to his ideas, but he still believed that Eden had opposed his policy outright believing that it would antagonize Russia, encourage American isolationism and divide Europe. Since 1944, however, Cooper pointed out, Soviet expansionism had continued, and the communist menace was now growing beyond the 'iron curtain' — in France, Belgium and Greece — whilst Britain had failed to take a lead in Europe, either at the political or economic level. The continentals remained weak and pessimistic, perhaps even likely to turn to Russia for aid. Duff Cooper was only too well aware that French policies, as well as the British, had caused problems for his vision of Anglo-European unity, but with de Gaulle gone and the Levant issue settled, he pleaded forcefully:

The time has come ... to count our friends, to fortify them, and to bind them closely to our side. Of purely European countries France remains, despite her failures and perplexities, potentially the strongest and richest on the continent, provided the mistake of allowing Germany to become powerful again is not repeated. An Anglo-French alliance would form a potent magnet for others who are now looking round rather wildly in search of security and salvation .

To Duff Cooper all his arguments of 1944 had proved correct; time had only served to reinforce them. It remained for Britain to learn the lesson and act quickly.[23]

It would be tempting indeed to see Duff Cooper, in this telegram, as a visionary, the exponent of a policy which, if pursued quickly, could have made Britain the leader of a united post-war Europe. Certainly, in retrospect, his belief that Western Europe could unite to become a major force in the world, was perceptive, and there had been no *visible* move by London to organize Western Europe as yet. Cooper was also right to assert that the Soviet Union was Britain's greatest potential menace, and he was right, in retrospect, to believe that the Anglo-French alliance was a strong basis on which to build wider European cooperation (in 1947, as will be seen below, this is just what occurred). His scepticism about the value of the United Nations in maintaining world peace was also justified. But in many other ways, his analysis of events and recommendations for action, were flawed, vague or simply mistaken.

After 1946, most importantly, it became increasingly clear despite Cooper's views that America *was* ready to abandon isolationism and stand forward as the defender of the West; furthermore, not only did the Americans involve themselves in Europe (economically via the Marshall Plan, and politically and militarily through NATO), they also proved willing to defend Britain's colonial interests where these were exposed to communist expansion, and, when compared to the weak and demoralized West Europeans, America was a much more impressive ally. Despite Cooper's high hopes of her, France under the Fourth Republic did *not* prove a very strong, stable or prosperous state, even after she entered the Western alliance. Cooper's talk of a European 'federation' furthermore was, at best, very imprecise: whether he conceived of an actual institutional structure and full-fledged economic union, or merely an evolutionary, step-by-step approach to continental cooperation was not clear. Eden, of course, had been more favourable to the 'Western bloc' proposal than Duff Cooper guessed, and in early 1946 Bevin and the Foreign Office *did* have a policy of greater cooperation with Western Europe in mind, as one possible option for the future. But officials in Whitehall, with a wider range of concerns than the Ambassador to Paris, could not have been expected to throw themselves wholeheartedly behind his policy. No one as yet could, predict whether America or the Europeans would prove the more reliable ally for Britain, but it would have been imprudent at best to put at risk cooperation with the first by an over-hasty pursuit of an alliance with the second. The doubts of 1944 about Duff Cooper's motivation also remained pertinent: a Western bloc overtly designed as 'reinsurance' against Russia *would* antagonize Moscow, divide Europe, and throw away any hope of keeping the world united. In early 1946 it still seemed worthwhile, for all the evidence of a growing Soviet threat, to try to preserve the wartime alliance wherever possible, and this of course had tempered Bevin's hopes for Western European cooperation since he came to office. Indeed, despite their support for an Anglo-French treaty itself, officials were, in early 1946, still reluctant to include proposals for a wider Western bloc in their draft Cabinet paper because of the likely Soviet reaction.[24]

There was one final, vital flaw in Cooper's arguments, however, and that concerned the role of Germany. Again, because of his parochial view of affairs from Paris, and his passionate desire for an Anglo-French alliance, the Ambassador had a very simple approach to the German problem: he favoured its control by the allies, broadly along the lines suggested by the French. But in the long term, of course, a revitalized Germany was to prove as vital to European security as was an American alliance: Germany, *not* France, was to provide the powerhouse for European recovery after 1947. And in the short term it was the German problem which put an end to the hopes of an early Anglo-French treaty. For, although in early 1946 the Levant problem was removed as a hindrance to a treaty, de Gaulle's old demand for an Anglo-French agreement on Germany remained. In late 1945 the French had made their 'thesis' on Germany perfectly clear: they wanted the Rhineland (the traditional invasion route into France) and the Ruhr (Germany's industrial heartland) to be separated from the rest of the country, the Saar (with its coal) to be made autonomous but linked in economic union with France, and what remained of Germany to become a federation of states, forever disarmed; in addition the Germans would have to pay large reparations.[25] The British had agreed to study these demands in September 1945, and Bevin had even seemed sympathetic to a loss of German territory in the West,[26] but by February 1946 the British, facing enormous financial burdens in their zone in Germany (which included the Ruhr), and concerned by the possible results of French plans on the European economy, as well as the dangers of provoking a German irredentist movement, were coming to view Germany's political destruction with disfavour. Bevin told Bidault that it was better to control Germany by economic controls on her industrial production.[27] The question in March was whether such divisions over Germany still made a treaty between Britain and France impossible.

There was some feeling in the Foreign Office at this time that the French treaty *must* await settlement of the differences over Germany, but other officials were not so certain. Many were increasingly concerned with the strength of the communists in France's coalition government, and hoped that an early Anglo-French treaty — which was known to be a popular idea in France — would encourage non-communist voters in the next elections, due in June. Otherwise there could be a communist 'landslide'. Furthermore the new French Premier, Felix Gouin, was now saying that a treaty might be possible before the German problem was resolved, and it was largely because of these suggestions that, in early April, Bevin sent one of his leading officials, Oliver Harvey, to Paris to explore the situation, assisted by Duff Cooper.[28] Hardly had Harvey arrived, however, that on 5 April the French Cabinet reaffirmed de Gaulle's policy, and a few days later it was confirmed that an Anglo-French treaty, too, required a prior agreement of the German problem. Harvey and the Foreign Office were very disappointed and decided they would not seek a treaty in such a way again: if the French wanted a treaty *they* must ask for it.[29] And on 17 April the British Cabinet formally decided to reject French plans for a truncated Germany in favour of economic controls on a united German state.[30] Official Anglo-French talks, begun in late April, to discuss Germany were only able to produce a catalogue of disagreements in May[31] and there then began a series of conferences in Paris — two sessions of a new CFM and then a conference on the European peace treaties — which lasted until October and made talks on an Anglo-French alliance impossible.

Duff Cooper was a lone voice during this period for progress on a French treaty, and his efforts confirm the determination of his search for greater Anglo-French understanding. His interpretation of the Harvey mission was different from that given in London. Although he had fully cooperated with the mission, Cooper later saw the effort as misguided and mistimed: if the Foreign Office had waited, and taken full account of the German problem, the whole fiasco need not have occurred. 'It must be borne in mind', he wrote to Bevin, 'that while other nations are beginning to fear Russia, France continues to fear Germany'.[32] He, of all people, wanted to see a treaty made quickly; he, too, was very fearful of communist influence in Paris, but — and in this he *was* far more realistic than the Foreign Office — Duff Cooper appreciated the strength of French feeling about Germany, after three invasions from across the Rhine since 1870, and France's craving for a lasting promise of security. It was all very well for the French Cabinet to settle the far-off Levant problem with Britain: a very different matter for them to end their deeply-felt concern with Germany. And on 29 May the Ambassador decided to state his views on this matter forcefully in a despatch to Berlin .

Again Cooper impressed the Foreign Secretary — the despatch was circulated as a full Cabinet paper — but again it was not seen as providing any possible guide for British policy, merely an interesting alternative view. Cooper in fact simply recommended that Britain should adopt the French policy of separating the Ruhr, *the* most important area of Germany in everyone's eyes, from the rest of the country. He mustered a series of arguments in support of this approach, apart from the obvious point that it would pave the way to a French treaty. Germany, Cooper insisted, *had* to be controlled as closely as possible: he refused to believe that Germans could ever be won over to the West. Given this, political separation would prove far more effective than economic controls which, in any case, would be hard to administer. A separation would prove far more effective than economic controls which, in any case, would be hard to administer. A separated Ruhr could, he believed, function as a successful economic unit. Certainly, such a policy could lead to German irredentism, but economic controls, too, were likely to arouse German opposition: the important thing was to avoid the mistakes of the inter-war years over Germany, which had led to the revival of German militarism, and which had undermined the Anglo-French alliance. But, in this despatch again, Cooper had gone rather too far towards the views of the country in which he served. British policy had already moved too far along alternate lines, embracing concerns beyond Anglo-French relations, and on 2 July Bevin replied to Duff Cooper with the Foreign Office view that the Ruhr's separation would harm the European economy, prove hard to enforce, and antagonize German popular opinion.[33] Later in July Cooper visited Bidault, and appealed to him to seek a treaty with Bevin, but he got a negative response. Then in despair he appealed once again to London for action, only to have it restated, by Harvey, that Britain would not 'run after' France.[34]

Events in the last months of 1946 seemed to promise no early Anglo-French alliance. Over Germany the two sides remained far apart, and any agreement was made less likely after the British, under great financial pressure, agreed to unite their zone with that of the Americans, in the so-called 'bizone'. In the wider world Bidault became very concerned about Britain's growing identification with America and suspicion of Russia, in contrast to French policy which — influenced by the presence of communists in government — still sought full agreement with Moscow.[35] Communist strength meanwhile continued to make Bevin and the Foreign Office suspicious of the French.[36] In September 1946 there were some positive moves in Anglo-French relations in the form of a general settlement of debts, the establishment of an 'economic committee' (to discuss problems in regular meetings), and a committment to reduce unnecessary economic competition between the two.[37] But this was hardly likely to appeal to the public imagination, and Conservative MPs continued to criticize the lack of real achievement in Western European cooperation.[38] Whitehall's commitment to such cooperation remained genuine enough: in December, Orme Sargent, the Permanent Under-Secretary, confirmed that the 'Western bloc' remained Britain's long-term policy;[39] and Bevin had already begun to press, on the economic side, for a study to be set up of a possible customs union with the continent (a study eventually estabished in 1947).[40] But for Duff Cooper, who still refused to believe that the Foreign Office took any real interest in France and Europe, the year closed on a pessimistic note: 'This has been a year far less eventful than last and far less satisfactory,' he noted in his diary '. . . There has been little, if any, improvement in Anglo-French relations, and the German difficulty is greater'[41] All the hopes raised earlier in the year, by the Levant settlement and the departure of de Gaulle, had come to nothing; the German problem, the strength of the French communists, and growing East-West divisions had combined to ruin any chances that his vision of a British-led continental union - so forcefully put in his telegram of 19 March — had of success.

And yet in December 1946 Duff Cooper was on the brink of his greatest triumph. The opportunity for an early improvement in Anglo-French relations was given by the advent in Paris of an all-

Socialist government, led by pre-war premier Leon Blum. The constitution of the new, Fourth Republic had now been approved and the Blum Government was an interim administration, designed to govern France until the President of the Republic was elected. The Socialists, however, were already known as the most 'anglophile' French party, feeling a certain affinity to the British Labour Government and — importantly — taking a more moderate line than the other main parties (the Communists and Bidault's Christian Democrats) on Germany: the Socialists, indeed, were willing to accept the British policy of *economic* controls, rather than political separation, in Germany. It was on Duff Cooper's personal initiative that anything else was made of the opportunity to advance Anglo-French relations. He contacted Blum's Deputy Foreign Minister, Pierre-Olivier Lapie, formerly one of the Free French exiles in London and a leading anglophile, and arranged to see Blum (who combined the roles of Premier and Foreign Minister) on 26 December. In the meeting Blum proved very keen to improve relations with Britain, but even he was suprised when the Ambassador went so far as to suggest that an Anglo-French treaty should be made. This seemed to go too far in taking advantage of a short-term opportunity. Blum was only too aware that his government would not last long. And besides, he was concerned to see at least one concession from Britain, to pave the way for a treaty specifically: he wanted the British to increase coal exports to France from their zone of Germany, so as to help France's economic recovery (coal supplies in France, despite the level of the Saar mines, were still struggling to reach their pre-war level). Blum and his advisers correctly guessed in fact that Cooper's approach was unofficial, and they were unwilling to give too much away to him. Despite the account in his memoirs, which draws a straight line from this meeting to the signature of a treaty in March, it is evident that Duff Cooper himself left the meeting doubtful about its likely results. His report to London actually suggested that it was *Blum* who had raised the treaty proposal first; and Cooper refused to discuss the idea further with any French officials over the next few days.[42]

Duff Cooper's approach, however, had its effect: it encouraged Blum and Lapie to go further. In early January the French Premier wrote to Clement Attlee, an old acquaintance, saying that he would like to visit London, and also saying that he was interested both in a treaty and in increased coal exports from the Ruhr. The Foreign Office decided to welcome the idea of a visit, *not* so much because officials hoped to carry through the Western bloc at last, but because they could see no reason to turn Blum away. Attlee sent off a warm invitation and the visit was arranged for 13-16 January.[43]

But the likely results seemed problematic. Duff Cooper sent a telegram to Bevin, pleading for real concessions to be made to France, possibly in the form of a treaty (or a least for a declaration that such a treaty would be negotiated)[44] but the Foreign Office refused to believe that, after two years of delays and French condition, a treaty was really possible. The French Ambassador, René Massigli, warned Cooper, that, if the visit came to nothing , *he* was responsible![45] It was only when the London meetings were actually held that the genuine desire for cooperation on both sides was revealed. Blum not only expressed himself willing to make a treaty, he also dropped all prior conditions on this; Bevin not only expressed himself willing to increase Ruhr coal exports, he also indulged in an extraordinary statement of faith in the French alliance which came close to endorsing Duff Cooper's philosophy. The Anglo-French treaty, declared Bevin, should prove an important means to control Germany and prevent future aggression, it must become the basis of British policy in Europe, and it should lead to a general '*entente*' between the two on world issues. Blum, Massigli and Duff Cooper were all delighted, and the decision to negotiate a treaty was formally publicized. Even the fall of Blum's government soon after failed to halt the forward momentum.[46] On 29 January the treaty negotiations began in London, headed by Sargent and Massigli. The final text was approved a month later and welcomed by a standing ovation in the French Chamber — with Duff Cooper present — when it was announced; the signature took place, in Dunkirk on 4 March, with Cooper as the second signatory for Britain, after Bevin.[47] The Ambassador's note in his diary reflected both his personal satisfaction with the treaty and its importance for his career: 'Nunc dimittis.'[48]

Duff Cooper's satisfaction with the events of early 1947, however, was tempered by disappointment with the treaty itself. Certainly the signature of the treaty marked a great personal achievement, and must be seen as the high point of his ambassadorial career, but as with his earlier ministerial performances the achievement proved less dramatic than he hoped. Even before the treaty was signed he had criticized it in form. The problem was that the terms of the Treaty of Dunkirk embodied nothing of the general 'entente' which Bevin had discussed with Blum. Instead, both the British and French had put forward drafts similar to their respective treaties of 1942 and 1944 with Russia, and based them upon a mutual commitment to oppose German aggression. There was not even a commitment to hold staff talks. Yet again, Cooper complained, concern with Russia was being allowed to tarnish Anglo-French cooperation: neither party to the new treaty was willing to antagonize Moscow by writing more into the new text than had been offered first to the Soviets. A commitment to resist Germany seemed unremarkable — it was surely taken for granted anyway — and Duff Cooper (despite his own wishes to see the Western bloc as 'reinsurance' against Russia) could still see no reason for Moscow to raise objections to closer Anglo-French links. The Ambassador was anxious to have Dunkirk recognized as 'a most momentous decision in British foreign policy', portending Anglo-French cooperation over Germany, in the colonial sphere and in military planning; the British and French Empires, he asserted, in a despatch of 7 February, could together equal either of the superpowers.[49] Yet again his craving for 'instant' and far-reaching cooperation jarred against the more evolutionary and gradualistic course favoured by the Foreign Office. There was no doubt which approach triumphed in the actual text of Dunkirk, and it is significant that the Foreign Office negotiated the treaty in London with Massigli rather than allowing Cooper to take charge of the talks in Paris.

The months after Dunkirk saw a pronounced strengthening of Anglo-French cooperation. Immediately after the treaty's signature Bevin and Bidault attended another foreign ministers' conference in Moscow, at which a German peace treaty was discussed. Here even Bidault became exasperated at Soviet behaviour, and seemed likely to turn in future towards Anglo-Saxon powers. The Russians refused even to discuss French plans for the future of Germany; but Bevin, in contrast, agreed to increase coal exports further to France from the Ruhr. In Paris, meanwhile, a growing crisis within the coalition government finally led to the expulsion of communist ministers by the Socialist Premier, Paul Ramadier, in May. These events seemed to confirm that greater West European cooperation was necessary, given the apparent threat from Russia and the communist movement. And in May 1947 the Foreign Office began moves towards a Belgian treaty, based on the Dunkirk model.[50] These preparations, however, were then interrupted in June by another major development for Eurpean cooperation, when the United States (fearful of growing communist support based on economic discontent) offered to finance a continental recovery programme. In responding to this, the so-called 'Marshall Plan', Bevin was careful to cooperate closely with Bidault. The two acted together, first to invite the Soviet Foreign Minister, Molotov, to discuss the plan, and then, when Molotov walked out of the talks, to call together a conference of West European states in July in Paris. By late September the officials of sixteen nations had drawn up a comprehensive recovery plan to put to Washington: Europe was divided, economically at least, between East and West, but Duff Cooper's vision of

West European cooperation led by Britain and France was being increasingly realized. In June, Bevin had gone so far as to tell Duff Cooper that Britain should try to create a customs union and common currency in Western Europe,[51] and the high point of Anglo-French relations was reached on 22 September when Bevin, accompanied by the Ambassador, visited Paul Ramadier and spoke of making 'the union of Britain and France': talks on further economic and colonial cooperation could, the Foreign Secretary declared, lead to an Anglo-French 'superpower', which could in turn bring peace between Russia and America. It was all very similar to what Bevin had earlier told Blum and may indeed have reflected one possible policy option in the Foreign Secretary's mind. Ramadier, fearful of an increasingly divided world, was much encouraged, and Duff Cooper was more determined than ever to press for concrete results from the meeting.[52] On 3 September, he had learnt that he was to be replaced as Ambassador to Paris at the end of the year, a piece of news which had long been expected but which, nonetheless, came as something of a shock. It seems likely that in any case, given such news, the Ambassador would have wanted to repeat all his arguments in favour of Anglo-French cooperation,[53] but the Bevin-Ramadier conversation could only have strengthened this desire. Unfortunately the next three months were generally to be ones of disappointment.

It was evident from talks in Whitehall after the Bevin-Ramadier meeting that, yet again, there would be no dramatic improvements in Anglo-French cooperation in the short term. Bevin himself still hoped that it would be possible to find agreement with the Russians at the next conference of foreign ministers (due in November in London), and he was unwilling to make any further moves, such as the beginning of military staff talks in France, which might antagonize Moscow. In the colonial sphere the preference in Whitehall was for the development of technical cooperation with France: differences of imperial outlook ensured that political 'unity' between the two Empires was unlikely. An inter-departmental meeting on greater Anglo-French economic cooperation, held on 8 October, showed that there could be little advance here either; the Treasury and Board of Trade argued that practical difficulties, and the need to preserve the Commonwealth trading system, made a customs union with France impossible; French commercial policies were heavily criticized; one-third of the time was spent discussing Eire![54] Again it was evident that only a gradualistic policy would be expected from London and Duff Cooper's protests were as great as ever. On 16 October, after reading an account of the 8 October meeting, he sent an angry despatch to Bevin complaining about the negative attitude of officials, insisting that the Americans and the British public were now fully behind European cooperation and asking that the Treasury and Board of Trade be given instructions to be more positive towards France. Playing on a favourite theme of Bevin's, the Ambassador suggested that major improvements in European tourism were possible, to help bind together the common people of Europe.

Duff Cooper made much of his 16 October telegram in his memoirs, and he did not hide from Bevin the fact that imminent removal made the telegram more frank than usual. And again, contrary to the impression given in his diary, the despatch *did* have some effect. Bevin saw the Chancellor of the Exchequer, Stafford Cripps, and complained about the lack of warmth shown by officials towards France. The Foreign Secretary also asked that an encouraging response be sent to the ambassador's despatch. But the Foreign Office took time to prepare their reply and it was not sent until 27 November. It was full of hopes for greater economic cooperation in future, but otherwise pointed out the practical problems over trading priorities, which made major short-term improvements impossible.[55] On 13 November Cooper wrote to Bevin to complain about the lack of progress on Anglo-French staff talks as well, which led the Foreign Secretary to minute that 'what we must get into the heads of our people is western security regionally and [a] less anti-attitude'. But again, in a reply to Paris on 28 November, Cooper was told by the Foreign Office of the practical problems with staff talks, including the unreliability of French security (which was suspected to be communist-infiltrated) and the naïvety of the French Chief-of-Staff, General Revers (who was reputed to have discussed an anti-Soviet alliance with one of Franco's generals!).[56] Undeterred as ever, Duff Cooper sent another despatch on 5 December insisting that: 'There is always the possibility that the worst may happen. Before it does we ought at least to have made up our minds upon some fundamental principles of defence.' By the time Bevin replied to this the British were indeed on the verge of a new policy in Europe. The London foreign ministers' conference had ended in complete disappointment over the future of Germany, between Russia and the West, and to Duff Cooper Bevin's despatch sounded a note of optimism: 'now that we have unhappily failed to reach agreement on a four-power basis, we shall not postpone any longer ... discussion of future security arrangements.' But Duff Cooper was not to see the results of this letter. Sent on 17 December, it was in fact Bevin's last despatch to him as Ambassador, and included a message of thanks for his services.[57]

The months following December 1947 did indeed see the adoption by Britain of a new foreign policy. The cooperation of the wartime Big Three had come to an end by 22 January 1948. Bevin told the Commons of his desire to create a 'Western union', for the defence of Western civilization; the British Commonwealth, the Western European nations and the United States were to be drawn together to resist the menace of Soviet communism. Over the next months this vision led to the creation of a West European alliance (the Brussels Pact), the decision to create a West German state, and then talks on an Atlantic Pact with America. Initially, Western union was very much centred on strengthening Western Europe. The Foreign Office went so far as to consider full political-economic unity with the continent, and Bevin again talked of forming a 'union' with Europe. Had Duff Cooper remained in Paris, the pressures in favour of maintaining this direction might have been greater. As it was, the original form of Western union broke down by 1950, for a number of reasons: the continental states, especially France, still seemed politically unstable, and economically and militarily weak; the Treasury and Board of Trade remained reluctant to see radical new steps in economic cooperation with the continent; and Bevin came to see America and the Commonwealth as more 'reliable' partners around which to build Britain's future security. When the continental states began steps towards a 'supranational' Europe with the Schuman Plan, Britain remained outside.[58]

The Paris Embassy was Duff Cooper's only ambassadorial position. It also marked the end of his active public life. He did retain his links with France, owning a flat in Paris, and in 1952 entered the Lords as First Viscount Norwich, but he never re-emerged as a leading Conservative. His memoirs, *Old men forget*, were published in 1953 and he died, suddenly, the following January. Any judgement of his diplomatic service under Bevin must necessarily concentrate on Cooper's advocacy of a close French alliance and wider cooperation with Western Europe, which formed the essence of his recommendations on foreign policy to the Foreign Office. His memoirs reflect exasperation with the Office for failing to pursue the course he outlined, an exasperation broken only by the Treaty of Dunkirk (which, in any case, the Ambassador saw largely as his own work).[59] In retrospect his views seemed to support the case that post-war British planners completely underestimated the potential for continental cooperation and lost the opportunity to make Britain the 'leader' of Western Europe.

The release of official documents from the period has taken away much of the force of these arguments, however: several facts emerge from a full consideration of the evidence from the 1940s which undermine the thesis of Duff Cooper's memoirs. First, though Cooper could not have been fully aware of it, the Foreign Office *did* see Western Europe as an important area with which to develop fuller cooperation. This was natural given the common interests – geographical, political, colonial – with the West Europeans. The Office did, consistently, hope for an Anglo-French treaty, around which might be built a wider 'Western' bloc. There were many good reasons why this course was not pursued more fully before Cooper was replaced: the 'conditions' laid down by the French, over the Middle East and Germany, were perhaps the most important complications for the Anglo-French treaty; other problems were added by the strength of the French communists; and the Office was always reluctant to pursue a full Western bloc until all chances of cooperation with Russia were lost. It was unfortunate that a more determined policy of European cooperation *was* taken up only after the Ambassador's departure. Duff Cooper certainly had some genuine reasons to complain about attitudes in Whitehall: the Treasury and Board of Trade, for example, seem to have adopted a critical approach as an almost 'automatic' response to ideas for European cooperation; in the Harvey mission of April 1946 the Foreign Office do seem to have misread French feeling regarding Germany; and the Ambassador's prescient warnings, that the continentals would seek unity among themselves in future and exclude Britain, were not apparently fully appreciated in London.

But generally speaking the differences between Cooper's policy and that of the Foreign Office were ones of degree. The Ambassador wanted swift results and saw events very much from a French perspective, he was anxious about the temporary nature of his own position, and was obsessed with the memory of the Anglo-French differences in the inter-war period (then, too, the Middle East and Germany had proved divisive issues and the price, Cooper believed, had been paid in 1940). The Foreign Office in contrast favoured a gradual, evolutionary approach to continental cooperation, took a global perspective on foreign policy-making, and were quicker to come to terms with the realities of French and European (though not, perhaps, British) decline since 1939. With the benefit of hindsight it may indeed be possible to argue that Britain ought to have made even greater efforts in the direction of European cooperation, but there can be little doubt, from the perspective of the 1940s, that the Foreign Office were correct in seeing America (not France) as the most valuable ally in the postwar world, correct to believe that a draconian policy in Germany would prove disastrous, and justified in 1945 in seeking cooperation with Russia where possible rather than antagonizing her.

In some respects Duff Cooper resembles Harold Nicolson's

description of the 'amateur diplomatist' who is apt 'owing to the shortness of his tenure to seek for rapid success . . . inclines to be far to zealous and to have bright ideas . . . arrives with a righteous contempt for the formalities of diplomacy and with some impatience of its conventions.'[60] Cooper also seemed unable to come to terms with change: his craving for an embassy to crown his career was reminiscent of the Edwardians, his belief in the French alliance owed too much to the 1920s. But to end with such criticisms would be harsh. There can be little doubt that, as with his political career, Cooper's diplomatic career never lived up to his own high hopes: it had its successes, principally the Treaty of Dunkirk, but ultimately failed to see a full Anglo-French *entente*, despite Bevin's insistence at times that this was his aim. However, there can equally be no doubt that he *was* a successful Ambassador to Paris. Bevin found his advice stimulating (even if it was not always followed); Cooper had an excellent, and sympathetic, understanding of French aspirations and fears; and his retention at Paris by the Labour Foreign Secretary, was itself evidence of Britain's desire for good relations with France. Duff and Diana Cooper together made the Embassy a centre of Parisian social life and the Ambassador proved very popular with the French:[61] to President Vincent Auriol he was 'le seul independent, qui a du caractère et grand ami de la France'.[62] For all his criticisms of the Foreign Office in his memoirs, Duff Cooper was nonetheless satisfied to have ended his public life in Paris. For all its failures to adopt fully his foreign policy recommendations, the Foreign Office nonetheless had in Duff Cooper a thoughtful and determined representative, whose views underlined the importance of Western Europe as one of the areas of vital concern for Britain's future international policy.

Notes

1. The official biography, *Duff Cooper*, 1986, is by John Charmley. Duff Cooper's memoirs, *Old men forget*, 1953, however, remain invaluable.
2. On the appointment see Charmley, op.cit., 165-71; Cooper, op. cit., 315; the discussion in E. Barker, *Churchill and Eden at War*, 1978, 90-2; Diana Cooper, *Trumpets from the steep*, 1960, 170-1; and the correspondence in Churchill College, Cambridge, Duff Cooper papers, DUFC, 4/4.
3. Public Record Office (P.R.O.), PREM. 3/273; copy in Cooper papers, DUFC, 4/4.
4. On Anglo-French Gaullist relations, see especially Barker, op. cit., II; Sir L. Woodward, *British foreign policy in the Second World War*, 5 vols, 1970-6, II, 320-60; and Charmley, op.cit, 172-81.

5. P.R.O., CAB 66/53, W.P. (44) 409; J. Charmley, 'Duff Cooper and Western European union, 1944-7', *Review of International Studies*, 1985, 56-7; Cooper, op.cit., 344-8; copy of memo in Cooper papers DUFC. 4/7.
6. V. Rothwell, *Britain and the Cold War, 1941-7*, 1982, 407.
7. On the Western bloc and French treaty in this period, see Woodward, op.cit., III, 95-103 and V, 181-97; Rothwell, op.cit., 406-13; and Charmley, op.cit., 182-94 and 202-3.
8. R. Butler (ed.), *Documents on British policy overseas (D.B.P.O.)*, Series 1, Vol. I, 1984, 873-81.
9. D.B.P.O., I, 181-92, and see, e.g., F.O. 371/49068/7882 (26 June); FO 371/49069/9196 (10 August) and 9639 (6 August).
10. On the meeting see FO 371/49069/9501 (8 August) and 9595 (13 August); Charmley, *op.cit.*, 361-2; Alexander Cadogan diary, Churchill College, Cambridge, 1/15, 13 August; and see also Ministère des Relations Extérieures (M.A.E.), Series 2, Europe 1944-9, sous-série Grande Bretagne (G.B.), file 35 (9 August).
11. Charmley, 'Duff Cooper', *International Studies*, op.cit., 58; Charmley, *Cooper, 204-5 and 207;* A. Bullock, *Ernest Bevin, Foreign Secretary*, 1984, 73-4; Cooper, *Trumpets from the steep* op.cit., 240 and 242; Cooper, *Old men forget*, op.cit., 361.
12. FO 371/49069/9382 (8 August) and see 9556 (13 August).
13. FO 371/49069/9525 (14 August); Cooper, *Old men forget*, op.cit., 362. The French Ambassador to London, René Massigli, was also keen to build Anglo-French cooperation at this time: FO 371/44581/6094 (16 August), and R. Massigli, *Une Comédie des erreurs*, Paris, 1978, 74-6.
14. FO 371/49069/9525 (21 August).
15. Cooper, *Trumpets from the steep*, op.cit., 171 and 216.
16. ibid., 244.
17. For a fuller discussion of the Levant settlement, see J.W. Young, *Britain, France and unity of Europe, 1945-51*, 1984, 18-25; Cooper's account (*Old men forget*), 363-4 is very short.
18. FO 371/45584/7806 (13 October) and 8206 (23 and 26 October).
19. J.W. Young, 'The Foreign Office and the department of General de Gaulle', *Historical Journal*, **25**, (1), 1982: 209-16.
20. Cooper, *Old men forget*, op.cit., 364-6; Charmley, *Cooper*, op.cit., 208; FO 371/59956/621, 630 and 690; FO 800/464/46/1-4.
21. On this period see S. Greenwood 'Ernest Bevin, France and Western union', *European History Quarterly*, **14**, 1984: 319-37, which, however, says too little on the Levant, overestimates the chances of Bevin accepting French plans for Germany, and underestimates the support for the Western bloc *on its own terms* (not just as an anti-communist device) in the Foreign Office after February 1946.
22. FO 371/59951/2411; and on this period see also M.A.E., Z, Europe, G.B., file 36.
23. FO 371/59952/2780; Cooper, op.cit., 366-7; Charmley, *Cooper*, op.cit., 209; Cooper papers, DUFC. 4/7.
24. FO 371/59952/2411.
25. On French plans in 1945 see especially C. de Gaulle, *War memoirs*, III,

1960, 49-51 and B. Ruhm von Oppen, *Documents on Germany under occupation*, 1955, 66-8.
26. e.g. FO 371/45582/6840 and 6960; PREM 8/43; and on Bevin's Ruhr policy see S. Greenwood's excellent 'Bevin, the Ruhr and the division of Germany', *Historical Journal* **29**, 1986.
27. FO 371/55399/1407; FO/ 371/55400/1963; M.A.E., Z, Europe, G.B., file 36 (18 February).
28. On Foreign Office considerations at this time (encouraged by Duff Cooper's despatch of 22 March), see especially FO 371/59952/2780 and 3308; and FO 371/59953/3625; M.A.E., Z, Europe, G.B., File 36 (24 and 31 March).
29. On the Harvey mission see especially FO 371/59952/3283, 3286, 3287 and 3308; FO 371/59953/3405, 3528 and 3612; Oliver Harvey papers, British Library, MS 56402; M.A.E., ibid. (3-24 April).
30. CAB 128/5, CP (46) 36; CAB 129/8, CP (46) 139 and CAB 129/9, CP (46) 156.
31. FO 371/55403/5256, 5375; FO 371/55404/6073
32. FO 371/59953/3612; Cooper, op.cit., 367.
33. FO 371/55404/6081; CAB 129/10, CP (46) 223; Charmley, op.cit., 209-10.
34. FO 371/59954/6814.
35. See e.g. FO 371/59955/8895 and 8989.
36. See e.g. FO 371/59956/9765.
37. See Young, *Unity of Europe*, op.cit., 37-42, for a full discussion.
38. See e.g. 423 H.C. Deb. 5 S., 1868-9 and 1949-52.
39. FO 371/67670/25. Charmley, 'Duff Cooper and Western European union', op.cit., 59-60, argues that 'confusion . . . reigned in the Foreign Office' over the Western bloc, but Charmley's evidence rests on the rejection by officials, late in 1946, of Sir Nigel Ronald's proposals for European cooperation. These proposals were actually very different from mainstream Foreign Office thinking about the bloc, a throwback in fact to Churchill's wartime ideas for a 'council of Europe' under United Nations auspices which would be just one of a number of regional 'councils' in the world. See the discussion in Rothwell, op.cit., 424-33. Foreign Office minute of January 1947 noted (after moves towards a French treaty began) that 'we are slowly progressing in European states without regard for any world-wide jigsaw of the kind contemplated by Sir N. Roland': FO 371/67670/25 (by Rumbold).
40. FO 371/59978/7116; CAB 128/6, CM (46) 91; and CAB 129/16, CP (47) 35.
41. Cooper, op.cit., 369.
42. FO 371/59967/10747; FO 371/67670/25; Cooper, op.cit., 369-70; P.O. Lapie, *De Leon Blum à de Gaulle*, Paris, 1971, 53-7.
43. PREM 8/516; FO 371/67670/25 and 291; FO 371/67686/269; Lapie, op.cit., 54-5 and 61-6; Charmley, op.cit., 211-12; M.A.E., Z, Europe, G.B., file 36 (27 December).
44. FO 371/67680/170; M.A.E., ibid., file 37 (4-9 January).
45. Cooper, *Old men forget*, op.cit., 371.
46. FO 371/67686/650 and 654; Cooper, op.cit., 371-2; Lapie, op.cit., 66-70;

and Massigli, op.cit., 88-90.
47. For fuller discussions on the treaty, see Young, *Unity of Europe*, op.cit., 47-51; S. Greenwood, 'Return to Dunkirk', *Journal of Strategic Studies*, **6**, 1983; J. Baylis, Britain and the Dunkirk Treaty', *Journal of Strategic Studies*, **5**, 1982; Charmley, op.cit., 212-13; and B. Zeeman, 'Britain and the Cold War', *European History Quarterly*, 16, 1986. Zeeman is an excellent general essay. Greenwood and Baylis are both somewhat teleological, the former determined to prove that Dunkirk was anti-communist in intent, the latter seeing the treaty as the forerunner of NATO.
48. Cooper, op.cit., 373.
49. FO 371/67673/8461, 8579 and 8652; Cooper, op.cit., 377-8; Massigli, op.cit., 104; see also Cooper papers, DUFC 4/6 (7 February).
50. On this period see particularly Rothwell, op.cit., 433-43; Young op.cit., 55-61; Charmley, op.cit., 213-14; M.A.E.,Z, Europe, G.B., file 37.
51. Cooper, op.cit., 376.
52. FO 371/67673/8461, 8579 and 8652; Cooper, op.cit., 377-8; Massigli, op.cit., 104.
53. Cooper, op.cit., 376-7.
54. On this meeting see FO 371/67673/9053; and, in general on the period, Young op.cit., 70-6; Charmley, op.cit., 217.
55. FO 371/67674/10270; Cooper, op.cit., 379-80.
56. FO 371/67674/10271; Cooper, op.cit., 380 Charmley, op.cit., 217-18.
57. FO 371/67674/10907; Cooper, op.cit., 381.
58. See G. Warner's essay in R. Ovendale (ed.), *The foreign policy of the British Labour governments, 1945-51*, 1984; Young, op.cit., chapters 9-17; and see Charmley, op.cit., 218-21, on the end of the ambassadorship.
59. In *Old men forget*, op.cit., 361 Cooper complained that 'I never received a letter from Bevin in his own handwriting . . . and I never wrote to him without suspecting that my letter would be laid before him together with the comments of the department'.
60. A. Nicholson, *Diplomacy*, 1939, 76-7.
61. On the Duff Coopers at the Paris Embassy, see Earl of Bessborough, *Return to the forest*, 1962, 126-9; W. Hayter, *A double life*, 1974; C. Gladwyn, *The Paris Embassy*, 1976, 234-9; P. Ziegler, *Diana Cooper*, 1981, chapters 11 and 12.
62. V. Auriol, *Journal de Septennat*, I, Paris, 1971, 233.

4 Sir Alec Kirkbride and the Anglo-Transjordanian alliance, 1945-50

Ilan Pappé

British policy towards the Arab-Israeli conflict and to a lesser extent towards the Middle East as a whole was based on a strong Anglo-Transjordanian alliance. Britain's firm commitment to the Hashemite rule in Transjordan dated back to 1921 when the Colonial Office decided to offer the rulership of that part of mandatory Palestine to the Amir Abdullah.

Britain's dominant role in Transjordan was due to Sir Alec Kirkbride's immense influence on King Abdullah. Kirkbride had been His Majesty's Government's representative in Transjordan since 1920: in other words he had arrived there even before the Hashemites and had spent more than thirty years in that place. Owing to Kirkbride's position in Transjordan and his personal impact on its policies, Britain could rely, unhesitatingly, on Transjordan's loyalty and cooperation. As one of the Foreign Office's senior officials had put it: 'We are by force of circumstances and in recognition of King Abdullah's loyalty to us, basing our policy on Palestine and in the Middle East generally, to a large extent on the maintenance of a stable Transjordan.'[1]

Sir Alec Kirkbride enjoyed a position similar to that of a Colonial High Commissioner and, together with Glubb Pasha, occupied the most important posts in the country after the King and his Prime Minister. Kirkbride's unique standing was quite exceptional in comparison with the other British diplomats in the area; to this can be attributed the fact that throughout the period under review his influence on the Foreign Office's policy towards the Arab-Jewish conflict in Palestine was so decisive. Nevertheless, his views were not always accepted by the officials and politicians in London and were usually opposed by his colleagues in the area itself. Some of his contemporaries, Middle Eastern as well as British and American, have continued to criticize him in their memoirs and autobiographies.[2]

Thus we find that at times he acted quite independently without consulting with or reporting to his superiors in London or Jerusalem. Yet he was the one who succeeded in convincing London in 1946 to abandon all its previously proposed solutions for the Arab–Jewish conflict and to adopt a new approach towards the problem. This new attitude was based upon a Jewish–Hashemite understanding over the partitioning of Mandatory Palestine between Transjordan and the future Jewish state, a solution which had become the cornerstone of British policy towards the conflict after the British Government had decided to withdraw from Palestine and refer the question to the United Nations. The understanding was in turn based upon Jewish approval for the annexation of the Arab-populated areas in Palestine to Transjordan in return for the latter's recognition of the Jewish state: an understanding which determined to a large extent the outcome of the 1948 war and the consequent peace and armistice negotiations.

In July 1920, Great Britain was granted a mandate over Palestine which included Transjordan. This latter territory, located east of the river Jordan, had formerly been part of the Ottoman province of Damascus. A barren land and scarcely populated, it had been until the late 1880s outside the control and authority of the central government. The northern parts of the country were inhabited by tribes which had been subsidized by the Turks in order to keep them away from the pilgrimage route to Mecca which passed through Transjordan. The same tribes came under British control when the mandate of Palestine was established.

A number of Arabic-speaking officers were sent as representatives of the Palestine Government to help administer these areas in the 1920s: it was a group of only four men, since most of the Palestine Government officials were preoccupied with the organization of the political and economic order in Palestine west of the river Jordan. These officials formed small autonomous administrative centres and each of them had his own 'Little Kingdom'. They were sent to Transjordan with the impossible task of 'making bricks without straw':[3] with no financial or administrative assistance from Palestine.

One of these officers was the young Alec Kirkbride, whom T.E. Lawrence described as 'A taciturn, enduring fellow, only a boy in years, but ruthless in action, who messed for eight months with the Arab officers, their silent companion'.[4] Alan Kirkbride, his younger brother, was appointed to Amman, while Alec was sent to Kerak, more than fifty miles to the south. It was not Alec Kirkbride's first visit to that area. He had spent a short time in Kerak during the reign of Abdullah's brother, the Amir Faisal in Damascus (1918–20). After the occupation of the Arab Middle East by the allied forces, the governorship over the Damascus province was given to Faisal. Both Faisal and Abdullah were sons of the Sharif Hussein from Mecca in the land of the Hejaz. Hussein was the head of the Hashemite dynasty which had cooperated with the British against the Turks in the First World War; in return for their cooperation the British had vaguely promised to give the Hashemites rulership over the former Arab Ottoman provinces. Abdullah was promised the throne of Baghdad and his younger brother Faisal the seat of Damascus. However, the promise to Faisal contradicted the Sykes-Picot agreement which granted direct French control over Syria. Nevertheless, before he was expelled by the French, Faisal had formed the Arab Government of Syria and was declared Greater King of Syria. The status of Transjordan was ambiguous during Faisal's reign: whereas Faisal ruled through his governor over the area, at the same time the Palestine Government had sent Kirkbride as its representative there. This ambiguity was resolved when Faisal was deposed and when Britain and France signed a new agreement in September 1919, reiterating the Sykes-Picot accord by including Palestine, Iraq and Transjordan under British control and leaving Syria and Lebanon within the French sphere of influence.

Thus Kirkbride's 'Royal Seat' in 1920 was the town of Kerak. Reminiscing about this period, Kirkbride recalls fondly in particular the primitive nature of the place: 'No motor roads, no telephones and no telegraph', and most important of all, 'no other British [officials]'.[5] All these virtues made Kerak an attractive place. He thought himself to be an expert on Arab affairs and displayed very little respect, if any, towards the British diplomats who served in the area without knowing the language or the history of the Arab people. Throughout his stay in Transjordan he would consistently and constantly disagree with his colleagues.

Kirkbride, discussing this period in his memoirs, mentions another aspect of his life which had made Kerak and later Transjordan as a whole such a pleasant and attractive place to be in: 'I was, in fact, truly my own master.'[6] Yet he never desired to be called King of Jordan or Ruler of Eastern Palestine. He was content with the honour of being the head of the 'National Government of Moab' (the ancient biblical state believed to be situated in that area).

In January 1921, the Amir Abdullah arrived at the southern border of Transjordan. Abdullah had initially been promised the throne of Iraq, but had to give it up after Faisal had been expelled from Damascus. Faisal was compensated by the Colonial Secretary, Winston Churchill, with the seat of Baghdad, and thus we find Abdullah in the winter of 1921 attempting to regain at least a part of his brother's lost kingdom of Greater Syria. The Amir came leading an army of 2,000 men. In fact, it was a primitive army which Abdullah hoped to use in order to launch an attack on Damascus and redeem it from the French. From these chronicles we learn that Kirkbride arrived in Transjordan before the founder of the Hashemite Kingdom of Jordan. Thus, Abdullah had been no less of a stranger and foreigner there than Kirkbride.

When Kirkbride first heard of Abdullah's plans, he doubted the sincerity of the Amir's scheme to reach Damascus and expel the French. However, the High Commissioner in Jerusalem, Kirkbride's superior, did not send clear instructions regarding the desired course of action in case the Amir progressed to the border with the intention of continuing to Damascus. Kirkbride therefore decided to refrain from any action. When Abdullah reached the kingdom of Kirkbride, the latter greeted him and received him as an honoured guest.[7] This cordial and generous reception enabled the Amir to achieve a new *fait accompli* in Transjordan. Kirkbride had not disobeyed any of his superiors' instructions, but he did decide to act without consulting them - a feature in his conduct which would recur many times in his future.

From their very first meeting, the two men took a liking to each other. In Kirkbride's eyes the Amir was charming, kind, amusing and somewhat flattering. In their first encounter, Abdullah expressed the hope that Kirkbride would remain so that he could 'give me your support and advice in the difficult days which are to come'. Most important of all was Kirkbride's acknowledgement of Abdullah's right to the land *before* the British administration did so.[8] With Kirkbride's help, a central administration was settled in Amman and the autonomous councils were abolished. For the six years that followed these events, Alec Kirkbride was posted to the secretariat of the High Commissioner in Jerusalem.

In the meantime, the new Colonial Secretary, Winston Churchill, had decided to establish Abdullah's rulership in Transjordan on a firm basis by bringing it under the British mandate in Palestine, but with special autonomous standing. T.E. Lawrence, who had been one of the architects of this arrangement, recommended that the Amir should be assisted by a British representative: he should be in sympathy with Arab self-government and one who should in addition have a commanding personality for an infrastructure of British administration.[9] Lawrence's candidate at the time was St.John Philby, but these virtues could equally well be applied to Alec Kirkbride.

After Kirkbride's return to Transjordan as a political adviser, the Emirate had concluded a new agreement with Britain in 1928, and an organic law was promulgated that year. In that law, the British representative was granted wide authorities and was allowed to intervene significantly in Transjordan's internal and external affairs.

In the years to come (1928-45), Kirkbride's position was strengthened and his friendship with Abdullah developed into one of close cooperation. There were many occasions when the two disagreed but, all in all, their relationship was harmonious. Thus, when the Second World War ended, Kirkbride joined Abdullah in the latter's request to terminate the British mandate and to grant Transjordan independence. As Abdullah had been the only loyal Arab ruler during the war and as he had sent his army to participate in the Allied operations against the pro-Nazi elements in Iraq and the Vichy forces in Syria, it is not surprising that his request was wholeheartedly granted in 1945.[10]

During the war, the Amir, who in 1945 had become King, presented his scheme for Greater Syria: a plan for the unification of Palestine, Transjordan, Syria and Lebanon under his rulership. This scheme was totally rejected by the countries involved and was regarded by London as unrealistic. The lack of Arab support and Britain's unwillingness to support it diminished the chances of such a plan ever being implemented. This did not, however, deter Abdullah, who continued to advocate his plan until 1947. It was mainly Winston Churchill, once Abdullah's chief protagonist, who opposed the king and who wished to see King Ibn Saud of Arabia - and not Abdullah - charged with the government of Greater Syria. In the final analysis, neither Abdullah nor Ibn Saud won the support of Britain and the British Government followed the advice of its Foreign Secretary, Anthony Eden, and decided to remain aloof as far as those Arab plans were concerned.[11]

Abdullah's main opponents amongst the British diplomats in the area were the high officials of the Palestine Government in Jerusalem, particularly the various High Commissioners. In 1942, one of them wrote that the political position in Syria was 'no legitimate business of the Amir and that any proposal that Transjordan should become part of a republic of Greater Syria would convert him [the King] into an ardent separatist'.[12] Kirkbride, at that time, joined this severe criticism of Abdullah's schemes. He and most of the subsequent Transjordanian ministers were to find some of Abdullah's policies and actions either premature or far too ambitious.

The final attempt to implement the Greater Syria plan had been made by Abdullah in July 1947, before the Syrian national elections. The King had been contemplating the annexation of Jabel Druz, the southern region of Syria, with the help of the rulers of the area, the Al-Arrash family. The scheme failed because of Glubb's firm opposition to use the Arab Legion in this adventure. Later, in December 1947, Abdullah sought the alliance of the Druzes of the Lebanon; he conveyed to their leader, Kamal Jumbalat, his readiness to grant them autonomy if they would assist him in realizing the dream of Greater Syria. Once again it was Glubb who, with Kirkbride, foiled the programme.[13]

However, notwithstanding these incidents, Kirkbride regarded Abdullah as Britain's most loyal ally in the Middle East. This view was shared by Glubb; both Britons advocated basing British policy in the area on Arab monarchs such as Abdullah and not on republics like Syria.[14] Needless to say, their colleagues serving as representatives of the British Government in the Arab republics rejected this theory: they found it hard to perceive the King and his likes being the pillars of British policy in the area. Abdullah however, did become the pillar of what remained of the British Empire in the Middle East. He was certainly one of the important pillars after Egypt had declared first a cold war and later an open war against Britain, and in any case he was the principal ally of the British Government in the area of Palestine.

It is possible, in fact, to argue that owing to the prominent role he had played in post-mandatory Palestine Abdullah strengthened his position in Whitehall. This achievement was not easily won. The King owed his new status to Sir Alec Kirkbride, and these two were to be preoccupied from 1948 to 1950 with the effort of convincing Britain to base its Palestine policy on a strong Anglo-Jordanian alliance. This alliance necessitated close coordination and British identification with Abdullah's ambitions in Palestine. The King's aim was to enlarge his kingdom by annexing parts of mandatory Palestine to Transjordan and so create a new state of Greater Transjordan; in other words, Abdullah was prepared to give up the idea of Greater Syria, provided he could be compensated with the formation of a Greater Transjordan.

The withdrawal from Palestine left Britain with the need to review its Middle East policy in general and its approach towards the question of Palestine in particular. Palestine itself remained a British interest despite the decision to leave it. It was perceived as a battleground in case of a Third World War and the Transjordanian army was regarded as the main local ally that would fight alongside the Western forces in a possible confrontation with the Russians. In order to prepare the Arab Legion for this task, Britain had immediately after the Second World War strengthened this force by adding new and substantial numbers of British officers to its core.[15] Indeed, in such a contingency it was felt both in London and Washington that the Middle East would turn into a secondary theatre and that in the initial stages of the fighting it would be possible to employ only local forces. Palestine and Transjordan would become the last line of defence in the path of a possible Russian invasion of the area which, according to British and American estimates, would be aimed at the Suez Canal and the oilfields of Arabia.[16]

The Foreign Office and the Colonial Office had little trust in the Jewish community in Palestine after 1945. It was Whitehall's view in particular that a future Jewish state would be at best neutral in its attitude towards the bipolar conflict and at worst pro-communist. At the same time the Office was confident about Transjordan's loyalty; this was due, very much, to Kirkbride's and Abdullah's efforts in this matter. Kirkbride's main success was to convince London that the stability of Transjordan depended on its ability to maintain control over Palestine after the termination of the British mandate and, furthermore, he conveyed the message that it was Britain's duty to assist Abdullah in his efforts to resist Jewish and non-Hashemite Arab dominance there.

It should be noted that the principal British effort at this time was aimed at securing its base in Egypt since this was considered the most important strategic asset in the Middle East. This meant that in time of war, with or without Egypt's acquiescence, Britain would enter and defend or reoccupy Egypt. The Egyptian position in 1948 indicated that this would have to be done without Egyptian approval. Kirkbride could thus convince at least some of the Foreign Office officials that in time of peace Transjordan was an important and vital interest, and probably of greater strategic value than the increasingly hostile Egypt. It is possible to say that a pro-Hashemite school was formed in the Office and that the school's main achievement was to deepen British involvement in Transjordan to such an extent that every Hashemite problem whether external or internal, became a British problem as well.

It seems that Transjordan became as important as it did because it was loyal in an area which had, to a certain extent, become xenophobic and unwilling to associate itself politically or militarily with the West. Britain represented in the area not only its own interests but also those of the West; however, it found it more and more difficult to do so in the face of Arab enmity. Thus, as Kirkbride put it: 'Britain is putting all its eggs in one basket since all the other baskets are unwilling to accommodate our eggs.'[17]

Winning such a position for Transjordan was Kirkbride's main accomplishment. It was an outstanding achievement if we bear in mind Abdullah's endless efforts, most of which failed, to prove his usefulness and importance to Britain, first by participating in the allied war effort in the Middle East and then by offering to protect British interests in Palestine.

Kirkbride's fruitful efforts were overshadowed, however, by the contempt and animosity directed at Abdullah by the rest of the Arab world. Kirkbride deemed it necessary for Britain to join forces with Abdullah in order to try to refute allegations that the King was Britain's protégé. The first step was to terminate the British mandate over Transjordan and the granting of independence to the Emirate. However, this rose of independence soon wilted under the heavy burden of 'British strategic interests in the area'. The declaration of independence was followed by a treaty of alliance between the parties. Whereas Transjordan's independence was perceived as an indication of Britain's willingness to leave the area, the treaty was condemned by the Arab governments. The cool reception accorded the treaty by the Arab world implied that Abdullah's image had not been improved. The main object of Arab criticism was the clause in the treaty which allowed Britain to station troops on Transjordan's soil.[18]

It was Abdullah who decided to exploit the reaction in the Arab world to his advantage. The King looked for an opportunity to discuss with Ernest Bevin and senior Foreign Office officials the desired policy towards the question of Palestine. He needed a face-to-face meeting with the Foreign Secretary and could not carry out these negotiations publicly. Abdullah wished to meet Bevin in close quarters since he knew the differences of opinion existing between them and one could not settle these disagreements by correspondence. He could not risk public announcements regarding his efforts to coordinate Britain's policy with his own since he had been committed to the Arab League decisions to oppose by force the United Nations partition resolution of 29 November 1947. In the event, he sent his Prime Minister, Tawfiq Abu Al-Huda, and Glubb Pasha to London in January 1948, ostensibly to negotiate the revision of the Anglo-Transjordanian treaty of 1946. The King explained that such a revision was needed in order to refute Arab allegations that Abdullah was a British puppet and that what was called for was a new treaty in which Transjordan's independence would be fully respected and recognized by Britain. However, the real purpose of this overture was to assess jointly with the British Foreign Minister the recent developments in Palestine.

In order to discuss Palestine, the Transjordan Premier asked for an exclusive interview with Bevin, that is, without his Minister for Foreign Affairs, who was considered more militant and nationalistic as far as accepting any deal on the future of Palestine was concerned. Already in Amman, Tawfiq Abu Al-Huda had hinted to Kirkbride that he wanted to discuss a 'very delicate relationship' that might develop after the termination of the mandate.[19] He was referring to the King's contacts with the

Jewish Agency and his attitude to the future Jewish state.

Already before the negotiations in London, Abdullah had warned Kirkbride that chaos in Palestine could harm his position. He urged the British to prevent hostilities between Jews and Arabs there. The alternative, from Abdullah's point of view, could only have been the annexation of the whole of Palestine, or the Arab parts of that country, to Transjordan. Abdullah had talked publicly about this possibility already in 1946 and for that purpose he had commenced negotiations with all the parties concerned, namely the Arab Palestinians, the Jews and the British. Abdullah, however, revealed his real motives only to the Jews and the British. He deemed it necessary to have an outlet to the Mediterranean and could not accept the idea of either an independent Palestine or a chaotic Palestine. Yet before sending his premier to London the King had told Kirkbride that he would occupy Palestine only if he were welcomed as its liberator by the Arab world and if the British guaranteed to assist him in the Security Council to the extent of using their veto. The British representative doubted Abdullah's chances of success in getting the blessing of the Arab world and asserted that the British Government would never agree to use their veto for such purposes.[20]

It is possible to assume that Abdullah did not expect the British to be enthusiastic about his plans. This is presumably the reason for his decision to give priority to contacts and agreements with the Jewish Agency. Indeed, few officials in the Foreign Office at that stage tended to support Abdullah's scheme. Harold Beeley was the main opponent of the plan to annex Arab Palestine to Transjordan. It would have meant, argued Beeley, the enforcement of the United Nations partition by the Transjordanians. He warned that this course of action would lead to the destruction of the Arab League and would cause clashes with the leader of the Arab Palestinians, Haj Amin Al-Husseini, the Mufti of Jerusalem. As regards the British position in the Arab world, it was Beeley's contention that supporting Abdullah would embarass the government since this would mean taking a stand against the majority of the Arab League.[21] Kirkbride shared Beeley's apprehensions about the possible damage to British interests stemming from such a course of action but could not suggest an alternative course since all other options would, apparently, harm British interests even more. He was strongly opposed to the idea of either an independent or a unitary Arab Palestine so, to his mind, this was the least of all evils.

Before discussing the issue with the Transjordanian Premier, the Foreign Secretary, Ernest Bevin, shared Beeley's opinion. However, there was a significant difference between Bevin's and

Beeley's outlook for the future. Beeley advocated that the Arab countries should let the local Arab forces in Palestine launch guerilla warfare against the Jews that would bring about the creation of an independent Arab Palestine, whereas Bevin still hoped that partition would eventually prove a failure and the parties would return to his own plan: the creation in Palestine of a provincial autonomy composed of Jewish and Arab provinces controlled by the High Commissioner's advisory council in which both the Jews and the Arabs would be represented, together with the proviso that after four years of restricted Jewish immigration the country would be granted its independence. Beeley had already observed during the London conference that had been convened in order to discuss the plan (September 1946) that the Arab leaders believed that any scheme of provincial autonomy would lead to partition.

This was the background for the Anglo-Transjordanian talks in February 1948. Until these talks, there was a lack of inclination on the British side to support the King's ambitions. However, when Tawfiq Abu Al-Huda requested British assistance for Abdullah's programme he found a very sympathetic Foreign Office and, moreover, he succeeded in gaining Bevin's approval for the plan.

What caused this shift in British policy and thinking? The most apparent feature that emerges from Bevin's behaviour on this issue was his pragmatism. The Foreign Secretary looked for ways of maintaining a dominant British strategic position in the area despite the termination of the mandate and Abdullah was the first to offer an outlet. Thus although it initially seemed a risky option, the direct meeting with Abu Al-Huda and further reflection on it convinced the Office and Bevin that this was a credible policy. After the Jewish successes in Palestine in April 1948, any doubts remaining about the desirability of this policy disappeared. It was also seen as the only way of leaving Palestine in an orderly manner. The Foreign Office adapted itself to Bevin's new Palestine policy with little difficulty as it was formulating its own re-evaluation of British policy in the Middle East.

The failure of the Foreign Office to effect a reorientation of the Arab League policy along pro-British lines serves as the best explanation for the Office's readiness to base its policy in the area on Abdullah. One of the gravest consequences of Abdullah's action would have been, as the anti-Hashemite school in London perceived it, the deterioritation of Transjordan's relations with the League. However, even before Tawfiq Abu Al-Hadu's visit to London the Foreign Office and Bevin had made up their minds about the future of Anglo-League relations. For them, the League was an unimportant political factor, merely a tool for Egyptian anti-British policies. Arab unity was regarded as pure utopia and the Office advised the government to treat Arab countries individually.[22] The implication of this attitude was that Abdullah could win British support even if he acted in defiance of the League's decisions.

Once Bevin had decided to back the Transjordanian option, it was quite easy for the Foreign Office to explore the advantages of this course for Britain. Annexation of Arab Palestine to Transjordan meant the extension of British rights contained in the Treaty to that area, thus compensating Britain for the loss of Palestine.[23]

After the discussion in London between Tawfiq Abu Al-Huda and Bevin, the Foreign Office made some practical decisions in preparation for the coming conflict. The officials in London thought that British officers serving in the Arab Legion should *not* be ordered out, and that Britain should continue its subsidy to that body. When the day of the fighting approached, Kirkbride suggested that, until open warfare developed, the British combatant officers accompany their units even if they moved into Palestine proper. The Foreign Office approved his recommendation, thus probably leading to some involvement by British officers.[24] In an interview he gave in the 1960s, Kirkbride admitted that even after the fighting had commenced, he ignored consecutive telegrams ordering the withdrawal of British officers since he believed that the Legion could not have done without them.[25] It was decided in the Foreign Office that the Legion be allowed into Arab areas without hindrance. Sir Alec Kirkbride did not expect the Transjordanians to be welcomed in those areas. However, he could not see any alternative course that could prevent the chaotic situation that might prevail in Palestine.[26]

The possible hostile reaction in Arab Palestine was not the only problem facing the implementation of such a plan. It was necessary to assess the Arab states' reactions as well. The Foreign Office and Kirkbride agreed that there was no need to declare that Transjordan intended defying the League's decisions. Whatever the rumours that had accompanied the talks in London and despite the long-standing knowledge of Abdullah's ambitions for a great Transjordan, the Arab world had difficulty in discovering the King's real intentions. Instead, the press and politicians in the Arab capitals talked about the occupation of the whole of Palestine as the ultimate goal in the coming war. As Kirkbride tells us in his memoirs, Azzam Pasha, the League's Secretary-General, had frequently visited Abdullah to ensure that the 'Jordanian authorities did not fail to play the part assigned to them in the plan drawn up by the Arab League'.[27] For this purpose, Azzam offered

Glubb the appointment by the League of the post of Commander-in-Chief of the Arab forces in Palestine. Kirkbride and Glubb were convinced that the offer was made in 'bad faith' and in order to find a scapegoat for any future failure.[28] Thus Azzam might have guessed Abdullah's real motives in entering Palestine but, for the sake of saving Palestine from the Jews, he was prepared to support him: or, for the sake of finding someone to blame in the future, he promised the King he would stand behind him.[29] Thus in April 1948, against the better judgement of Kirkbride, Abdullah accepted the title of Supreme Commander of the Arab forced in Palestine.

The head of the Eastern Department, nevertheless, was aware of Abdullah's need to toe the general Arab line; he thus favoured a close Iraqi-Transjordanian cooperation in Arab Palestine. A joint control of Arab Palestine by the two Hashemite kingdoms was encouraged also by one of the King's most intimate Palestinian associates, Musa Al-Alami. This cooperation was deemed a necessary step in preventing the creation of what the Foreign Office called 'a Mufti state'. Musa Al-Alami conveyed to Alec Kirkbride the impression that was acceptable in London, that if Abdullah entered Palestine the Syrians and the Mufti would together work against him. Therefore, Kirkbride advocated close cooperation with Fawzi Al-Qawqji, who was an Iraqi protégé and one of the Mufti's main rivals in Arab Palestine. This attitude accounts for the ease with which Al-Qawqji entered Arab Palestine before May 15, despite the protests of the High Commissioner of Palestine, Sir Alan Cunningham, in Jerusalem.[30]

The assessment of the prospects of Abdullah's policy had to take into account the reactions of the United Nations, the Americans and the Jews. It seemed in London that there was no risk of United Nations opposition since it was the easiest way to enforce its decision from November 1947. Bevin told the Foreign Office that he was confident of American support as it promised the establishment of a Jewish state. He hoped his plan might even bring the Americans to pressure the Jews in the future state to give up a reasonable amount of their customs revenues to support the Transjordanian economy.[31] Given Bevin's point of view, it is understandable why the Foreign Office regarded favourably the Transjordanian contacts with the Jewish leadership. Bevin was satisfied with Abu Al-Huda's assurances that the Legion would not enter Jewish areas unless the Jews invaded Arab areas.[32]

There was, however, a significant deterioration in the King's relations with the Jewish Agency between March and May 1948. During March some of the main Jewish protagonists of the Hashemite–Jewish understandings were dissatisfied with the lack of clear commitment on the part of Abdullah to reach an agreement with the Agency over the partition of Palestine. They advocated a delay in the termination of the mandate for a year and a search either for new partners or an attempt to negotiate a new accord.[33]

Abdullah, for his part, felt that after the successive Jewish achievements in the March–April civil war, namely the Jewish occupation of Jaffa, Haifa, Tiberias and Zefat, he would have to reconsider his position, and when at the end of April the Jewish Agency offered to continue negotiations he refused, claiming that the Jews were responsible for the publicity given to previous contacts. Abdullah had continued to insist publicly on a solution that proposed only autonomy to the Jews.[34]

Despite this deadlock, at the beginning of May a meeting took place between two senior Hagana and British Legion officers (Colonel Goldie and Major Crocker). Both sides expressed their desire to prevent a war between the two armies. The main outcome of this meeting was the Hagana realization that the Legion had no plans to go beyond occupying the Arab areas, even though it would have to participate in the Arab war effort. It was further understood that the Legion, as well as the Jewish forces, would try to decide the future of Jerusalem on the battlefield first.[35]

It should be remembered that by this time it was clear Abdullah would enter Palestine as the Supreme Commander of the Arab forces. Kirkbride, however, reported to the Foreign Secretary that the Office should pay attention only to the fact that 'It is understood that the objectives of these top secret negotiations is to define the areas of Palestine to be occupied by the two forces.'[36] Bevin, upon learning of such an agreement, remarked that a good reason to retain the British combatant officers on the battlefield was that they would ensure that the Hagana–Legion understanding would be maintained. He further wrote that 'I am reluctant to do anything which might prejudice the success of these negotiations, which appear to aim at avoiding hostilities between Arabs and Jews.'[37]

It seems that the two parties had no intentions of departing from the original understanding. This is in spite of incidents such as the one that occurred two days before the war broke out. This incident, which would have provoked full-scale Jewish–Legion fighting, was the Gush Etzion affair.[38] Sir Alec Kirkbride was pressed by the Foreign Office to find out in the last week before the war if any changes had occurred in Abdullah's plan. Kirkbride reported that Abdullah would not attack the Jewish state and that the British legation still hoped that Jerusalem would be excluded from the fighting by a truce. The British Legion officers informed Kirkbride that a similar tendency to avoid clashes was implied in their meeting with the Hagana officers. Like Bevin, the British minister in Amman relied on the British officers to restrain the King.[39]

The outcome of this first week of fighting indicated that, intentionally or out of necessity, and in the final analysis, the Legion operation did not constitute a breach of the Jewish-Transjordan understanding. The basis for the agreement was a promise given by King Abdullah to the Head of the Political Division of the Jewish Agency, Golda Meir and Moshe Sharett, not to attack the Jewish state. Nevertheless, it should not be overlooked that there was no written or binding agreement. The Legion attacks on the Jewish Potash plant and the Jewish Electricity project, as well as the two armies engaged in the bloody battle over Jerusalem, seem to prove this point.

We have explored the issue of the Jewish–Hashemite understanding beyond the chronological order of events in order to emphasize the significance of the Anglo-Transjordanian talks which took place in London in February 1948. In this connection it should be added that, although it was the King who suggested the division of Palestine between the future Jewish state and Transjordan, it was Bevin who first introduced the idea of annexing to Transjordan the very same areas allotted to the Arab Palestinians in the 29 November 1947 partition resolution. This was suggested in order to enlist the support of the United Nations and the Americans. This new Anglo-Transjordanian accord, namely the creation of a Greater Transjordan, became Kirkbride's main concern and ambition between 1947 and 1951.

The revision of the Anglo-Transjordanian treaty was also discussed at the meeting in London. The revised treaty served to strengthen British control over Transjordan. Whereas the British negotiations with other Arab countries for the conclusion of similar revised treaties had proved an ordeal for the Foreign Office and the Chiefs-of-Staff, the talks with Transjordan were a comparatively easy task. Owing to Britain's dominant role in Transjordan, the army had little problem in agreeing to the revision of the 1946 treaty. In fact, the Chiefs-of-Staff recommended to Ernest Bevin the revision of the treaty and the compliance with the Transjordanian request since the army realized that the treaty substance and spirit would not be changed.[40]

The main amendment in the 1948 treaty concerned the relationship of the British Army with the Legion. Direct British control over the Legion was replaced by a joint board of defence. The British hoped to reduce the impression of complete British control by excluding Glubb Pasha from this body. Its chairman was nevertheless a British officer. In practice, then, nothing had changed. Moreover, after the treaty had been concluded the Chiefs-of-Staff sent two directives to the board itself, emphasizing the relevant article in the treaty which called for cooperation; the second was sent only to the British members of the board. This latter directive stated that the board was incorporated in the British military organization in the Middle East, and that it had become subordinated to the British Middle East Forces.[41] There was no intention of involving the board in the preparation for the war in Palestine. In fact, British officers rejected Abdullah's appeal to convene the board before the termination of the British mandate as they, unlike Abdullah, had no inclination of becoming militarily involved in the fighting.

As might have been anticipated, the treaty was widely condemned in the Arab world. After all, almost the same draft treaty had been rejected by the Iraqi Parliament. In the summer of 1947, combined nationalistic pressure and the desire of Nuri As-Said (the prominent pro-British politician) to strengthen the alliance with Britain contributed to the Iraqi determination to negotiate a revision of the Anglo-Iraqi treaty. In January 1948, the revised treaty was agreed upon in Portsmouth but was rejected by a coalition of Iraqi politicians who had not participated in the discussions; they convinced the Parliament not to ratify the treaty. The main Iraqi argument was that the revised treaty did not differ from the Anglo-Iraqi treaty of 1930. This is to say, it still left Britain in a paramount position in Iraq and would prevent Iraq from gaining full independence.[42]

Why then did the Foreign Office offer the same treaty to the Transjordanians? It seems that the Office was convinced that the unpopularity of the Iraqi Government, and not that of the treaty, was behind the violent rejection of it. Furthermore, as the Transjordanian Premier explained in a letter to Bevin: in Trasjordan there was no need to bring treaties for ratification to the Parliament.[43] In general, this British decision manifested the Foreign Office tendency to play down the importance of the nationalistic Arab opposition to a continued British presence and influence in the Arab lands.

However important the treaty was for Britain's position in Transjordan, it was not as valuable as Kirkbride's presence in the country. The treaty and the British contingent in Transjordan ensured a military dominance there, but Kirkbride's residence promised continued political influence in the kingdom. It was due to Sir Alec Kirkbride's immense importance that Britain could rely without hesitation on Transjordan's loyalty and cooperation. As Elizabeth Monroe has summarized it: since Jordan was an absolute monarchy, an agreement with Abdullah was an agreement with Jordan.⁴⁴ This was certainly the case until 1949, when the King's position was considerably undermined owing to the emergence of a Palestinian Public opinion in the country.

Kirkbride enjoyed a position similar to that of a colonial high commissioner and together with Glubb Pasha occupied the most important posts in the country after the King and his Prime Minister. In a letter to the head of the Eastern Department, Bernard Burrows, Kirkbride admitted that he was so well informed about the King's state of mind and could influence his decisions to such an extent that it caused him embarrassment. As he explained: 'As a result of our long association (twenty-seven years) King Abdullah had got into the habit of informing me of what he had in mind, in both official and private matters with such frankness which is something startling.'⁴⁵ It seems that Kirkbride was embarrassed since he conveyed Abdullah's thoughts to London, and this information was sometimes used to rebuke the King.

Both in London and in Amman it was realized that a British representative with a similar standing should be found to replace Kirkbride. Furthermore, every effort was made so that Abdullah's heir apparent, Prince Talal, would be under British influence as much as his father had been. In October 1948, Kirkbride reported that Talal, who in the early years of the Second World War had displayed an anti-British attitude and had therefore been excluded from the succession the the throne, had considerably mended his ways and could be trusted to be pro-British. In any event, London had to have faith in Talal as Naif, the second son, could not be relied upon owing to his involvement in 'disgraceful escapades' (blackmail and smuggling). Incidentally, Hector Bolitho, who had spent a considerable time with the Hashemites in Jordan, refuted British allegations about Talal's hostile attitude.⁴⁶

Kirkbride advised that a Foreign Office official who spoke Arabic should be sent to win the confidence of Talal since, as he himself put it, 'Kirkbride will not last forever'. And in his opinion, the establishment of personal influence by a Briton over Talal would be the principal safeguard against the decline of British control over Transjordan. This last assumption was well founded and influence lasted as long as Kirkbride remained in Transjordan. With his departure, however, Britain ceased to play an important role in Transjordanian politics. But he, and Britain, were still there when the UN debated post-mandate Palestine.

When the United Nations General Assembly recommended the partition of Palestine, Britain could have pursued one of two distinct policies. As the mandatory power, the British Government could have, and some might argue should have, cooperated in enforcing the resolution on behalf of the United Nations — or at least facilitated the transition of mandatory Palestine to its successors, the Jewish and Arab communities. Alternatively, the British Government could have chosen to do nothing, ignoring the United Nations resolution; that is, Britain could have resisted the implementation of the resolution, at least for as long as it was the sole authority in Palestine. In many respects, Britain's decision to refer the Palestine problem to the United Nations was meant to extricate the Government from a position in which it would have to make a decision. As Bevin pointed out in the House of Commons in February 1947, while announcing the decision to withdraw from Palestine, Britain was unable to find a solution acceptable to both parties.[47] The proposal by the United Nations General Assembly to partition Palestine into two states was accepted only by the Jews; Britain could therefore not take part in its enforcement but neither could it not oppose it as it was committed to accept any resolution by the United Nations.

It is no wonder then that both the Foreign Office and the War Office were preoccupied with the possible consequences of the British Government's decision to adopt a neutral posture towards the Arab-Jewish conflict in Palestine. The main question asked in London in December 1947 was: how important and vital was post-Mandatory Palestine to Britain's interests in the Middle East?

The Chiefs of Staff could not envisage the exclusion of Palestine from the British sphere of influence. Their committee ruled in January 1948 that one of the basic and essential British requirements was the maintenance of strategic rights in Palestine.[48] Most of the British diplomats in the area shared this view, but only Kirkbride maintained that this could be achieved by coordinating Britain's Palestine policy with that of King Abdullah. His major success was convincing London that, unless Britain could assure itself of some impact, or indeed a decisive impact, on the course of events in Palestine, after the termination of the mandate, it could not be confident of its ability to preserve its strategic rights in that country. Thus, it was mainly through Kirkbride's and Abdullah's eyes that the British policy-makers concerned themselves with questions such as the outcome of the Palestine war, its implications for British interests in the area and, finally, with the dilemma of the most desirable solution for the Arab-Jewish conflict from the British viewpoint.

This led to the emergence of a British policy to solve the Arab-Jewish conflict while at the same time preserving British interests in the area. As has been pointed out, this policy was formulated during the Anglo-Transjordanian negotiations in London in February 1948. The gist of this solution was British approval for a Jewish-Hashemite understanding about the implementation of the United Nations partition plan. However, whereas the United Nations recommended the partition of Palestine into a Jewish state and an independent Arab state, the new solution advocated dividing Palestine between Transjordan and a future Jewish state. This formula had first been suggested by Abdullah to the Jews; only later did it win the blessing of Kirkbride and the Foreign Office.

The factor which united the three parties concerned (the Jewish Agency, Britain and Transjordan) in their suport for this concept was their opposition to the establishment of an independent Arab Palestine state as provided for by the United Nations partition resolution. The Foreign Office, like the two other advocates of this concept, believed that such a state would be led by the Mufti of Jerusalem and the Chairman of the Arab Higher Committee, Haj Amin Al-Husseini. In general terms, one could say that its creation would have prevented both Abdullah and the Jews from implementing their territorial and national ambitions in Palestine, and in particular from the point of view of the Jewish state such an entity would have perpetuated the Arab-Jewish conflict in Palestine. An agreement with Abdullah, on the other hand, seemed more feasible and workable. As for the British, in such a case they would have to reconcile themselves to the division of Palestine between the local Arabs and the Jews. These two communities were perceived by the Government at the time as strongly opposed to Britain's influence in the area.

This approach ignored two important factors in the Palestine conflict. In the first instance, it disregarded the demands and the aspirations of the Arab Palestinians. This was, however, hardly a new phenomenon. Since the active involvement of the Arab countries in Palestine's affairs (from 1936 onwards) this seems to have been the attitude of everyone concerned. The Palestinian inability to present a united and independent or a moderate position contributed to this state of affairs. Thus, British satisfaction of Arab demands did not necessarily mean satisfaction of those of the Arab Palestinians. This concept was also unacceptable to the Arab League: it antagonized Egypt and Syria in particular. It thus caused a serious deterioration in Anglo-Arab relations, which had already been considerably weakened by the emergence of a new trend of anti-British Arab nationalism.

Notwithstanding these problems, the Foreign Office regarded this solution as the lesser of two evils. It seems that the United Nations and the Americans viewed the situation in very similar terms. Nevertheless, it took some British persuasion before this concept was accepted by the United Nations as the best solution for the Palestine problem and before the Americans had abandoned their own ideas about a desirable peace settlement.

Thus, one has to differentiate between two main currents in Britain's Palestine policy during the Arab-Israeli war of 1948. There was, on the one hand, a concern to safeguard British withdrawal; this was accompanied by a policy of non-interference in the developing Arab-Jewish confrontations. On the other hand, there were the British plans and ideas about post-Mandatory Palestine. This last effort was based primarily on the greater Transjordanian concept — this is to say, the enlarging of Transjordanian territory at the expense of the United Nations' Arab Palestine. This meant that London had to coordinate its policy with Abdullah — a mission entrusted to the experienced hands of Sir Alec Kirkbride.

During the last days of British rule in Palestine, Kirkbride's main concern was to prevent the Arab incursions into Palestine from turning into a campaign against King Abdullah. In the months from January to May 1948, Arab irregulars entered Palestine, most of them via Transjordan. They came from Syria, Iraq and Lebanon and were trained by officers from the Syrian army. There is no wonder, then, that Kirkbride perceived them as immensely dangerous to the stability of Transjordan.[49]

The British policy of non-interference was applied to the Arab incursions as well; that is, as long as these operations did not undermine the efforts for a safe evacuation, they were ignored. This British insistence on limiting the maintenance of law and order to British areas alone led to some absurd decisions: while London did not mind the infiltration of Palestine by small Arab groups it refused to cooperate with the United Nations and objected to the arrival in Palestine of a United Nations group of experts who wished to examine the means for a gradual British civil and military evacuation.[50] Instead the British Cabinet decided to maintain its administrative control until 15 May 1948, thus not allowing any period of transition. This British policy, which was not accompanied by an effort to maintain law and order, was a formula for future chaos. The United Nations experts suggested gradual evacuation of the civil administration but this was not achieved owing to the lack of transitional period. The British Cabinet itself realized what its policy would mean in the final analysis. A Cabinet minute accurately described the collapse of the civil, legislative and security systems in Palestine if the policy of non-interference were maintained.[51] Ten years later Kirkbride pointed out that the main British 'crime' was the refusal to hand over authority to the United Nations; in his words, this was 'inexcusable'. Like many other Britons serving in the Middle East at the time he asserted with hindsight that the Government should have sought ways for handing over the responsibility and the liabilities of the mandate to a United Nations authority.[52]

As for Kirkbride's main task, the coordination of British and Transjordanian policies during the war, this was accomplished with little difficulty. Without his despatches from Amman during the war, London could not have assessed the Arab intentions and plans in Palestine. The Foreign Office had learned through Kirkbride about the proceedings of the Arab leaders' meetings during the war. However, even more important was Kirkbride's ability to know in advance the forethoughts and schemes of the most able and potent of the Arab forces fighting in the war — the Arab Legion. An examination of the estimated strength of the parties involved in terms of manpower, equipment and ammunition proved that the Arab Legion was in fact the most significant force facing the Jews in 1948. Therefore, a priori knowledge about Abdullah's decision to restrict his effort to the area of Jerusalem and about his prior understanding with the Jewish Agency on the annexation to Transjordan of the West Bank[53] enabled Kirkbride to predict almost to an inch the final outcome of the war. No other British diplomat had such an insight and the Chiefs of Staff who, unlike the Foreign Office, did not benefit from Kirkbride's services, had totally misjudged the results of the Palestine war since they had based their assumptions on purely military considerations.[54]

Nevertheless, during the war itself Kirkbride realized that even some of his predictions were wrong. He estimated that the 7,400 Legionnaires would be able to stay in the battlefield for eight months at least. Militarily speaking, it was reasonable to expect the well-organized and equipped Legion with its mechanized regiments to fulfil these anticipations.[55] However, the Legion's arsenal depended on the British who stopped supplying arms and ammunition in the early stages of the war. To Kirkbride's surprise and dismay, Bevin had reciprocated an American decision to exercise an arms embargo on the parties fighting in Palestine with a British decision to suspend all deliveries of arms to the three Arab countries which had military contracts with Great Britain: Transjordan, Egypt and Iraq.[56] Bevin acted in this way not only for the sake of Anglo-American coordination, but he wished also to perpetuate the situation that had emerged after the first week of fighting. After five days of fighting the Syrians and Lebanese were expelled from the United Nations Jewish state, the Egyptians had moved mainly into the United Nations Arab state, and the Legion had consolidated its control over the West Bank and tightened its siege on Jerusalem. Palestine was thus divided between the Hashemites, the Egyptians and the Jews. The Foreign office could not ask for more.

Kirkbride's apprehensions stemmed from the Arab League's decision to resume the war effort after the end of the first truce in June 1948. It meant that the Arab armies would find themselves without spare ammunition in the next stages.[57] At the same time, the Jews were able to circumvent the embargo by purchasing arms in the Eastern bloc and tipping the strategic balance in their favour.[58]

Kirkbride thus found himself at loggerheads with the British Government since he saw no point in exposing Transjordan to a Jewish attack. He further argued that an arms embargo was sensible only as long as the cease-fire was kept. Otherwise, maintained Kirkbride, it would be the end not only of Greater Transjordan but of the Hashemite Kingdom altogether.[59] But his difficulties were not confined to the dispute he had with London. King Abdullah was determined to continue the war effort in the city of Jerusalem, sending his troops to the battlefield lacking artillery and mortar ammunition.[60]

Kirkbride felt that Abdullah was forced to enter the battle of Jerusalem owing to the earlier Jewish occupation of the Arab quarters in the city. He therefore pleaded with London to allow further shipments of arms to the Legion in spite of the arms embargo. He was undoubtedly encouraged by Abdullah's success in capturing the Jewish quarter in the Old City, and sensed that at least parts of Arab Jerusalem could be annexed to Transjordan. Such an achievement could have been the feather in Abdullah's cap since by that he would assume the ancient role of his family, namely that of protecting the holy places of Islam. Moreover, it was anticipated in Amman that this sacred prize would guarantee Arab recognition for the occupation of the Arab areas of Palestine. However, Bevin and the Foreign Office were adamant in their refusal to allow further shipments and all Kirkbride's and Glubb's desperate appeals fell on deaf ears.[61]

Thus Abdullah resumed the fighting after the end of the first truce in June 1948. However, by the beginning of August that year the King was out of the circle of violence. In September he signed a *de facto* agreement with Israel on the partitioning of the city of Jerusalem.[62] The Israeli demand that the Iraqi forces in Samaria should be repatriated and the Israeli advance towards the Gulf of Aqaba in March 1949 had prolonged the negotiations over an armistice between the two countries and thus the agreement was concluded only in April 1949.

When the fighting was over and the dust storm that had swept through Palestine faded away, it became apparent that only Israel and Transjordan had emerged victorious from the battle. Adbullah had annexed most of the Arab areas of Palestine and occupied the two holy mosques of Jerusalem and many Arab neighbourhoods in the city. The other Arab regimes suffered political as well as military defeat from which they would never recover. Sir Alec's little kingdom had become the leading Arab state in the confrontation with Israel, and was saved for the time being from the hands of all its external enemies.

The main outcome of the Palestine war was the annexation of parts of Palestine to Egypt and Transjordan, and the creation of the state of Israel. Transjordan had in fact incorporated the largest number of Palestinians: this included both the inhabitants resident on the West Bank and more than 250,000 refugees on the West Bank and about 100,000 on the Eastern Bank. In other words, more than half of the Palestinian population in the Middle East were under Jordanian rule. As there were few proper Hashemites (those who had come with Abdullah from the Hejas) and a few other minority groups, it would be safe to say that three quarters of the population of the enlarged kingdom were Palestinians.[63]

This new demographic reality meant that Transjordan, now the Hashemite Kingdom of Jordan,[64] could have easily been turned into a Palestinian state. Such a development would have meant for Britain that its most loyal ally in the area, King Abdullah, would be replaced by a hostile entity. The Hashemites could have been deposed by the former Mufti of Jerusalem, Haj Amin Al-Husseini, Britain's worst enemy in the Arab world during the 1930s and 1940s. Such a proposal was even worse for Kirkbride. The edifice he had built in Transjordan and which he believed to be the basis for the whole British infrastructure in the Middle East would have collapsed in front of his very eyes.

The Transjordanian effort in the years from 1948 to 1950 was therefore to ensure that the annexation of Arab Palestine to Transjordan would not undermine the Hashemite control over that country. It meant that what was needed was a consent — international, regional and Israeli — for the annexation. In addition, Abdullah had to ensure that all existing manifestations of irridentist Palestinian identity in the area occupied and outside it, in the Arab world, should be either eliminated or reduced.

In Transjordan this effort was carried out by the King, the Government and his political advisers, in particular Tawfiq Abu Al-Huda who had served most of the period under review as the Premier. But it was only Kirkbride who had been aware that the main challenge to the Hashemite hegemony in the newly formed kingdom did not come from without, from Israel or the Arab world, but from within. Thus he alone occupied himself with questions relating to the possible impact the Palestinians would have on the national character of Jordan and on its political inclinations.

The King was mainly obsessed with reaching a firm and open understanding with the Israelis. He had therefore strived to conclude an armistice with Israel which would include an offical Israeli consent for the annexation of Arab Palestine to Transjordan. It is beyond the scope of this article to enter into the details of the Israeli-Transjordanian negotiations (December 1948 – April 1949) but it will suffice for our purposes to note that Kirkbride had supported the idea of an armistice with Israel since the principle of armistice had been accepted by the Arab League (Syria, Egypt and Lebanon had signed similar agreements with Israel). However, Kirkbride believed that the King in his eagerness to obtain an official Israeli recognition in the new enlarged kingdom had gone far too far in order to satisfy the Israelis' demands. The main Israeli condition for granting this consent was the annexation to Israel of the area known as the 'Little Triangle'. This was an area in which more than 15,000 Palestinians lived; the final demarcation line of that 'Triangle' had divided some villages into two and separated others from their cultivated lands.[65]

During the process of negotiations, Kirkbride urged the King not to concede to this Israeli demand which he saw as an act of pure blackmail.[66] However, the King feared that his refusal would lead to an Israeli attack on the West Bank; an attack which would have found the Jordanians defenceless. The Arab Legion was unable at the time to defend the West Bank by itself. The Iraqis had already withdrawn in accordance with a previous Israeli demand and there was very little hope that Britain would come to the rescue. Both Kirkbride and the King realized that the British would not hasten to intervene militarily as long as British lives were not endangered and as long as the Israelis did not attack Transjordan proper. In fact, the British Cabinet took a decision to that effect, namely that His Majesty's Government was committed by its treaties with Egypt and Jordan to protect the integrity and sovereignty of these countries should they be attacked by a third party (i.e. Israel). This commitment, however, did not relate to territories annexed, either by Egypt or Jordan (i.e. the West Bank and the Gaza Strip).[67] Neither government was informed at the time of this British decision. Nevertheless, British behaviour during the war itself indicated the disinclination of the Government to become involved in any act of fighting. There was nothing therefore that Kirkbride could offer the King towards strengthening his position *vis à vis* Israel. Furthermore, the Americans for their part refused to exert pressure on Israel in order to moderate its demands.[68]

In these most unfavourable conditions it is no wonder that the British representative in Amman chose to describe the meeting at which the Israeli demand had been made as taking place in circumstances 'strongly reminiscent of Hitler and the late Czech President'.[69] Undoubtedly he had used such strong language in order to convey to London the dire straits the King was in. One might note that the account by the American representative in Amman who had generally shared Kirkbride's apprehensions did not correspond with this description.[70] Nevertheless, it should be noted that at earlier stages of the negotiations the Israelis had indeed threatened the King that any delay in the conclusion of an armistice might lead to the renewal of fighting between the two countries.

Kirkbride's disapproval of the King's conduct in the negotiations stemmed not only from differences of opinion about the tactics used in negotiations. In his contacts with the Israelis, Abdullah, who had hitherto always consulted the British representative on every political issue, chose this time to deal with the Israelis without sharing his thoughts, worries and plans with Kirkbride. Thus, for the first time since he had come to Transjordan, Sir Alec Kirkbride learned about the King's policies only after they had been implemented. He therefore could not have informed London *beforehand* of most of the Israeli–Jordanian meetings. This was the case during the period that followed the armistice agreement (signed on April 3 1949), a period in which the King sought a proper peace treaty with Israel.

The King was not content with the armistice agreement as a means of ensuring Israeli acquiescence with his rule over the West Bank. He therefore looked for a formal peace pact between the two countries. It is quite probable that Abdullah wished to enter history as the peacemaker of the Arab–Israeli conflict and as the guardian of stability in the area of Palestine. This role could have guaranteed Western support and recognition as NATO's bastion in the Middle East. Such a position could have compensated him for the growing isolation of Jordan in the Arab world. Kirkbride did not underestimate these considerations; he felt, however, that a *de facto* agreement with Israel, namely the armistice accord, was sufficient for obtaining this very goal.[71] In particular, the armistic between Israel and Transjordan was tolerated by the Arab world, notwithstanding the inclusion in the agreement of apparent violations of previous Arab League decisions about Palestine. These decisions had been taken by the League already in February 1948. The League declared that any part of Palestine that was 'liberated' should be tranferred to its people so that they themselves could determine the desirable solution to their problem. It had further decided on the establishment of a Palestinian administration that was subordinate to the League and whose role was to prepare the ground for the formation of an independent Palestinian entity after the war.⁷² The Arab defeat had voided all such resolutions of any substance and therefore apart from verbal protestations there was very little that the Arab League could do in order to prevent the annexation of Arab Palestine to Transjordan. Only the Egyptians went as far as creating a Palestinian government in exile in Gaza in September 1948 as a countermeasure to Abdullah's policies, but, as will be elaborated below, this venture failed and was never attempted again. Kirkbride sensed that the Arab reaction to a separate treaty between Israel and Transjordan would be even stronger.⁷³ Indeed it seems that whereas the League had not taken any action against the unification of the two banks of the Jordan river by the Hashemites, it had nevertheless adopted an Egyptian draft resolution that any member of the League concluding a bilateral agreement with Israel would be expelled from the League. It is the irony of history that this very clause was exercised by the League years later in 1979, in order to oust Egypt from the organization following the Camp David accord.

However, the possible severance between Jordan and the Arab League did not trouble Kirdbride. As mentioned before, he, like most of the Foreign Office officials including Bevin, had formed a very low opinion of the League at the beginning of 1948. In their eyes, the League had ceased to represent Arab unity and had become merely a tool in Egyptian hands in their struggle against Britain. Kirkbride's source of worry was identification with and support for the general Arab line by the Jordanian ministers and in particular by the Prime Minister, Abu Al-Huda. Their opposition to the King's *rapprochement* with Israel stemmed both from practical and ideological grounds. They asserted that the Palestinian population in the West Bank would resent any official agreement with the Israelis and could be easily instigated by Arab countries such as Syria, Saudia and Egypt.⁷⁴ Moreover, the ministers, who since 1949 had included three notables⁷⁵ from the West Bank, had regarded themselves as part of the Arab national movement and not as pawns in the hands of Britain, or any other power, in the international chess game.

Thus the Transjordanian Government in Amman joined Kirkbride in his criticism of the King's enthusiastic and ambitious plans for a separate peace with Israel. The King had almost succeeded in outflanking his opponent when after lengthy and tiring negotiations he offered the Israeli representatives who came to his winter Palace in Shuneh a non-aggression pact for five years which, *mutatis mutandis*, was a formal peace treaty which included proper commercial relations and a Jordanian corridor to the Mediterranean via Israeli territory. This was in February 1950, two months before the designated date for the formal unification of the two banks of the river Jordan, the euphemism used by the King for the annexation of the West Bank. It was Kirkbride who turned up trumps and foiled the agreement by convincing the King to stipulate the final ratification of the non-aggression pact on its approval by a newly elected government, namely the one that would be formed after the unification, composing representatives from both Banks. Kirkbride had anticipated that the Palestinians from the West Bank would firmly reject the pact, as indeed they did in April 1950.[76] However, it would be erroneous to conclude from this summary that the King's efforts were wasted, since in the final analysis the Israelis had abandoned their plans for occupying the West Bank.

Elsewhere, the Jordanians had obtained recognition for their act of annexation when the United Nations mediator, Count Folke Bernadotte, recommended in his final conclusions that the best solution for the Arab–Israeli conflict would be the division of Palestine between the Hashemites and Israel.[77] Although his recommendations were not accepted as an official United Nations peace plan, owing to the Count's untimely death (he had been assassinated by Jewish extremists in September 1948), they were regarded as his sacrosanct will and secured the *de facto* American and European recognition for the annexation.[78]

As for the need to eliminate any secessionist Palestinian tendencies in the area, one might question the effectiveness of the Hashemites' efforts on that score; at least Kirkbride did, and so do we in hindsight. In the short term, however, the Jordanians dealt most effectively with this problem. In the first two years after the occupation they abolished all the remaining independent Palestinian organizations.[79] Abdullah had successfully countered the Egyptian attempt to undermine his pretensions to represent the Palestinians. The Egyptians had established an exile Palestinian government in Gaza in September 1948. Abdullah reacted by forming his own two Palestinian assemblies: a refugee congress in Amman in October 1948 and a local residents' conference in Jericho in December that year. With considerable assistance from the British legation in Amman, these two conventions were carefully staged in order to portray the impression of overriding Palestinian support for the King's policies.[80] Furthermore, the King added two members from the West Bank to the Jordanian mission to the Arab League, thus claiming that the Palestinian cause was represented in the League by the Jordanians alone.[81]

But it is mainly Abdullah's *fait accompli* policies which tipped the balance in his favour. He completed the administrative and political annexation in less than two years and correctly surmised that Arab support for the Palestinians would not go beyond verbal protestations. However, in retrospect we might add that he did overlook the radical political and social transformations that were sweeping through his newly enlarged kingdom. Kirkbride, who was not unaware of developments, discovered that this issue had become the main bone of contention between him and his old-time companion, Abdullah of the Hejaz.

For the sake of clarity it should be noted that Kirkbride was completely in favour of the annexation of the West Bank as the best means of stabilizing the Kingdom of Jordan and by so doing protecting British interests. This could have been achieved if the autocratic character of the Jordanian Kingdom had been preserved, that is, that all political decisions, both external and domestic, should be taken by the Hashemite family. To his bewilderment and astonishment this notion was not shared by King Abdullah, who believed that a flavour of democracy should be added to the process of annexation. As mentioned above, the King had always looked for legitimacy for his fictitious Kingdom created by Churchill in 1921 on the soil of Palestine. International legitimacy was not hard to obtain; he now wanted at least the appearance of internal legitimacy — the public support of the Palestinian population. As long as this process of democratization was controlled by the Hashemite authorities, as in the cases of the congresses of Amman and Jericho, Kirkbride went along with the King's schemes. But when Abdulla suggested that the new enlarged Kingdom should have proper, that is Western, legislative judical and executive powers he was, in Kirkbride's eyes, acting in the most bizarre way.

Abdullah allowed a committee of Palestinian and Jordanian jurists to prepare jointly a new constitution for the Kingdom.[82] Had not Abdullah's grandson, Hussein, suspended this constitution, Jordan would have become a constitutional monarchy. Abdullah created a new legislative system, which included a House of Commons to which members were elected in the April 1950 election on a regional basis, and thus the Palestinians had an overall majority in it. The system also provided for a Senate to which the King selected in parity senators from both banks of the river Jordan.[83] Needless to say, Palestinian politicians, merchants and activists at the time supported the annexation provided it would be followed by a process of democratization. Abdullah had never intended turning Jordan into a republic or a democracy; he wanted the appearance of democracy. In, fact, generally speaking he had pursued a discriminatory fiscal and political policy towards the West Bank.[84] But Kirkbride did not believe in semi-democratic regimes. In his view, such regimes were bound to become democracies. Before analysing Kirkbride's perceptions and apprehensions about Abdullah's quasi-democratic acts, it is important to note that the King's actions were accompanied by a public declaraction about his willingness to resettle a large number of Palestinian refugees in Transjordan and the West Bank.[85] Even if only the refugees in the West Bank could have been resettled, it would have meant that fewer than 100,000 Hashemites and their allies would have ruled over more than 750,000 Palestinians.[86] Hence Kirkbride insisted on precluding the possibility of a large-scale resettlement project for the refugees in Jordan. He succeeded in dissuading London from accepting this concept of a large-scale resettlement in the West Bank. Thus, the Foreign Office advocated the resettlement of most of the refugees in Syria and Iraq.[87]

With the refugees or without them, the Palestinians of the West Bank were regarded by Kirkbride as a political group that endangered the existence of the Hashemites in Jordan and, by that, the whole British edifice in the Middle East. Not everyone in the Foreign Office shared Kirkbride's advocacy for a strong Anglo-Hashemite alliance but it was shared by the senior policy-makers and thus became the main feature of British policy at the time.[88]

Kirkbride used frequently at that period the term 'Palestinization of Greater Jordan', namely the overthrow of the Hashemites. In his mind what would follow would have been a communist state since he and Glubb believed that most of the Palestinians were susceptible to communism in Jordan. Consequently he convinced the King to declare the Communist Party illegal and most of its leaders were arrested. Kirkbride warned that its influence would rise once again if the country went through an economic crisis.[89]

There is confusion in Kirkbride's analysis of the situation; at times he talked about the communist danger and at times about the perils of democratization. The crux of the matter was that as a result of the new geopolitical situation that emerged after the Palestine war of 1948, Kirkbride's authority was diminished considerably and was mainly affected by the union and the presence of anti-British Palestinians in the Jordanian Government and Parliament. After the union was completed he found no other words in which to describe the new political situation other than 'throes of revolution'.[90] The revolutionary forces were the political-minded Palestinians who were about to revolt against the King. Kirkbride attributed to himself, with a great measure of justice, the preservation of a Hashemite control over the executive authorities and in the army. However, he concluded in the end of 1950 that the Palestinians dominated the legislative bodies and therefore had won the preliminary battle against the executive. Consequently, Kirkbride's own impact declined and he was unable to exert much influence on either side. This was due mainly to what he called the negative Palestinian attitude to all British suggestions. Moreover, the British representative complained: 'The Palestinians were people with whom I never worked before'.[91]

Kirkbride's solution was to form a new government with a smaller number of Palestinian ministers; otherwise, he warned, Jordan would collapse and the place would be abandoned and divided by its neighbours. The inevitable result, Kirkbride predicted at the end of a desperate letter to the head of the Eastern Department, would be the collapse of Britain's most vital stronghold in the area, which he (Sir Alec) had been building up over the previous twenty-six years.[92]

The head of the Eastern Department and most of the officials in Whitehall believed it was only a matter of time before the Palestinians would see things in the same way as the King did.[93] The Foreign Office's more optimistic point of view proved to be more to the point, not so much because of the emergence of a more pro-British or pro-Hashemite Palestinian public opinion, but rather owing to Kirkbride's own initiative to 'Jordanize' the West Bank. For his part, Kirkbride was right. During the first years after the annexation there was certainly a danger of Palestinization of the united state. Kirkbride thus acted in order to allay his own fears and misgivings and prevented the formation of a new enlightened legislative system that had been promised to the Palestinians by the King. The new system that emerged was based on a mixture of old British mandatory regulations with Jordanian martial law.[94] In August 1950, Kirkbride took another precaution against Palestinization and warned the King that the post of the chief administrator of the West Bank, which had been held by a notable from Nablus, Jamal Toukan, was granting the area a quasi-autonomous position. Thus, the post was abolished and the various departments in the West Bank had to deal directly with Amman.[95]

Yet the Palestinian identity remained alive both on the West Bank and outside it. In theory, the seats in both Houses of Parliament were divided equally between representatives from both halves of the Kingdom but, in practice, persons from the West Bank dominated the Houses since several Eastern constituencies were represented by Palestinians. In December 1950, Kirkbride came to the conclusion that the presence of representatives from the West Bank in the House 'was affecting this institution so profoundly that the King and his ministers could no longer depend on an obedient legislature as they had done in the past'.[96] Then he noted that the first ever anti-British statements had been made in Parliament.

In the concluding remarks of his annual report for 1950, Kirkbride noted that the agitation against the unification throughout that year had been fostered by followers of Haj Amin Al-Husseini, aided by some Arab states and communists.[97] Therefore, in the period preceding the assassination of Abdullah, the legation to Amman followed closely the activities of the former Mufti. The latter had moved from Cairo to Syria in May 1951 where he instigated disturbances on the West Bank and remained in Syria with other former members of the Arab High Committee there.[98] Thus when the King was murdered in Jerusalem on 20 July 1951, Sir Alec had little doubt about those who were to blame for the assassination. It was, after all, the same group that caused his own decline: 'This crime was a notable manifestation of the fact that the once peaceful and amiable state of Transjordan had largely been taken by the Palestinians.'[99] He reported that the parliamentary elections following the King's death were dominated by 'loud anti-British nationalists from the West Bank who had also won the election there'.[100]

For Sir Alec Kirkbride, Jordan after Abdullah's death was a state which moved closer to the pattern of the other Arab countries. As he himself put it, 'it was no longer in a fearlessly independent position within the Arab League'.[101] However, for Kirkbride it was even worse than that. It was a serious blow to his position within the Hashemite Kingdom. The British representative in Amman who had spent almost thirty years in the place, felt that a new era in the Middle East had begun in which Britain would have only a marginal role to play.

The Foreign Office did not view things in such a gloomy way. The Office did not sense any change in the strength of the Anglo-Jordanian alliance (the only Anglo-Arab alliance left in the Middle East after the abrogation of the Anglo-Egyptian treaty in October 1950). Nevertheless, the Eastern Department did not ignore Kirkbride's warning and advocated a more sensitive policy towards the nationalists in Jordan. However, the Conservative Governments from 1951 onwards only hardened the British attitude towards Arab nationalism which in turn became more and more anti-Western and it was thus inevitable that British officers were expelled from Jordan.

It is impossible to write off, in one sweep, a life's work. Thus, as long as the Hashemites continue to rule in Transjordan and the West Bank, their regime owes its own existence to two people: King Abdullah and Sir Alec Kirkbride. Despite his expulsion, Kirkbride was regarded for many years as one of the Hashemites' forefathers in the Jordanian historiography. A former British officer in the Arab Legion wrote about him in 1956: 'His name is still one to conjure with throughout Jordan, Desert and Sown alike, and it is not impossible that, if he had still been in Amman at the time of Glubb's dismissal, things would have turned out differently. People in Jordan still say about big things and small: "Ah! If Kirkbride had been here, it would not have happened".'[102]

Thus, in spite of the problems caused by the annexation and the danger of Palestinization of Jordan, the principal aim of the British Palestine policy in the period was achieved very much as a result of Kirkbride's presence in Amman. Britain's loyal ally in the Middle East had fulfilled its territorial ambitions, which coincided with British strategic interest and with what was believed by the Foreign Office to be the beginning of a solution for the Arab-Israeli conflict.

What had begun as an act to forestall a larger Jewish state turned almost into a crusade against an independent Palestinian state by the British, the Jordanians and the Israelis. The short-term fruits of this policy were evident: they included an Israeli-Jordanian *modus vivendi* with merely verbal protestations from the Arab world, and implicit American and UN approval. Moreover, this policy ensured the strengthening of Abdullah and justification for his rule and existence as protecting British interests in Palestine. Kirkbride and Britain had saved Jordan for the time being as a British bastion but the West Bank would re-emerge as a thorny problem long after the British had left the area. As for Kirkbride himself, his departure marked the end of what Elizabeth Monroe has so neatly summarized in the phrase, 'Britain's moment in the Middle East'.

Notes

1. The head of the Eastern Department in FO 371/68864 E13842, FO minute, 8 October 1948.
2. It seems that Sir John Troutbeck, Sir Harold Beeley and Sir Ronald Campbell were his main opponents.
3. A. Kirkbride, *A crackle of thorns*, 1956, 20.
4. T.E. Lawrence, *Seven pillars of wisdom*, Vol.2, 1953, 511.
5. Kirkbride, op.cit., 20.
6. ibid., 20.
7. ibid., 26.
8. ibid., 27.
9. U. Dann *Studies in the history of Transjordan, 1920-1949, the making of a state*, Westview, Boulder, Colo., 1984, 42-3.
10. ibid., 117-19. Professor Dann interviewed Sir Alec shortly before his death. Kirkbride referred to Abdullah's flirtations with the German legislation in Ankara in 1940. Professor Dann did not, however, find any evidence to support this allegation.

11. FO 371/27043 E2685 and E2716, FO minutes, May 1941.
12. Y. Porath, *In search of Arab unity, 1930-1945*, Hebrew, Jerusalem, 1985, 316.
13. FO 371/68403 E300 and E2001, Glubb's and Kirkbride's memoranda, December 1947.
14. CO 537/856, Glubb's memorandum, August 1946.
15. E. Monroe, 'Mr Bevin's Arab policy', *St Anthony's Papers*, **11**, 1961, 13.
16. FO 371/68378 E4319, notes on Intermezzo, an exercise on Russian invasion of the Middle East.
17. FO 371/68864, Kirkbride to Burrows, 21 October 1948.
18. FO 371/68383, FO memorandum, 1 March 1948.
19. FO 371/68366 E1739, Amman to FO, 6 February 1948.
20. FO 371/68365 E548, Amman to FO, 11 January 1948.
21. FO 371/68364 E504, FO minute, Beeley, 22 December 1947.
22. FO 371/68381, 68382 (E8103), 68443, 75051 (E13522).
23. FO 371/68818 E1899, FO minute, Pyman, 3 February 1948.
24. FO 371/68852 E6008, Amman to FO, 8 May 1948.
25. Interview with Kirkbride by E. Monroe, September 1959 in *Monroe papers*, Middle East Centre, Private Papers Archives, St Anthony's College, Oxford.
26. FO 371/68367 E2046, Amman to FO, 11 February 1948.
27. A. Kirkbride, *From the wings: Amman memoirs, 1947-1951*, 1976, 22
28. J.B. Glubb, *A soldier with the Arabs*, 1958, 286-7.
29. The first possibility is explored by W. Ad-Daly, *Asrar Al-Jami'ya Al-Arabiya* (The Secrets of the Arab League), Cairo, 1982, 233-5, and the second in J.B. Glubb, op.cit., 23, and A. Kirkbride, op.cit., 22.
30. FO 371/68367 E2120, FO minute, Burrows, 21 February 1948.
31. FO 371/68368 E2696, FO minute, Burrows, 9 February 1948.
32. FO 371/68367 E1980, FO minute, Wright, 11 February 1948.
33. Zionist Central Archives, file S/25/9383, Sasson memorandum, March 1948.
34. FO 816/123, Amman to FO, 9 June 1948.
35. FO 371/68852 E6008, Amman to FO, 8 May 1948.
36. FO 800/477, FS 48/7, 13 May 1948.
37. ibid.
38. The local Arab bands had imposed a seige on these Jewish settlements south of Jerusalem.
39. FO 371/68852 E6008, Amman to FO, 8 May 1948.
40. FO 371/68818, brief for Mr Bevin's meeting with Abu Al-Huda, 6 February 1948.
41. The Anglo-Transjordanian Treaty in FO 371/68818 E1899 and E2994, March 1948.
42. FO 816/113, Abu Al-Huda to Bevin, 20 March 1948.
43. ibid.
44. Monroe, Mr Bevin's Arab policy, op.cit.,
45. FO 371/68818 E2832, Kirkbride to Burrows, 16 February 1948.
46. FO 371/68864 E13842, Kirkbride to Burrows, 21 Octover 1948; see also R. Bolitho, *The angry neighbours: a diary of Palestine and*

Transjordan, 1957, 118-19.
47. FO 371/68864 E13843, Kirkbride to Burrows, 21 October 1948.
48. ibid.
49. FO 371/68365 E1165, Amman to FO, 21 January 1948.
50. As the Foreign Secretary explained in a minute he wrote to the Cabinet, the arrival of the United Nations group would have gravely affected the security situation in Palestine. However, the main reason for this British attitude was its disinclination to appear in Arab eyes as cooperating with the United Nations. See CAB 128/12, CM (48) 2, Bevin, 5 February 1948.
51. CAB 128/12, CM (48) 12, Bevin, 5 February 1948.
52. *Monroe papers*, op.cit.
53. The Term was used by the Foreign Office from 1949 onwards.
54. DEFE 4/12, CoS (48) 48, 1 April 1948.
55. FO 371/68822 E11049, Transjordan situation by Glubb and Kirkbride, 20 April 1948 and DEFE 4/12, op. cit.
56. B.G. Glubb, op.cit., 101, and J. Lunt *Glubb Pasha*, 1984, 139, See also FO 371/68375 E2917, Cairo to FO, 9 July 1948.
57. FO 371/68375 E9168, FO minute, Bevin, 5 July 1948.
58. Israeli Defence Forces, *Toldot Milchemet Ha-A'zmaut* (The Israeli Independence War), Tel Aviv, 239. Thus, the British decision had complicated Kirkbride's main task of preserving the Transjordanian achievements in the first week of the war. From the second week on, the Arabs had to admit not only their failure to liberate Palestine but they were faced with the possibility of a Jewish offensive on the Arab lands themselves.
59. FO 371/68822, Adbullah to Bevin, 12 August 1948.
60. FO 371/68822 E11409, Kirkbride to Bevin, 12 August 1948.
61. FO 371/68822, FO minute, Burrows, 17 August 1948.
62. FO 817/142, FO to Amman, 16 December 1948.
63. There are two important sources for the number of Palestinians: the first is S.G. Thicknesse, *Arab refugees: a survey of resettlement possibilities*, 1949, and *The U.N. Economic Survey Mission Final Report* (a body formed by the Palestine Conciliation Commission to explore the economic possibilities for the resettlement of the refugees). The Eastern Bank population was 450,000 local inhabitants (half of them Palestinians) and 400,000 resided on the West Bank. There were about 400,000 refugees on the West Bank and 100,000 on the East Bank.
64. In May 1949, the Transjordanian Ministry of Foreign Affairs sent a note to all diplomatic representatives in Amman to correct the name of the country to the Hashemite Kingdom of Jordan.
65. The little triangle was the area around Wadi Arara (The Valley of Arara) and the road running through it which connected the Jewish towns, Afula and Hadera. The Israelis also demanded the strategic high places overlooking the Wadi. D. Ben-Gurion, *Yoman Ha-Milchama* (War Diary), Rivlin and Orren, Israel Defence Ministry, Tel Aviv, 1983, 977.
66. FO 371/85386 E679, Amman to FO, 21 March 1949.

67. FO 371/82715 E1501/2, Sir Eric Beckett memorandum, 18 March 1950.
68. *Foreign relations of the U.S.*, (1949), 5, 863, Secretary of State's memorandum, 24 March 1949.
69. FO 371/75386 E3844, Amman to FO, 24 March 1949.
70. *FRUS*, op. cit., 49, Stabler to SoS, 23 March 1949, 861.
71. FO 816/142, Amman to FO, 17 December 1949.
72. H. Hassouna, *The League of Arab States and regional disputes: a study of Middle East conflicts*, New York, 1975, 34-5.
73. *FRUS*, 49, Fritzlan to Secretary of state reporting a conversation with Kirkbride, 4 November 1949, 1468.
74. The unrest was caused by the loss of land to Israel in the Armistice agreement, FO 371/75273 E8621, report on the month of June 1949.
75. They were Ruhi Al-Hadi, Khulsi Al-Khairy and Musa Nasir.
76. FO 371/82715 E1015/18, Amman to FO, 6 March 1950.
77. The Count had presented his first proposals in June 1948 and his second in September that year. He was assassinated at the end of September.
78. The Foreign Office wanted to pass the Bernadotte plan as a UN resolution that would replace the November 1947 resolution on partition. However, the Americans disinclination to abandon the latter as a basis for negotiations had foiled this scheme. Nevertheless in December 1948, the UN General Assembly adopted a new resolution on the Arab-Israeli conflict which included, *inter alia*, elements from the Bernadotte proposals.
79. FO 371/68641 E7589, Jerusalem to FO, 25 May 1948.
80. FO 816/142, political report, Palestine, 6 December 1949.
81. A. At-Tal, *Karithat Filastin* (The Palestine Catastrophy), Cairo, 1959, 343.
82. FO 371/82706, E1017/2, Kirkbride to Bevin, 2 August 1950.
83. FO 371/75329 E13636, summary report of Arab Palestine, October 1949.
84. The economic problems were caused by unwise financial and administrative policies which discriminated against the more effective and progressive West Bankers. Details can be found in the final report of the Economic Survey Mission in Appendix 2, 8: 'An approach to economic development in the Middle East' and CAB 134/501, 27 May 1949.
85. *FRUS*, 49, **6**, Bevin to the American SoS, June 1949, 1123.
86. See note 64.
87. I. Pappe, 'Britain and the Palestinian refugees, 1949-1950', *Middle East Focus*, **9**, (2), 19-26.
88. The two main antagonists of the Hashemites were Sir John Troutbeck, head of the British Middle East Office and Sir Ronald Campbell, British Ambassador to Cairo.
89. FO 371/82703 E1013/4, Kirkbride to Younger, 27 July 1950.
90. FO 371/82716 E1053/2, Kirkbride to Furlonge, 30 November 1950.
91. ibid.
92. ibid.

93. ibid., Furlonge to Kirkbride.
94. FO 371/82706 E1017/2, Kirkbride to Bevin, 2 August 1950.
95. ibid.
96. FO 371/91788, E1011/1, annual report for Jordan, 1950.
97. FO 371/91788, ibid.
98. FO 371/91796 E10389/1, Kirkbride to FO, 17 May 1951.
99. FO 371/98856, Jordan annual report for 1951.
100. ibid.
101. ibid.
102. G. Lias, *Glubb's Legion*, 1956, 105.

5 Robin Hankey
Victor Rothwell

Robin Hankey was associated, as Anthony Eden's private secretary from 1933 to 1936, with the policy of drawing the Soviet Union into the League of Nations as a preliminary to the possibility of Russian inclusion in a system of collective security against German expansion. In Moscow they met Stalin and Litvinov and afterwards visited Poland and Czechoslovakia. His career between 1945 and 1949 was divided into two unequal stages: eight months (July 1945–March 1946) as counsellor at the reopened British Embassy in Warsaw, and over three years as head of the Northern Department at the Foreign Office which handled British relations with the Soviet Union and several North and Central European countries including Poland, and which therefore had a major role in policy formulation in the early Cold War. (In November 1949 he was transferred to the Embassy in Madrid, a phase in his career which will not be considered here.) Before turning to Hankey's own actions it is necessary to discuss the situation in Poland.

Poland was a country which British people and British foreign policy-makers had learned to take seriously just before and during the Second World War. Entry into war in 1939 as Poland's ally, playing host to Poland's exile government after it was forced to flee France in 1940, and the presence in Britain and with the British forces on various fronts of hundreds of thousands of Polish servicemen and civilians, had made the British very conscious of Poland. Informed opinion saw the difficulties in the resolution of Polish–Soviet differences in the light of Soviet participation in the partition of the country in partnership with Germany in 1939 and refusal after 1941 to return the 1939 conquests as among the most formidable of the obstacles in the way of preserving the wartime grand alliance in peacetime, when it might be reduced to Britain and Russia only, if the United States reverted to isolationism. Yet such preservation was one of the main aims of wartime British foreign policy continuing on into the peace.[1] Nor can this aim be dismissed as simply deluded. Available evidence suggests that it was shared by Stalin providing his terms were met.[2]

By February 1944 Churchill was publicly acknowledging, to the delight of Goebbels's propaganda machine, the existence of serious disagreements between Moscow and the London Polish Government over frontiers, the right of the Soviet Government to interfere with the composition of the Polish Government with which it had broken off diplomatic relations the previous year over the affair of the Katyn graves, and the use which Russia would make of the 'Union of Polish Patriots', including a revived Polish Communist Party calling itself the Polish Workers' Party, which had been set up in the Soviet Union in 1942. As the Red Army advanced into the country in 1944, the intransigence of the London Poles on frontiers gave Stalin a good excuse to transfer power in Poland to the Union and to the less congenial 'native' communists like Wladyslaw Gomulka who had remained in Poland during the German occupation. The communists' Lublin Committee was recognized by the Soviet Union at the beginning of 1945 as the Government of Poland, and at the Yalta conference in February Churchill was unable to gain more for the non-communist Poles than an agreement that the Lublin Cabinet should be broadened, and that the Soviet Foreign Minister and the British and American Ambassadors in Moscow should form a commission, normally meeting in the Soviet capital, to oversee free elections in Poland which were to be held within a year. These were extremely weak guarantees of a democratic future for Poland, and a distinct note of fatalism had crept into the British effort to secure for Poland control over its own destiny. However, there was one sign of hope in that the former London Polish Government Prime Minister, the Peasant Party leader, Stalinslaw Mikolajczyk, was accepted as a member of the broadened government.[3]

In addition, when the British Ambassador to Moscow, Sir Archibald Clark Kerr, visited Warsaw in late June he was warmly welcomed by Boleslaw Bierut, chairman of the National Council of the Homeland, the communist-controlled provisional parliament, and, to all appearances, the leading 'Muscovite' communist in the country. Bierut promised that everything possible would be done to facilitate the work of the British Embassy when it returned, and to house its staff in as much comfort as the Polish capital, reduced to rubble by the Germans, could offer.[4] Hankey was asked to fly to Warsaw and see that these promises were kept prior to the despatch of an ambassador. He was a natural choice in that he knew Poland well from having served there in the late 1930s. In September 1939, as a member of the British Embassy staff, he had shared the agony of the Polish people as their country fell before German and Soviet invaders. Serving during the war in Romania, Egypt and Iran he had extensive dealings with Polish problems, especially with the exodus of General Anders and his Polish army from Russia with many families and civilians to Iran, where he also had many dealings with the Soviet embassy.[5] He was to write in his first report that Bierut's promises were being kept; he and his staff were in comfortable quarters in the Hotel Polonia in which the British Embassy had been installed, the 'relative comfort of which is in striking contrast to the ruin, desolation and misery on every hand'. But there was also a darker side. He reported that, although unofficial Poles, drawn mostly from 'the lower classes', were visiting the mission's offices quite freely, they warned of frequent arrests still taking place, particularly of members of the main anti-Nazis resistance, the former Home Army, whom one communist cabinet minister, after spending the war in the safety of the Soviet hinterland, had described as 'dung'. Poland at this time was suspended between freedom and totalitarianism, and Hankey's arrival had been preceded by a turn towards the former with the Polish communists lessening their use of terror and allowing the inauguration of a genuine multiparty system in May and June.[6]

Hankey and the Ambassador, Victor Cavendish-Bentinck, who arrived in August, were aware that many Poles would expect them to do more than sit back in the tolerable quarters which the communists had provided. At his famous conference with Stalin in Moscow in October 1944, at which Mikolajczyk as Polish Prime Minster had accompanied him, Churchill, desperate to offer the Polish leader some safeguard of Polish independence, had said that he would send an ambassador to Warsaw. Mikolajczyk had replied bitterly that he would rather die in action before the war ended 'than be hanged later by Russians in full view of your British ambassador'. This was a challenge to Britain's representatives in post-war Poland to be more than spectators at the execution of Polish democracy, and not to confine themselves to the defence of British interests in a narrow sense, though Mikolajczyk's strategy for attaining power in post-war Poland was not crucially dependent on Western support.[7]

In late June, before leaving London, Hankey asked a series of questions about the line he should take in Warsaw. 'Do you wish to let the Russians play a leading hand in Warsaw, or is our Embassy to help the Poles to get real independence while encouraging friendship with Russia?' With a hint of fellow feeling towards another imperial power, he went on to ask whether Britain should accept Soviet control of Polish financial affairs 'as Great Britain does in the sterling area'. British interests in the narrow sense found expression in a question about the attitude to be adopted if Polish coal exports made British coal uncompetitive in the Scandinavian market. Finally, Hankey asked whether he should offer help to people who claimed that their lives were in danger, and who could make out a case that they had helped Britain during the war. In the subsequent discussion with four colleagues, including Sir Orme Sargent who was soon to become Permanent Under-Secretary, and Christopher Warner, head of the Northern Department, Hankey was instructed to proceed with great caution except in the matter of demanding rights of free travel not only for embassy staff, but also for British journalists in Poland who should be allowed to send their reports in the diplomatic bag and to use embassy planes. The Foreign Office attached considerable importance to enabling the British public to be well informed about how Anglo-Soviet relations were faring in this key country. On curbing the activities of the Polish security police and the Soviet NKVD, who were known to be present in Poland on a large scale, the colleagues did not think that Britain could do much; and on helping individuals Warner for one took a negative stand. He used the rather strange argument that since Britain had not been able to do much to help individuals in the Polish resistance under German occupation, it would be appropriate to maintain continuity by not helping them in the future.

Two more features clearly emerged from the discussion. The first was a near-hopelessness about relations with the United States. Sargent saw them as wishing to keep Britain at arm's length everywhere as part of a general unwillingness to concern themselves with the problems of lesser powers: 'There was a tendency at the present time for the United States of America to regard themselves and the Union of Soviet Socialist Republics as the two first-rank powers in the world and to wish to keep clear of what they regarded as intra-European squabbles.' The Poles were likely to look to America rather than to Britain, in the first place, for support and to be bitterly disappointed, making Britain's position somewhat easier. Secondly, the meeting struck several notes of irritation against the Poles, by implication in case they expected Britain to do more for freedom in their country than it could, and explicitly over frontiers and the repatriation of Poles in Britain and with the British forces abroad. The Foreign Office were unhappy that even the London Poles had accepted Stalin's plan to extend Poland's Western frontier to the Oder and Western Neisse rivers, giving Poland over one-fifth of Germany's 1937 territory, from which the German populations were being expelled except such of them as the Poles were retaining for their labour. Britain still hoped that at the forthcoming summit conference at Potsdam German territorial losses might be scaled down, but that was not going to be made easier by the absence of any Polish voices of moderation. On the expatriate Poles, the British did not see a future for a great number of them in Britain itself, and hoped that many of them would return to Poland, though there was no question of compulsory repatriation. Hankey said that 'if a large proportion did not return it would not look good for us.' His meaning is not clear. Such refusal might surely have been seen as a compliment to Britain or an embarrassment to the predominantly communist Polish Government or both. The British reasoning was that the United Kingdom was already desperately short of housing, other durables and food and would probably soon be short of jobs as well. In addition, there were doubts about the willingness and ability of the Poles to integrate into British society. Finally, it was hoped that Poles returning from the West would have imbibed democracy, and would be an obstacle to authoritarianism of the right or left. Under all these circumstances a significant Polish admixture to the population of the United Kingdom was not desired.[8]

Hankey thus travelled to Warsaw to carry out a rather cautious role in a country where the Soviet Union had virtually a free hand and in which its intentions could therefore be tested. This was made explicit to him in a letter from a Cabinet minister, Sir John Anderson, though it also advised him that he might be instructed to take a more interventionist line if Anglo-Soviet relations deteriorated.[9] Soon afterwards, the results of the British general election were announced, and Hankey reported dismay among the non-communist Poles who assumed that the incoming Labour Government would be completely indifferent to their fate.[10] This fear proved to be unfounded. The new Foreign Secretary, Ernest Bevin, sent the Warsaw Embassy a message of personal support for Mikolajczyk, repeating what Churchill had said to him at Potsdam: 'I will back you up to the limit of my strength; this was a matter which went further than politics.'[11] It made life easier for the embassy staff not only that Bevin took this view but also, in a sense, that Anglo-Soviet relations did soon deteriorate, quite spectacularly to those in the know at the London Conference of Foreign Ministers in September.[12] They could not feel indifference to what was happening to the non-communist majority of the Polish people and, while they were personally annoyed by the harrying activities of what Bentinck called 'the irresponsible collection of corner boys, pimps and thimble-riggers who now staff the Polish Security Police',[13] they were well aware that that was insignificant compared with the tragedy which might befall Poland. (Unfortunately, because of a wartime remark by Eden to Molotov, the communists probably thought that Bentinck, who had been chairman of an important intelligence committee during the war, was really a spy, not a diplomat.)[14]

The Soviet Union and the Polish communists did not rely exclusively on terror in establishing their autocracy over Poland. As Mikolajczyk, who would almost certainly have been the country's leader under a democratic system, ruefully noted, they took account of 'the moods and undercurrents' of the Polish nation.[15] They pushed through populist social and economic reforms, though those would have encountered little resistance in the radicalized post-war atmosphere in any case, and, paradoxically, were able to make a successful appeal to Polish nationalism over the Western frontiers. However, police terror was used openly against opponents and against entire communities by way of reprisals. (It is only fair to add that some of this was counter-terror in reprisal for the harassment and murder of communist cadres.) The Soviet NKVD were heavily involved, in the later stages often in Polish uniforms as what the Poles called POPs, an acronym from the Polish words meaning 'people fulfilling the functions of Poles'.[16] The Embassy in Warsaw received ample information, some of it no doubt one-sided and unreliable (as Lord Bethell noted, both sides in this civil war had 'a vested interest in exaggeration'), on what was happening from their contacts in the Peasant and Socialist Parties, and in December 1945 sent a large quantity of papers on the police terror and also on Soviet exploitation of Polish economic resources to Bevin for use in scheduled conversations with the Polish Vice-Foreign Minister, Modzelewski, when he visited London in February for the meeting there of the United Nations General Assembly.[17]

As the winter drew towards its close, Hankey left Poland and became head of the Northern Department in succession to Warner in March. He was served by an efficient and devoted staff. The Russian desk was in the hands of Thomas Brimelow, a Soviet expert and Russian speaker and later head of the Diplomatic Service. The Polish desk was for most of the time headed by Patrick Hancock. Hankey reported to his predecessor Warner and later to Charles Bateman as Assistant Under-Secretaries and in matters concerning Soviet policy and intentions also to Gladwyn Jebb, the chairman of the Russia Committee. This team reported through the Permanent Under-Secretary to Bevin or, when he was away from London, very often to Attlee. Both his new duties and his sympathies called for continued heavy involvement in Polish affairs, and he and Bentinck, who remained as Ambassador and with whom he was on the most cordial terms, agreed that, without interfering in Polish internal affairs, Britain should take an avowed interest in the rule of law there and in the implementation of the Yalta agreement, and should not hesitate to condemn such things as electoral fraud. This meant gritting one's teeth, endeavouring to work with the Polish Government and, as Bentinck wrote to Hankey in April 1946, giving them 'as few excuses as possible for justifiable complaint'. Hankey agreed and noted, 'This is difficult as they are so contentious'.[18]

Hankey's concern with Polish affairs in the Northern Department reached its peak with the fraudulent January 1947 elections after which there was no hope that Poland would not be an outright totalitarian Soviet client state. Before considering these elections, certain other features of Anglo-Polish relations with which he was involved merit attention. The first was that the terror and intimidation so prevalent in Poland had an overspill into London. One Pole in the British capital who was anxious to see Hankey begged for a meeting in a café rather than in the Foreign Office on the grounds that he was under NKVD surveillance, and that it would be a black mark against him to be seen entering such a stronghold of capitalist imperialism. The Polish Ambassador in London, Strasburger, told Hankey that he was resigning and not returning home because communists on the embassy staff had made conditions impossible for him, even making communication with his own wife difficult.[19]

A second was the favourable reception which this, to Hankey, deeply flawed regime was getting from much of the non communist left in Britain. The reconstruction of Poland aroused much interest in Britain, and in 1945-6 Warsaw became something of a Mecca for British parliamentary delegations, naturally predominantly Labour because of that party's huge majority. Many of these politicians were impervious to the advice which the Embassy gave them about the true situation and returned full of praise for the popular and radical policies of the communists and their allies in the bloc of parties which they were constructing to fight elections, and for the restraint with which the Soviet Union was abstaining from interference in Polish affairs. These people had an intellectual high priest in a man who knew that it was more than his life was worth to return to his native land. This was the Polish-born, London-based, Marxist-Trotskyist journalist Isaac Deutscher, who was assiduous in propagating the message that the new regimes in East Central Europe, if imperfect, were 'historically progressive': a vast improvement on their predecessors and vastly better than anything else which those benighted societies were capable of producing. In 1946 Hankey heard that Deutscher was spreading the word among political and media contacts in London that the British Embassy in Warsaw was a nest of reactionaries which stood in need of change. (Perhaps appropriately, one Foreign Office official who found Deutscher intellectually stimulating was Guy Burgess.)[20]

Thirdly, Hankey was uncomfortably aware that the communists had one unmatchable asset. That was the new Polish Western frontier, and the universal Polish conviction that the Germans would be obsessed with recovering the lost lands east of the Oder and Western Neisse rivers and, in all probability, with putting paid once and for all to the Polish nation. All Poles were aware of how narrowly they had escaped the fate of genocide which the Nazis had in store for them as part of the 'racial restructuring of Europe' which was the Third Reich's fundamental aim,[21] and which they had begun to practise against the Poles even as priority was given to the murder of the Jews. Beginning to think of the Germans as possible future allies, the American Secretary of State, James Byrnes, made a speech in Stuttgart in September 1946 in which he hinted at revision of the Oder-Neisse frontier in Germany's favour. This created a deplorable impression in Poland, as, to a lesser extent, did an apparent repudiation of the new frontier by Churchill in his Fulton speech and a Delphic utterance by Bevin in the House of Commons that the new Polish frontier was conditional on free elections there. These speeches played a part in the extinction of Polish democracy. They were one factor in the Polish Socialist Party's decision to throw in its lot completely with the communists, after which the latter felt strong enough to indulge in a saturnalia of police regression and election-rigging.[22] In January 1947, as elections of a most unfree character were being held, the Polish Government sent to London an envoy to plead for British support for the Oder-Neisse frontier. This was Stanislaw Grabski, a member of the wartime London Government whose unique postwar achievement was to retain the respect of Western foreign ministries while remaining 'tolerable', as Stalin had described him during the Yalta debate on Poland, to the Polish communists. Grabski argued to Hankey that the question was not one of frontiers in any traditional sense but of national survival since 'the Poles could not possibly afford being overrun by the Germans again. The Germans would not make the same mistake a second time of exterminating the Poles so relatively slowly'. Hankey himself was convinced — wrongly as it ultimately transpired — that such a German threat existed, but felt that he could only reply that since Poland was now wholly under communist control it would have to look wholly to Russia for protection against this danger. Bevin was equally unforthcoming beyond a hint that if the Polish Government could persuade the mass of Poles in the West to return on the promise of farms in the new Western territories, then 'British opinion would be favourably impressed'.[23] For many years the Oder-Neisse frontier was to provide Polish communism with a trump card.

These interviews took place immediately after the wholly fraudulent Polish elections of 19 January 1947 in which the Government bloc were declared to have won 394 out of 444 seats. The Polish and Soviet Governments had ignored British and American pleas in the weeks before the election, based on their rights under the Yalta and Potsdam agreements, to allow a test of opinion which, if not wholly free, was not ludicrously unfair. The Polish Government countered by alleging British breaches of obligation to Poland, particularly in regard to the return of gold, ships and other assets belonging to the Polish state but under the control of the London Poles and thus allegedly under British stewardship since the end of the war, and by protests over the British attitude to the Oder-Neisse frontier and treatment of Poles in Britain. More dramatically, they arrested a friend of Bentinck, Count Grocholski, subjected him to a show trial on charges of treasonable contacts with the agent of a foreign power, and executed him a few days before the election. It was a snub for Britain and a warning to the Polish people to have no dealings with foreigners. Bentinck wrote to the Foreign Office that the nearest Grocholski had come to improper dealings with him was to give him a few underground political leaflets which were in any case circulating widely in Warsaw diplomatic circles, and, in Bentinck's presence, to make an offer to the journalist Sefton Delmer, who has been accused of being a Soviet agent, to introduce him to some underground figures, an offer which actually came to nothing.[24] Yet some Labour MPs took it for granted that the accusations of skulduggery against the Ambassador were true, and the accusation of improper interference in Polish affairs was to give the Foreign Office trouble for some time even though their consciences were clear. In January 1948 Hankey referred to the Grocholski episode, which was still figuring in Communist propaganda, by writing that the service was 'proud' to have maintained contacts with the Peasant and Socialist Parties in both the pre-war Poland of the colonels' regime and in the post-war period, just as its representatives in Spain were still trying to ascertain what anti-Franco Spaniards were thinking: 'But that does not mean to say that we have ever given aid and countenance to subversive or terrorist organizations in countries with which we preserve diplomatic relations. That accusation is completely untrue and has only been made in order to use the processes of justice for propaganda'.[25]

As for the Soviet Government, Molotov stonewalled amiably in the weeks before the election when the Ambassador in Moscow, now Sir Maurice Peterson, pleaded for them to 'use their great influence' with the Polish Government to bring about elections in which there was an element of free choice. When Peterson said that Britain and America desired governments in Eastern Europe that were not anti-Soviet and would have nothing to do with even a freely elected government in Poland that adopted anti-Soviet policies, the Russian Foreign Minister mockingly replied that the Soviet Union felt an equal degree of concern that there should be no governments in that area that were anti-British or anti-American.[26] Molotov would have felt even more confident if he had known that Bevin had been unwilling to protest as evidence mounted that the elections would be fraudulent. After originally adopting a 'wait and see' standpoint, Hankey had by November become convinced that it would be 'gross appeasement' to turn a blind eye to the preparations for ballot-rigging.[27] This sort of advice and the fact that the United States were determined to protest forced Bevin to reverse his original decision that there should be no protest as it would be 'a wild goose chase after one Party', whatever precisely that meant.[28]

Anticipating the results of the elections, Hankey in early January had drawn up a detailed blueprint for future Anglo-Polish relations which was in fact to be closely followed. There would have to be a protest against the election rigging, but it should not be so strong as to cause a breach in relations. Polish assets in Britain should be returned. Trade relations should be developed 'with Poland as a potential soft currency source of foodstuffs'. Poles in Britain should continue to be encouraged to return home. If all this was looking to British interests, Hankey thought that it would 'bring us into contempt' to do that and nothing else. Britain should make it clear to the Polish people that it remained keenly interested in their fate, and should give moral encouragement to non-communist politicians as long as they were allowed any vestige of freedom to pursue their activities, though 'we should not get entangled with the Polish underground movement or encourage active opposition to Russia in the future any more than we have done in the past'.[29]

Hankey's recommendations were based on Bevin's policy in the winter of 1946-7, which was still to deny that a 'Cold War' situation existed, including a refusal to attack Russia in British propaganda, or, as the Foreign Secretary told Grabski, to hold out any false hopes that Britain could 'deliver' (Grabski's word) a country like Poland to freedom. Putting it as diplomatically as possible, Bevin warned the Polish minister that the British 'would never indulge in efforts to set Poland against Russia nor would they ever use European states as pawns against other Great Powers for their own purposes'.[30]

Hankey found this policy somewhat frustrating. In February

1947 the visiting head of the British Commonwealth desk at the Polish Foreign Ministry, Zebrowski, was an overnight guest at Hankey's country house. Hankey recorded that he had known him from his own time in Warsaw, and that he was a charming man whose kindnesses included securing permission for Hankey's cook (who, incidentally, was to remain a valued friend of the Hankey family after she had left their service) to leave Poland, 'but I am sorry to report the view that he is completely faithful to the Communist Party line ... and, so far as I can judge, the party decrees that there shall be no accommodation except on full Communist Party terms between the Polish and British Governments', including that Britain should suffer in silence offensive anti-British propaganda from the Polish media, though to Hankey's amazement Zebrowski insisted that the allegation that the Western powers were already rearming the Germans was fact, not propaganda.[31]

Poland inevitably became less important in Hankey's work after this time. However, to his great pride, he continued to expend a great deal of energy in helping the resettlement, so far as possible in places of their choice around the world, of Poles who had been Britain's wartime allies.[32] He was also anxious that when Britain did finally begin a policy of vigorously answering the Polish regime's anti-British propaganda, there should be no naming of individual victims of injustice if their position might be made worse.[33] Widening the argument, Hankey urged in the spring of 1948 that there should be no question of encouraging a rising in Poland as it would lead to the deportation of the country's young men, and that there would be a catastrophe 'unless it could be given immediate military support, which is excluded.'[34]

It was Hankey's involvement in Polish affairs that did more than anything else to form his wider attitude to policy-making in the Cold War. The influences were threefold. First, he had been a helpless spectator while a gifted people who, for the first time in their history, stood a real chance of constructing a modern, democratic state, were, owing to a Soviet intervention, subjected to a 'tyrannical and unrepresentative' communist autocracy[35] which was not even efficient in non-police matters. In 1948 he looked back on the communist takeover of Poland as 'a filthy process' made more sinister in its lessons by the unusual courage of the Poles as a people and by their traditional ungovernability. It made him doubt whether any people in the world would be able to resist communism if pitted against the NKVD before which he had witnessed the Polish underground fail pitiably. (Hankey overstated his case; coercion was the main instrument by which the Polish communists consolidated their rule but not the only one.)[36] All this made the desire to do something effective against communism very strong. Secondly, he became convinced that communism was uncompromising in its determination to overthrow all other forms of society, but that it was also predictable, and therefore resistable, in the light of its history and of the communist scriptures of the time which he set about studying diligently, particularly Stalin's *Problems of Leninism*.[37] Thirdly, he had become acutely aware of how difficult it was to persuade many people, especially of course liberals and democratic socialists, of the truth, as he saw it, about the aims and nature of communism. The visiting Labour MPs who had been so impressed by the nascent Polish police state were following in the footsteps of Albert Einstein when, in 1934, he explained his refusal to sign a petition of protest against the reprisal execution of a number of political prisoners in the Soviet Union by saying that such a 'blunder' should not be allowed to conceal the essential benevolence of the Soviet rulers who had 'proved that their only aim is really the improvement of the lot of the Russian people'.[38] This belief, stretching from some of the loftiest intellects of the age to millions of more ordinary people, in the existence of a solid core of humanity and justice in Soviet and world communism, was, as much as Soviet aggression itself, the supreme danger which the Northern Department of the Foreign Office under Hankey's leadership sought to combat. It was a task in which they felt that they were greatly aided by Stalin's own acts.

Turning to Hankey's wider work in the Northern Department, he commented in March 1946, on taking up its headship: 'It is all too obvious the Treaty of Alliance [of 1942 between Britain and Russia] does not correspond to the present situation in spite of our ardent desire that it should.'[39] At the same time as he worried about electoral fraud in Poland, Hankey noted the communist grip on key ministries (Interior and Propaganda) in Poland's southern neighbour, Czechoslovakia, whose relations with Britain his department also handled; and, stretching a point since the Russians had evacuated nearly all their troops from Czechoslovakia in December 1945, wrote that where the Red Army went in Central Eastern Europe communism seemed ineluctably to follow. He thus paraphrased a remark, which was later to become famous, by Stalin to the Yugoslav leader, Marshal Tito.[40] At this stage Hankey did not see the Soviet Union as necessarily having unlimited ambitions. In September 1946 he wrote: 'I doubt myself if the Russians trust the Germans much. I think their fundamental idea is to draw a defensive line, mostly Slav, from Stettin to Trieste behind which the eastern bloc will consolidate.'[41] He urged that the West should take advantage of Soviet doubts about whether they could control a united communist Germany, even if it could be achieved, and press ahead with the creation of a state on Western lines in the Western occupation zones. If the West did choose to challenge Russia in an all-German context, the result might as easily be a reunited Germany which owed allegiance to neither Russia nor the West or a communist Germany as a pro-Western Germany. The first of these possible Germanys 'will almost inevitably start serious trouble', while the second would be a 'mortal danger' to Britain. The third would be a much more certain prospect in the context of the three Western zones alone, and should be striven for as a matter of British national survival: 'Unpleasant as it may seem, our frontier would really seem to be nearer the Elbe than the Rhine nowadays, if we are to take account of new weapons.' He conceded that Russia would 'perhaps rightly' see a united pro-Western Germany as an intolerable threat to itself. Sargent singled out Hankey's minute as one which Bevin should 'hear', but it may be that, as Hankey himself anticipated, the Foreign Secretary found it to reek too much of the 'old Adam'. More than a year was to elapse before Bevin became convinced of the futility of seeking renewed East-West cooperation over Germany.[42]

As Hankey got into his stride in his new job, he chafed at having to resign himself to a fatalistic acceptance of the 'indefinite continuance of the present state of tension and propaganda aggression'.[43] Unwilling to abandon all hope of cooperation with Russia and fearful that his own party might disown him if he did so, and uncertain about what help, if any, could be expected from the United States or the West European continental democracies, Bevin pursued a cautious course, causing his biographer to remark that he would have been accounted a failure if he had left the Foreign Office at the end of 1946.[44] It should be said that Hankey was, of course, aware of his chief's difficulties, was proud to serve under him, and paid tribute to him for being 'instrumental in the international discussions so far in standing up to the Soviet attempt to wear us all down.'[45] Even if Bevin's policy was a little less dynamic than Hankey would have wished, it was free from appeasement, and compared very favourably with the foreign policies of the other two leading Western countries, the United States and France.

Despite the almost cruel burden of work in the department, Hankey, with the aid of Thomas Brimelow, was well embarked on his study of Leninist-Stalinist ideology and, in particular, of its influence on Stalin's foreign policy. Hankey found Stalin to be both an ideologue and a ruthless opportunist so that his regime, while genuinely influenced by ideological notions about capitalism, was capable of 'doing almost anything however ruthless or inconsistent if it happens to suit their book'.⁴⁶ These studies, and what the Soviet Union was actually doing contributed to his growing belief that Soviet ambitions were insatiable, and that any display of goodwill by them would be by definition a sham. In the Foreign Office discussion on how Britain should respond to American Secretary of State Marshall's Harvard speech on economic aid to Europe, Hankey, encouraged by a remark by Bevin at a recent meeting of officials that he was convinced that the West European communist parties were preparing to change to a policy of revolution, took the lead in arguing that any Soviet offer to participate would be motivated by a desire to wreck any scheme from within. However, he had to accept that British public opinion would not be ready to support a refusal from the outset to exclude Russia, as well as Bevin's decision to await what attitude the Soviets actually adopted.⁴⁷ Indeed, Bevin ordered a continuation of negotiations with Russia on a Soviet proposal for a revised and revitalized version of the wartime treaty of alliance;⁴⁸ and vetoed a suggestion that British representatives should cease to be silent when the Foreign Secretary was the subject of personal abuse.⁴⁹ However, just how strained the situation was is shown by the fear in the Foreign Office in September that the Soviets were manoeuvring to induce the British and Americans to evacuate Trieste with its important rail communications in order to be able to use it themselves to send supplies to aid communist risings in northern Italy and France.⁵⁰

As it transpired, Molotov stormed out of the Paris conference on American economic aid, and the West Europeans and Americans, while finding it difficult enough among themselves to work out a scheme which the Congress would be likely to accept, were spared Soviet obstructionism. Hankey hoped that the Western countries were not far from the stage where they would not even make offers of cooperation in which what they thought was best for themselves was modified to meet Soviet complaints. He saw the founding of a new international body of communist parties, the Cominform, at a conference in Poland in October 1947 as new evidence of what he called 'the violent aggressiveness' of Soviet policy. He was inclined to see the inclusion of two non-governing parties, the French and Italian, as portending an onslaught against the governments of those countries before American aid could improve their economies and living standards, as well as spelling out the imminent extinction of non-communist political activity in Czechoslovakia and Hungary.⁵¹

Hankey remarked that it was odd that the Kremlin should have thrown down the gauntlet of the Cominform the month before an East-West foreign ministers' conference on Germany was due to open in London.⁵² This conference, which ended in deadlock, caused Bevin to abandon his quest for cooperation with the Soviet Union, and took Britain and the Western World a significant step nearer Hankey's view of how the West should conduct its relations with the Soviet Union. This was, in his own words nearly forty years later, 'to be realistic in resisting Soviet attempts to divide, subvert and undermine Western Europe including Western Germany from cohesive prosperity, but never to miss a chance of settling differences and disputes with the Soviet Union', all in accordance with Bevin's views.⁵³ Thus, 1948 opened auspiciously, but many problems remained. Bevin had little reason to feel confident of the full support of his Cabinet colleagues for an acceptance of Cold War realities. He feared that psychologically they simply were not ready for the message that Europe was irrevocably split into two camps, and that war between them was a real possibility. He therefore struck a cautious note at Cabinet meetings,⁵⁴ including an emphasis on the economic and social aspects of Western Union about which, Hankey somewhat impatiently minuted in February, if it led anywhere at all, 'the process will be long-drawn-out over many decades'.⁵⁵

Bevin's trump card was the support which he could usually expect from the Prime Minister. However, on the eve of the Foreign Secretary's notable speech on Western union in the Commons on 22 January, Attlee wrote to him urging a conciliatory note on Anglo-Soviet relations. Having read the notes to help Bevin in framing his speech, he minuted to him: 'I suggest that you might include a passage stating that we believe that countries with different ideologies can cooperate. (I believe that Stalin said something to this effect which might be quoted).' Indirectly, this was a rebuke for Hankey who had prepared the notes in question, and whose constant message was that any Soviet pretence of belief that it would cooperate with countries upholding other ideologies was a sham. He singled out Soviet support for the communist insurrection in Greece as the most outrageous current Soviet activity against international morality and Western interests; and the special venom which communism reserved for social democracy, and especially for the Labour Party, was also emphasized. As a footnote it was pointed out that the Soviet Union (in the pages of *Pravda*) had just initiated personal attacks against Attlee, putting him alongside Bevin who had long been under such attack.⁵⁶ (Shortly afterwards, Hankey was disgusted by a Russian press attack on one of his former chiefs, Lord Halifax, Foreign Secretary in 1939.)⁵⁷

Hankey and those who shared his views in the Foreign Office feared that most of their political masters simply did not understand the dangers in the situation or the nature of the communist threat. They took refuge in the hopes that purely symptomatic features, such as the boorish nastiness with which Molotov had been recently conducting himself, and evidence that Soviet children's textbooks were propagating hatred of the West, might change this state of affairs; and that the ever-cautious Soviets would restrain themselves until the forthcoming April elections in Italy in which Foreign Office intelligence anticipated that they and their Nenni socialist allies would poll 40 per cent of the vote, considerably more than the two parties were, in the event, to win.[58]

Within days the situation changed dramatically on one of the two fronts on which Hankey was labouring, that of convincing others of the communist danger, because of an event on the other front, that of actual communist expansion. On 25 February a new government took office in Czechoslovakia, giving the communists there an effective monopoly of power. This had an electrifying effect on left and liberal opinion throughout Western Europe. Bevin was not exempt. He remarked to the American Ambassador: 'It was no good our going on talking about Communism. Action was needed to prevent the further spread of dictatorship and totalitarian ideas.'[59] Among the rest of the Cabinet the change was even more marked, including a particularly gratifying realization of the irreconcilability of British social democracy and communism; the Cabinet now thought that the former should seek to undermine communist rule in the new 'people's democracies' rather than to build bridges between it and the West.[60]

By March 1948 Hankey could at last feel that his views were closely reflected in British policy towards the Soviet Union and communism. Yet he remained acutely aware of how easily many Westerners could relapse into what he regarded as wishful thinking (so that missionary work needed to be continued), and he pressed for British Cold War policy to become more vigorous and, in some respects, as he himself admitted, less scrupulous. The Northern Department and the British Embassy in Moscow were particularly relieved that the pendulum of Western opinion had swung their way despite the absence of a really serious threat of imminent war. (The Soviet Union had, after all, not been openly or directly involved in the communist coup in Czechoslovakia.) There was another source of relief in that — or so the Foreign Office policy-makers believed — the Kremlin had absolute control of the international communist movement since the blame for any communist adventure which threatened to misfire could be pinned on non-Soviet communists, who would be unlikely to protest, thus saving the Kremlin's face. If the most likely cause of war was Soviet miscalculation, as the Foreign Office believed, the danger was lessened by this state of affairs, which made a reassuring contrast with the relatively equal relationship between Berlin and Vienna in 1914.[61] Hankey did not himself absolutely rule out a 1939 scenario of deliberate Soviet aggression provoking war, and noted that the lines between East and West were still fluid in a large number of important places (Germany, Italy, Greece, Scandinavia, Turkey, Iran, and Palestine where some Zionists were believed to lean towards a Soviet orientation), so that the temptation to the Soviet to overstep any mark which the West could regard as tolerable was dangerously great. Even so the dangers were lessened by Bevin's policy of ignoring any 'soothing assurances' from Russia of its good intentions while Western Union was built up.[62] The Brussels treaty with France and the Benelux countries was signed in March, and discussion began on a defence arrangement with the United States. This both warned the Soviets against current risk-taking and made it possible to envisage eventually negotiating with them from a position of strength what would later be called *détente,* but what at this time was usually referred to by a term from the language which had preceded French as that of diplomacy — a *modus vivendi.*[63]

The spring of 1948 was marked by a lull in East–West tension, though there were ominous warnings that Western positions in Germany, and especially in Berlin, might come under pressure.[64] Noting that any hope for an internal breakdown of the Soviet regime was 'just wishful thinking', and that the new Soviet empire in Eastern Europe was almost equally invulnerable,[65] Hankey sought stepped up anti-communist measures at home and in countries threatened by Red takeovers. He initiated a campaign to make other government departments 'more Communism-conscious than they are at present'. The Colonial Office in particular, with its responsibility for Malaya where a major communist insurrection would soon start, was regarded as having its head in the clouds.[66] He also recommended a 50 per cent reduction in the size of Soviet Embassy personnel in London, but that was turned down by Bevin 'on the grounds that we cannot know where a policy of reprisals may not lead us'.[67] His most ambitious and controversial proposal was for an assault on the communist leaders of trade unionism in France and Italy, especially the latter. He noted that the governments in these two countries were weak, and that the workers there had plenty of genuine grievances for the communists to play upon. It was this which justified a British role:

The failure of continental democracy is the real crisis of our time. The fact is that totalitarian government, which is more bestial, is stronger. And 'bad money drives out good' in the old bi-mettalist jargon.

The answer is that Western Democracy may not be perfect, but *it must be strong*. So must we. If we are strong, our friends will look to us for help whatever our faults. If we are weak, they will compound with our enemies whatever our virtues. God knows how we are to do it.

He expanded his thoughts a few days later. He called for the British TUC to be asked to give active help to non-communist unionists in France and Italy (and also to withdraw from the World Federation of Trade Unions if they could not wrest control of it from communist hands). This would be a herculean task in Italy where the equivalent of the TUC, the CGIL, was under exclusive communist control. To aid in setting up a significant rival:

It might be necessary to give the Communists some of their own medicine by arresting some of the C.G.I.L. leaders and trying them on charges of tax evasion or black marketeering (of which most Italians are guilty) and getting them replaced by reliable Socialists. If the key positions in the C.G.I.L. could be secured even by such relatively unscrupulous methods (used every day by our opponents) the C.G.I.L. might possibly be wrested from the Communists intact.

One of Hankey's colleagues wrote an outspoken denunciation of these proposals on the grounds that ends could not justify means, and that democratic governments had to respect the autonomy of trade unions. Hankey himself, two months later, wrote that his proposal 'is now rather out of date. But the danger will remain'.[68]

Hankey may have meant that the 'bourgeois' parties in France and Italy were showing unexpected vigour, or he may have meant that there were more pressing problems. He certainly did feel that Stalin was concentrating his expansionist designs on Germany. In late June he had imposed the blockade on West Berlin; and at that point the defence talks with the United States were making slow progress, and their complete failure was not ruled out.[69] The very senior figure of Gladwyn Jebb wrote in a memorandum of 'general impressions' on the Washington defence talks in late July that 'it is entirely evident that the Brussels Powers could not successfully defend themselves against an attack by Russia except with the full military support of the United States.'[70] It was in this atmosphere that Hankey contemplated the eventual abandonment of West Berlin. He saw it as necessary at all costs to hold on to the city until West Germany had been organized on Western lines: 'When that is done efficiently, I cannot see ... what further actions we can fulfil in Berlin.'[71]

Then the talks which were to produce the North Atlantic Pact recovered momentum, and the successful airlift of supplies to West

Berlin promised to keep the city from falling at least during the summer months. The West (including not a few bewildered Western communists) was also presented with the spectacle of the break in party relations between the Soviet and Yugoslav communist regimes. Hankey's role in these stirring events was to issue advice against either complacency or euphoria. He joined with Jebb and William Hayter in warning the American Ambassador, Douglas, against regarding the Tito–Stalin split as more than 'a family quarrel' which might soon be patched up, while noting that the small size of Soviet forces in Eastern Europe — only half a million men — indicated both a lack of intention to start a war and confidence in the ability of the satellite regimes to hold down their own populations.[72] To Sargent, Hankey made a vigorous plea in late July against relying on Soviet promises 'until we are able and prepared to prevent and suppress Communist infiltration outside the Orbit'. ('The Orbit' was the term commonly used in the Foreign Office at this time to designate the new Soviet empire in Eastern Europe.) Even then he doubted whether it would make sense to discuss a *modus vivendi* since the Soviets would treat those of its provisions favourable to themselves as sacrosanct while treating those which favoured the West as no more than a basis for discussion and further concessions.[73]

In August Hankey cited the complete exclusion of Western interest from one of the great rivers of Europe, the Danube, as an example of Soviet 'cuckoo policy', participating in what started as a genuine international organization only to cast out others who were not its puppets, as well as being 'one more step in the ruthless consolidation of the Soviet Zone.'[74] To another colleague, F.A. Warner, at the Embassy in Paris, he used the metaphor of the blood-sucker: the Soviets 'tend to use and exploit people for their own purposes, and when they have sucked them dry they cast them out and trample on their rights.' Czech democrats and socialists throughout Eastern Europe had found this out to their cost: 'It is useless to be friends with the Communists; they just exploit their friends so long as they are useful, and then turn and rend them for their own purposes.'[75] Shortly before this Hankey had travelled to Germany to give a lecture which set out most fully his understanding of the aims of Soviet communism based on his theoretical studies and practical experience. In it he predicted that war might break out in Korea in view of the stated American intention to evacuate its forces from the south of that country. The communists would inevitably move into the vacuum thus created, and, since the United States position in Japan would be threatened, they would have to resist.[76]

He spent some time on the not very important problem, though it was one which worried Bevin, of reconciling the Atlantic Pact, as it became probable that there would be such an instrument, with the moribund Anglo-Soviet alliance treaty of 1942. Trouble from left-wing Labour MPs could be anticipated, though in fact there was to be very little.[77] In the winter of 1949 he drew up a paper to demonstrate that the pact and the 1942 treaty were compatible in law, and that if the former was anti-Soviet politically it was justifiably so; Britain had tried to cooperate with Russia 'till we found that we were being had for mugs.'[78] With misgivings because it came from what could be regarded as a confidential source, Hankey was willing to publicize a remark by Stalin to a delegation of Labour MPs led by Konni Zilliacus in October 1947 that the treaty had become 'a mere scrap of paper'.[79] Another problem stemming from the past which worried him was the danger from Soviet propaganda, especially films, aimed at convincing Westerners that during the war Britain and the United States had needlessly delayed the Second Front to bleed Russia dry. Fortunately, purges were apparently taking place in the Soviet film industry that were likely to impede the propaganda effort.[80]

In all this what stands out is that Hankey was helping to implement a British Cold War policy in which he passionately believed. By late 1948 he could feel happy that, within the Western camp, problems were increasingly on the margins. Internationally, a few countries like Denmark presented difficulties, requiring a major British effort to instil in them 'sufficient confidence to resist the bully'.[81] Domestically, he suggested in November that the time had come to give adverse publicity to left MPs and others who toured the East European satellites at the local regimes' expense and made anti-British statements, though 'it would be unfair and undesirable to say anything which could damage independent people like Mr A.J.P. Taylor who went to Breslau[82] and put up a very good show there.' Bevin was unwilling to travel far along that road. Another official recorded that he had rejected a suggestion that words should be placed in British passports warning their holders of the harm which criticisms of the country could do when made abroad. It had been decided instead to instruct British overseas missions 'to keep a record of disloyal utterances abroad.'[83]

To keep Western public opinion in general content, Hankey was reluctantly reconciled to the British and American Governments having to indulge in 'periodical bouts of fish-bowl diplomacy or at least fairly serious United Nations discussions (such as the Paris talks on Berlin and Greece)' to convince their peoples that Russia was to blame for the East–West tension.[84] Meanwhile, despite being wholly confident about the nature of the Soviet regime and its implacable hostility to the West, he preserved a healthy scepticism about his own or anybody else's ability to explain the exact meaning of Russian actions. In late November he confided to Geoffrey Harrison, minister at the Embassy in Moscow, that he had reservations about the Government's instructions, though naturally they had to be obeyed, to the Russia Committee of which he was a leading member to draw up twice-monthly summaries of Soviet foreign policy, 'popularly known here as the "crystal Gazer" ', adding: 'I have always maintained that one should never "crystal gaze" where Russia is concerned, but that is what the department is asked to do once a fortnight, and we do it with very great reserve and hesitation.' [85]

The winter of 1949 was a relatively quiescent one in East–West relations in which the Soviets placed increasing stress on propaganda in their contest with the West. Such tangible Western victories as the impending signing of the North Atlantic treaty (including its signature by Norway whom the Soviets had tried very hard to dissuade from such a step), the complete success of the Berlin airlift and the prospect that it could be continued indefinitely if necessary, and the evidence that Yugoslavia was surviving in its defiance of Moscow, plus the 'resignation' in March of Molotov whom the world had come to associate with Soviet expansionism, caused Gladwyn Jebb to wonder whether Stalin had become convinced of the need for a period of retrenchment in which 'capitalist contradictions', would be left to 'result in the strongholds of the bourgeoisie surrendering, not so much to the flourish of the Soviet sword as to the mere blast of the Soviet trumpet.' [86]

Hankey advocated extreme caution before breathing any more freely about Soviet short-term intentions. He was completely loyal to Bevin's policy of patient firmness and of adherence to the notion that 'it would be playing the Kremlin game to devote so much of the available resources of the western democracies to arms as seriously to delay or permanently to impair economic recovery.' [87] Yet, with his strong interest in ideological motivation in Soviet foreign policy, the Soviet emphasis on capitalist weaknesses and impending crises worried him. In the medium term he was not actually wholly confident that the Marxist–Stalinist scenario would not unfold: 'We aren't [sic] too sure what will happen in 1952 ourselves', he wrote in May 1949 about the economic prospects of the West.[88] In the much shorter term, he feared the communists believing their own propaganda and taking risks which might precipitate war in the belief that Western economic weaknesses would preclude the sort of response which the West would actually be bound to make.[89] His second fear was of Russia doing something desperate to prevent the setting up of the new West German state, on which progress was very advanced, or of succeeding with their propaganda in persuading some Western governments to draw back from accepting West German statehood at almost the last minute. As late as May, with Germany still 'in the melting pot', Hankey advised against giving serious consideration to even the most sweeping Soviet offer possible on Germany — giving up the East zone — since its purpose would only be to facilitate the 'infiltration and undermining' of the entire country to bring about a united communist Germany.[90] In June he expressed fears about the imminent institution of 'a policy of direct subversion and terrorism' by German communists, acting on Soviet orders, to force the Western powers out of the country.[91]

Developments in another part of the world gave Hankey pause for thought in 1949. This was China where it was becoming increasingly likely that the communist forces of Mao Tse-tung would soon rule the entire mainland. Sometimes Hankey did not dissent from the widespread view in British officialdom that Mao was a potential Tito who would have no wish to become a Soviet puppet and who, even if that was his desire, would have difficulty in achieving it in a country in which xenophobia was as rampant as it was in China.[92] Yet he could also speak of Mao's triumphs as part of a world communist blueprint, designed by Stalin whom Hankey thought to be in the habit of preparing plans for some new aggression in case an existing one failed:

This was his strategy during the war, and it has been his strategy in the political war which he has conducted since the end of hostilities with Germany. He has nearly been brought to a halt in Europe — the process will be more or less complete when we have formed an effective Western German Government — and in proportion as Stalin is stopped in Europe I expect to see him devote more and more attention to other areas, and especially to the Far East, and especially to south-east Asia. There is no doubt that by communizing south-east Asia he could deal a mortal blow to the economy of the Western world, to our air communications with Australia and, indeed, largely nullify the success of the Marshall Plan, quite apart from the effect on India, Burma and Ceylon.
It strikes me that the communization of China is Stalin's real answer to the Atlantic Pact — and hardly one we can laugh off![93]

Yet as a memorandum for the Russia Committee noted at this time, there was no evidence for a Soviet hand in China: 'the spectacular successes of the Communists, on all the evidence available, have been due to the general corruption and inefficiency of the National Government, rather than to a diversion of Soviet effort.' Work by historians has only confirmed this assessment.[94]

Hankey's rather unbalanced comment was perhaps only human after three years in so gruelling a post, and indicated an obsession with communist malevolence which could warp judgement, as did his comment that Soviet setbacks in Europe and over the Atlantic Pact were 'little' compared with the 'colossal expansion in the Far East.'[95]

Whatever the import of Far Eastern events, Hankey did not, by the end of the winter, deny the evidence of new tactics in Soviet foreign policy based on stirring up pacifist sentiments in the West so that, even as militarism was glorified in the Soviet Union itself, 'The Communists of Western countries conduct violent campaigns against rearmament and recruiting, employing the most grotesque pacifist sob-stuff propaganda about boys being torn from their mothers' arms for the forces.'[96] Hankey did differ from even as close a colleague as Geoffrey Harrison in not thinking that any of this involved even a 'breathing space' in Soviet policy, let alone a genuine change as after 1933.[97] It must, however, be emphasized that no one on the Foreign Office staff believed that the basic Soviet hostility to the West had abated in the slightest; every voice that was raised was adverse to any such theory.[98] Hankey would therefore not have been the only official to feel some disquiet that Bevin attached some credence to the theory of a conflict in the Kremlin leadership between moderates, including Vyshinsky and Malik, and hardliners, including Molotov and Gromyko. His own thought was:

Admittedly, we must be able to recognize a *real* peace offer if ever one is made. I do not believe that the Soviets are preparing a real peace offer at the present moment. This is not the implication of the increased pressure on our Missions in Prague and Sofia and on our Legation and Consulates in Roumania; nor of the intensified communist propaganda in the May Day slogans, in the Cominform journal, at the Peace Congress [*sic*] in Paris and elsewhere appealing to the Western peoples to resist their governments who are the 'instigators of a new war'.[99]

His reference to the 'Peace Congress' at Paris was to the conference of the Soviet and the three Western foreign ministers there in May at which, predictably, his great concern was that all the Western participants should be under no illusion that any Soviet display of goodwill would be genuine.[100] In this connection, in early 1949 Hankey drew up guidelines for British diplomats and ministers travelling abroad on how they should conduct themselves in social gatherings at which Soviet and satellite diplomats were present. They should normally be cool and reserved, but they should be affable if there seemed a chance of acquiring useful information, or should observe 'a more than ordinary frigidity' on occasions 'where there has been a particularly flagrant violation of human rights' in the Soviet bloc.[101]

Another point of general agreement from which Hankey would not have dissented was that the 'peace offensive' threatened one of the West's greatest assets in the Cold War, namely the clumsy, provocative way in which Soviet diplomacy had been conducted in recent years. Some notes drawn up in the Northern Department in March 1949 paid tribute to how much the imminent signature of the Atlantic Pact owed to the Russian diplomatic service: 'More than any other factor, except Hitler's aggression, Soviet diplomacy is responsible for the final demise of American isolationism.' [102] The new smiles on the faces of Soviet spokesmen were perceived as a threat to the cohesion of the Western alliance at the very moment of its birth.

One of Hankey's last actions before leaving the Northern Department was in connection with instructions for the new British Ambassador to the Soviet Union, Sir David Kelly, who had been promised an interview with Stalin. Hankey, while describing Kelly's proposals about what he should say to Stalin as 'about right', was actually alarmed by some of them. He did not see how a plea for greater Anglo-Soviet personal contacts could serve much purpose 'in a situation where the only Russians allowed to come abroad are hand-picked communists while, on the other hand, only people like Mr Zilliacus are likely to be let into the USSR'. In addition, it would be 'completely unreal' not to mention 'the openly declared intention of the Cominform, backed by the Soviet Government, to wreck the Marshall Plan and with it the economic reconstruction necessary for the well-being of the people of Western Europe.'

The instructions which Bevin sent to Kelly were probably milder than Hankey would have wished. Kelly should ask Stalin whether he had any ideas about how the two countries could live together. He should offer to discuss earnestly any 'misunderstandings'. He should avoid criticizing anti-British propaganda which had been discussed 'so many times, and the Soviet Government go their own way whatever you may say.' Stalin should be addressed 'in a very kindly and courteous way'. He should be reminded that, whatever their differences, 'we are united in our determination never to allow Germany to attack either of us again.' Hankey had argued against that last instruction as both outmoded and dangerous since the Soviets might quote it against Britain in their efforts to win support among the Germans. However, he would have been gratified by Bevin's order that Kelly should not raise the subject of Anglo-Soviet personal contacts since Stalin's only interest would be in 'causing embarrassment' to the British Government. After the interview had taken place and been reported to London, Hankey felt that it had been 'fairly anodyne', and had at least not made Anglo-Soviet relations worse. But, unlike Kelly, he found Stalin's remark that 'in the long run our two countries will understand each other' to be 'a sinister one if read in the light of Communist historical dialectic and Stalin's principle that the Western peoples want peace, but their governments are warmongering.' [103]

On one issue — trade — Hankey was called upon to work for cooperation with Russia for the present. The British Government were intent on buying Soviet-block raw materials, especially grain, as a very acceptable alternative to the hard-currency United States market. Even as the Cold War reached its height, Britain sought a dramatic increase in its trade with the communist countries; and it was Hankey himself who remarked at the Russia Committee in January 1949 that it was policy to sell tractors to Eastern Europe because the increase in agricultural production which might be expected to result would allow a long-term increase in the surplus available for export of which Britain would hope to buy a substantial portion. The Northern Department impatiently rejected a proposal by the former Foreign Office Permanent Under-Secretary, Lord Vansittart, that Soviet trade representation in London should be scaled down.[104] Hankey also spoke the language of conciliation in pronouncing against further souring of the Anglo-Soviet atmosphere by 'making publicity points out of Stalin's conversations with British ministers or public servants', perhaps most notably Field Marshal Montgomery whom Stalin had entertained in January 1947, because 'a time might come when we needed the atmosphere to be right for a frank and confidential talk with Stalin. If this view is maintained we should not use the conversations with Lord Montgomery publicly.' [105]

It is, however, fitting to conclude this survey of Hankey's work with an episode in the summer of 1949 in which he questioned whether Britain could afford to tolerate the misuse of its free society by the agents, in this case the Soviet Union's Tass news agency, of communist totalitarianism. He was dismayed by the outcome of a court case in which an exiled Czechoslovak university professor and hero of the wartime resistance against the Nazis, Krajina, had sued Tass in London for libel for accusing him of betraying allied parachutists to the Germans. The court declared that Tass was an agency of the Soviet Government, and that it could not be sued because it enjoyed diplomatic immunity. On 25 July Hankey, while noting that the British Government were 'the main protagonists of the rule of law in the world', questioned whether a country like Russia which was waging 'political warfare' against Britain should be allowed diplomatic immunity not only for its embassy, but also for its commercial and 'information' agencies. (The individual personnel of these agencies did not, of course, enjoy immunity as did diplomats.) He suggested that it should be demanded of the Soviets that they should formally make themselves responsible for ensuring that Tass observed the restraints which diplomats normally observed, thereby refraining from anything likely 'to interfere in British affairs, to stir up political or industrial ill-will in this country or still less to endeavour to bring discredit on His Majesty's Government.' He conceded that Russia might well respond by closing down the Tass office in Britain, and went on: 'It may be objected that to close down Tass Agency would be contrary to our principles of freedom of information. But it may be argued that our principles do not involve any obligation to grant freedom to commit libel or otherwise defy the law, and that the essential features of our principles would not be affected by such action.' He ended that if the Soviets did accept it would merely restore Tass to the situation which had been generally understood to prevail before the court case.

Hankey had already been worried about Tass's efforts to foment labour unrest in Britain, and especially about its role in the dock strike which was currently taking place in London. It had circulated an inflammatory *Pravda* article and the text of a Moscow radio broadcast, supplementing the work of the British communists who were following Soviet orders in the first place: 'The *Daily Worker* has, of course, been doing this for some time. In this connection it should be remembered that the duty of obedience to the wishes of the Kremlin is absolutely fundamental in the Communist Party organization, and there can be no doubt that the Communist line would have been altered already if it was not in accordance with Kremlin directives.' One Foreign Office legal adviser was favourable to Hankey's proposal and another one was adverse, remarking fatalistically that there would always be abuses of a system of freedom of information. Hankey riposted that it made no sense to treat Tass both as a press agency and as a government department. The Permanent Under-Secretary, Strang, pronounced against any action, partly because of the danger of the Soviets making conditions even worse for British diplomats in Moscow 'if indeed that were possible'. The Minister of State, Hector McNeil, agreed with Strang, and also thought that Hankey's proposal did not stand up 'in law and general practice'.

Hankey returned to this question a month later, in late August. This time even his colleague, Bateman, was not persuaded and

McNeil minuted, 'Agree with Mr Bateman otherwise we shall beat the air.' Hankey's final word was to 'Lie in wait for Tass *permanently* please and scrutinize their staff carefully' in case they did something so outrageous as to cause the Foreign Office leadership to reconsider their view. Hankey's opinions were actually probably nearer those of the British people. The Krajina case was debated in the House of Lords, and considerable outrage was expressed at the way in which Tass had been able to libel him with impunity. Furthermore, the Cabinet set up a committee to discover any discrepancies in treatment between Soviet-bloc missions in London and British missions in Moscow and the satellite capitals with a view to the abolition of any one-sided arrangements which favoured the communist states.[106]

Hankey found his work in the Northern Department too negative to be completely satisfying to 'a positive go-getter, which I do claim to be.' It involved providing a shield behind which others could carry out the more constructive work of rebuilding Western Europe and above all Western Germany which he increasingly saw as the key to a viable non-communist Western half of the continent. His work was made more painful by his lifelong admiration for the Russian people (but not their rulers), and somewhat easier by his lack of distress at the division of Germany after Soviet action had made that step inevitable. He regarded that division as a fair response to legitimate Soviet concern about their security whose existence, beneath the excesses of Soviet Cold War policies, he never denied. At the time he shared none of the confidence of some later commentators that the risks of the Cold War turning into a real war were always negligible, particularly in view of the advent of nuclear weapons.[107] He admits that he 'did not at that time foresee the immense force of mutual nuclear deterrence.' This accounts for his uncharacteristic readiness for a brief period to abandon West Berlin after West German statehood had been achieved because 'West Berlin might at some time easily provide the spark to start another world war.' [108] In this and in all his work in the Northern Department his overriding concern was to play a modest part in saving Britain and the emerging Western alliance from having to choose between war and the surrender of essential interests.

Notes

1. V. Rothwell, 'Germany and Anglo-Soviet relations during the Second World War', *Crossroads* (New York), no. 25, 1987, 1-18.
2. Wm. O. McCagg, *Stalin embattled, 1943-1948*, Detroit, Mich., 1978,

48-9, 62-8, 192-3; Paolo Spriano, *Stalin and the European Communists*, 1985, 166-9, 209-10, 214; S. Mikolajczyk *The pattern of Soviet domination*, 1948, 87, 144.
3. On Poland in the Second World War and the communist takeover of that country, there are magisterial surveys in the second half of J. Karski, *The Great Powers and Poland, 1919-1945*, 1985, and in J. Coutouvidis and J. Reynolds, *Poland, 1939-1947*, 1986. Also useful are S.S. Lotarski, 'The Communist takeover in Poland', in T.T. Hammond (ed.), *The anatomy of Communist takeovers*, 1975, 339-67; A. Polonsky (ed.), *The Great Powers and the Polish question, 1941-1945*, 1976; and the invaluable A. Polonsky and B. Drukier (eds), *The beginnings of communist rule in Poland, 1943-1945*, 1980. On Yalta see D.S. Clemens, *Yalta*, 1970. See also M. Kitchen, *British policy towards the Soviet Union during the Second World War*, 1986, 242-6, 249-53.
4. Clark Kerr to F(oreign) O(ffice), 27 June 1945, FO 371/47705/7608 and 8746.
5. S. Roskill, *Hankey, man of secrets*, 3 vols, 1970-4, III, 432-3; information from Lord Hankey.
6. Hankey to FO, 16 July 1945, FO 371/47705/8688; Polonsky and Drukier, op.cit., 59, 144, 159, 171-2; Coutouvidis and Reynolds, op.cit., 170-89, 192-6.
7. Mikolajczyk, op.cit., 109-11; Coutouvidis and Reynolds, op.cit., 202-9.
8. Minute by Hankey, 27 June, and record of meeting, 10 July 1945, FO 371/47705/7652; Mikolajczyk, op.cit., 158 (on Polish coal); information from Lord Hankey.
9. Sir J. Anderson to Hankey, 16 July 1945, FO 371/47705/8615.
10. Hankey to FO, 28 July 1945, FO 371/47706/9400.
11. FO to Bentinck, 23 August 1945, FO 371/47706/10656.
12. V. Rothwell, *Britain and the Cold War, 1941-1947*, 1982, 236-9, 414-5; J. Knight, 'Russia's search for peace: the London Conference of Foreign Ministers, 1945,' *Journal of Contemporary History*, XIII, 1978, 137-63.
13. Bentinck to Warner, 24 October 1945, FO 371/47707/14864.
14. P. Howarth, *Intelligence chief extraordinary: the life of the Ninth Duke of Portland*, 1986, 180.
15. Mikolajczyk, op.cit., 280.
16. Mikolajczyk, op.cit., 166-8, 171-2, 177-9, 192-200, 259-61; N. Davies, 'Poland', in M. McCauley (ed.), *Communist power in Europe, 1944-1949*, 1977, 44; Polonsky and Drukier, op.cit., 29, 31, 53-5, 63-5, 93, 106-9, for the early stages of terror before the arrival of the British Embassy.
17. Documents from Warsaw in FO 371/47708/17368; record of meeting between Bevin and Modzelewski, 9 February 1946, FO 371/56354/19731; N. Bethell, *Gomulka, his Poland and his communism*, 1969, 92; Coutouvidis and Reynolds, op.cit., 215-21, 240-1.
18. Bentinck to Hankey, 9 April 1946, FO 371/56355/5248; information from Lord Hankey.
19. Hankey to Bentinck, 18 April 1946, FO 371/56355/5500; Bentinck to

Hankey, 23 August 1946, FO 371/56357/11016; Hankey to Sargent, 8 November 1946, FO 371/56359/15647.

20. Howarth, op.cit., 215-17; Bentinck to Hankey as in note 19 above where Deutscher was stated to be the Polish communists' 'most useful ally' in London; minute by Burgess, 20 September 1949, FO 371/77564/6926. At least one parliamentary visitor to Warsaw soon became thoroughly contrite and convinced that he had been duped: G. Thomas, *Mr Speaker: the memoirs of Viscount Tonypandy*, 1986 edition, 57-8, 62-7.
21. G.L. Weinberg, *World in the balance: behind the scenes of World War II*, 1981, 19; R.C. Lukas, *Forgotten holocaust: the Poles under German occupation, 1939-1944*, 1986.
22. A.B. Lane, *I saw freedom betrayed*, 1949, 166-9; Rothwell, op.cit., 301-7, for British policy on the Oder-Neisse frontier; J.F. Byrnes, *Speaking frankly*, 1947, 190-2; Bethell, op.cit., 130-1; Coutouvidis and Reynolds, op.cit., 266-7, 278-87.
23. Minutes by Hankey, 20 January, and record of conversation between Grabski and Bevin, 24 January 1947, FO 371/66152/1119 and 1328. For Hankey's conviction that the Germans would never accept the Oder-Neisse losses, see his minute of 25 October 1946, FO 371/55592/11995; Karski, op.cit., 548-9, 588.
24. Lane, op.cit., 181-2; Howarth, op.cit., 219-20; cable from Bentinck, 10 January, and minute by Hankey, 15 January 1947, FO 371/66152/449 and 569; Anthony Glees in *The Observer*, 15 March 1987 (on Delmer).
25. Minute by Hankey, 21 January 1948, FO 371/71629/1141.
26. FO to Moscow Embassy, 9 January, and Peterson to FO, 11 January 1947, FO 371/66089/231 and 500.
27. Minute by Hankey, 25 May 1946, FO 371/56412/6738; Hankey to Sargent, 9 November 1946, FO 371/56359/15646; Coutouvidis and Reynolds, op.cit., 350, note 31.
28. Minute by Bevin, c., 31 December 1946, FO 371/66089/6.
29. Memorandum by Hankey, 10 January 1947, FO 371/66153/1639.
30. Minutes of FO Meeting on policy in Eastern Europe, 17 January 1947, FO 371/66090/658; Bevin-Grabski conversation as in note 23 above.
31. Minute by Hankey, 7 February 1947, FO 371/66153/1985; information from Lord Hankey. Comparisons with Stalin's 'gift' of his Russian manservant to Sir Archibald Clark Kerr when he left the British Embassy in Moscow in 1946 (as described by Frank Giles in *The Sunday Times*, 6 January 1980) would for several reasons be misleading!
32. Information from Lord Hankey; his work in this area is touched on in K.R. Sword, 'Their prospects will not be bright': British responses to the problem of the Polish recalcitrants, 1946-49, *Journal of Contemporary History*, **XXI**, 1986, 367-90.
33. Minute cited in note 25 above; nauseatingly, this minute contains a notation by Guy Burgess that Bevin, in recent speeches, had duly refrained from mentioning a Polish woman whom Hankey had named as vulnerable.

34. Minute by Hankey, 20 May 1948, FO 371/71650/5623.
35. Memorandum cited in note 29 above.
36. 'Russia's attitude towards the outside world', lecture given by Mr R.M.A. Hankey to the Control Council for Germany College, Brunswick, 22 September 1948, copy of text in FO 371/71671/10522; Coutouvidis and Reynolds, op.cit., 272, 290, 314.
37. Information from Lord Hankey.
38. Einstein's letter to Isaac Don Levine in W.R. Corson and R.T. Crowley, *The new KGB: engine of Soviet power*, 1986, 104. This may be compared with the Orwellian view of the Soviet proletariat offered in a despatch from the embassy in Moscow (Peterson to Bevin, 30 December 1947, FO 371/71667/96) on the apparent indifference of the Kremlin leadership to 'the mass of the population as a living and conscious entity. The classes which matter, from the Party point of view, are the Party functionaries and members, the State's administrative employees and the intellegentsia, while the workers are merely "labour", no more than a factor in production like raw materials or climatic vagaries'.
39. Minute by Hankey, 15 March 1946, FO 371/56840/3369, quoted in Rothwell, op.cit., 255. In this book I described Foreign Office policy in relation to the emerging Cold War in 1946-7 including Hankey's role, though without singling him out for special consideration. Accordingly, this middle portion of the period under consideration is, excluding Polish affairs, dealt with in somewhat abbreviated form here.
40. Minute by Hankey, 28 May 1946, FO 371/56008/6865 (quoted in Rothwell, op.cit., 370); minute by Hankey, 15 November 1946, FO 371/56013/15241. In April 1945 Stalin remarked to Tito that, 'Everyone imposes his own system as far as his army has power to do so. It cannot be otherwise'. M. Djilas, *Conversations with Stalin*, 1963, 90.
41. Minute by Hankey, 13 September 1946, FO 371/56414/11441.
42. Minutes by Hankey, 25 October, and Sargent, 5 November 1946, FO 371/55592/11995. This is quoted at several points in Rothwell, op.cit., where British policy on the future of Germany is examined in some detail.
43. Quoted in Rothwell, op.cit., 265.
44. A. Bullock, *Ernest Bevin: Foreign Secretary*, 1983, 345.
45. Minute by Hankey, 16 January 1947, FO 371/66279/503 (quoted in Rothwell, op.cit., 272).
46. Minute by Hankey, 5 February 1947, FO 371/66363/1373 (quoted at greater length in Rothwell, op.cit., 272).
47. Meeting in FO, 5 June 1947, FO 371/62399/4781; Hankey's record of meeting presided over by Bevin, 25 June 1947, FO 371/66370/7458; Rothwell, op.cit., 279-82; information from Lord Hankey.
48. See minute by Hankey, 25 June 1947, FO 371/66370/7532.
49. Rothwell, op.cit., 395.
50. Information from Lord Hankey.
51. Rothwell, op.cit., 276, 285-7, 373-4; see also minute by Hankey, 5 December 1947, FO 371/65767/13844.

52. Memorandum, 8 October 1947, FO 371/66475/11554.
53. Letter from Lord Hankey, 1 September 1986.
54. cf. minute by Frank Roberts for Bevin, 6 January 1948, FO 371/71670/207; Cabinet minutes, 8 January and 12 and 23 February 1948, CAB 128/12.
55. Minute by Hankey, 5 February 1948, FO 371/71629/1935.
56. Attlee to Bevin, 21 January 1948, and Hankey's notes for Bevin's speech, FO 371/71629/878 and 1141.
57. Minute by Hankey, 7 April 1948, FO 371/71630/4066. The press attack was 'complete muck'.
58. Roberts to Brimelow, 7 February 1948, and minute by Hector McNeil, FO 371/71629/2123 (on children's textbooks); minute by Hankey, 19 February and his marginal comment on minute by C.H. Bateman, 20 February 1948, FO 371/71670/1759 and 2305.
59. Record of meeting between British and American Ambassadors, 25 February 1948, FO 371/73069/2642.
60. Cabinet minutes, 5 March 1948, CAB 128/12.
61. Geoffrey Harrison (Moscow Embassy) to Hankey, 12 March 1948, FO 371/71671/3449.
62. Hankey to Harrison, 19 and 30 March 1948 as cited in note 61 above; minute by Hankey, 25 March 1948, FO 371/71630/3535.
63. cf. Sargent to Peterson, 19 April 1948, FO 371/71670/3910.
64. Report received from US Embassy in Paris, 26 April 1948, and minute by C.R.A. Rae, 5 May 1948, FO 371/71650/5036 and 5115.
65. Minute by Hankey, 30 April 1948, FO 371/71671/6295.
66. cf. papers, April 1948, in FO 371/71649/4671-2; see also J. Bloch and P. Fitzgerald, *British intelligence and covert action*, Dingle, Irish Republic, 1983, 71.
67. Minute by Hankey, 4 May 1948, FO 371/71630/5122.
68. Minutes by Hankey, 28 April and 3 May 1948, FO 371/71650/5410; minutes by H.G. Gee, 3 June, and Hankey, 4 August 1948, FO 371/71651/9029.
69. cf. the minutes in FO 371/73071.
70. Memorandum, 28 July 1948, FO 371/73073/6140.
71. Minute by Hankey, 22 July 1948, FO 371/70648A. Quoted in E. Barker, *The British between the Superpowers, 1945-50*, 1983, 123. Information from Lord Hankey who emphasizes the momentary nature of this thought, and adds (letter of 7 October 1986) that it was also never the collective view of the Foreign Office, for which see R. Ovendale, *The English-speaking alliance*, 1985, 78-9.
72. Record by Hankey of conversation, 15 July 1948, FO 371/71651/8294.
73. Hankey to Sargent, 21 July 1948, FO 371/71671/8568.
74. Minute by Hankey, 21 August 1948, FO 371/71630/9580.
75. Hankey to F.A. Warner, 14 October 1948, FO 371/71672/11137.
76. This is the lecture cited in note 36 above.
77. Minutes by Hankey, 6 August and 9 October 1948, FO 371/71638/8944 and 371/11776; minute by Bevin, November 1948, FO 371/73081/29539.
78. Memorandum, n.d. but February 1949, FO 371/77626/3199.

79. Minute by Hankey, 7 April 1949, FO 371/77626/3202.
80. Minutes by Hankey and others, November 1948, FO 371/71631/12286.
81. Minute by Hankey, 5 October 1948, FO 371/71672/10581.
82. Breslau was by this time the Polish city of Wroclaw. In August 1948 it was the location of a 'World Congress of Intellectuals for Peace' which, in so far as one event did so, inaugurated the 'peace movement' which has continued in the Western World, in one form or another, ever since.
83. Minutes by Hankey and N. Reddaway, 4 and 9 November 1948, FO 371/71653/12284.
84. Minute by Hankey, 11 January 1949, FO 371/68015A/4592.
85. Hankey to Harrison, 29 November 1948, FO 371/71672/12666.
86. Memorandum by Jebb, 14 March 1949, FO 371/77601/2456.
87. Minute by Hankey, 29 January 1949, FO 371/77609/769.
88. Minute by Hankey, 10 May 1949, FO 371/77612/4164.
89. Hankey to Radice, 25 January, and minute by Hankey, 3 February 1949, FO 371/77566/597.
90. Minute by Hankey, 24 March 1949, FO 371/77612/2790; remarks by Hankey at Russia Committee, 10 May 1949, FO 371/77623/4342; Hankey to Harrison, 5 May 1949, FO 371/77602/3999.
91. Minute by Hankey, 8 June 1949, FO 371/77604/5832.
92. Hankey at Russia Committee, 12 April 1949, FO 371/77623/3583; minute by J.Y. Mackenzie, 26 January 1949, FO 371/77566/597.
93. Minute by Hankey, 5 April 1949, FO 371/77568/4711.
94. Memorandum, 13 May 1949, FO 371/77603/4488; cf. J. Gittings, *The world and China, 1922-1972,* 1974, 141-2, 150-2.
95. Minute by Hankey, 17 March 1949, FO 371/77612/2798.
96. Notes compiled in Northern Department for House of Lords debate, March 1949, FO 371/77600/2453.
97. Minute cited in note 95 above; minute by Hankey on dispatch from Harrison, 28 June 1949, FO 371/77613/5696; minute by Hankey, 8 June 1949, FO 371/77604/5832.
98. cf. minute by Jebb at Russia Committee, 10 May 1949, FO 371/77623/4342. Strang, the Permanent Under-Secretary, was so impressed by a memorandum from this committee, arguing that the Soviet peace offensive was only a tactical deviation, that he ordered that copies should be sent to all Commonwealth prime ministers and to Acheson and Schuman. In particular, 'It would do Pandit Nehru good to read it'. Minute by Strang, 14 May 1949, FO 371/77603/4536. This is not the place to enter into the origins of the 'peace movement' on which see M.D. Shulman, *Stalin's foreign policy reappraised,* 1963, and R.H. Schultz and R. Godson, *Dezinformatsia: active measures in Soviet strategy,* 1984.
99. Hankey to Harrison, 5 May 1949, FO 371/77602/3999.
100. Minute by Hankey, 14 May 1949, FO 371/77612/4276.
101. Hankey to H. Farquhar (Ambassador to Sweden), 30 March 1949, and copy of guidelines, FO 371/77616/2717 and 2719.
102. Notes as cited in note 96 above.

103. Minutes by Hankey and Bateman, 29 June 1949, and correspondence between Kelly and FO, 28 June and 2 July 1949, FO 371/77618/5822 and 6025; minute by Hankey, 20 July 1949, FO 371/77619/6550; cf. *The ruling few: the memoirs of Sir David Kelly*, n.d., 429-30.
104. Hankey at Russia Committee, 21 January 1949, FO 371/77623/847; notes referred to in note 96 above.
105. Minute by Hankey, 7 April 1949, FO 371/77626/3202; Rothwell, op.cit., 270-2, for Montgomery's visit to the Soviet Union.
106. Documents relating to this episode in FO 371/77693/7023, 7060 and 7728.
107. cf. F.H. Hinsley, *Power and the pursuit of peace,* 1963, 346-53.
108. Information from Lord Hankey to whom I am indebted for his careful reading of and comments upon the preliminary draft of this essay.

6 Oliver Franks and the Washington Embassy, 1948-52

Peter G. Boyle

In April 1948, shortly before taking up his appointment as British Ambassador to the United States, Oliver Franks had dinner one evening with Winston Churchill. Churchill said to him that there were three interconnecting aspects of British foreign policy, namely, relations with the Commonwealth, relations with Europe, and relations with the United States.[1] From May 1948 to December 1952, Franks played a key role in the conduct of British foreign policy in the crucial area of relations with the United States in his capacity as British Ambassador in Washington.

Franks was, in some ways, a surprising choice for such an important diplomatic appointment. He was not a professional diplomat, but an academic. Born in Bristol in 1905, he attended Bristol Grammar School and went to Queen's College, Oxford. Much of his life was associated with Oxford University, and his period in diplomatic service was a temporary departure from academic life, rather than a permanent change of career. After graduation from Oxford in 1927, he was a praelector in Philosophy at Queen's College, 1927-37, and was appointed University Lecturer in Philosophy in 1937, the same year in which he was appointed Professor of Moral Philosophy at Glasgow University. In 1935 he taught as a visiting professor at the University of Chicago. With the outbreak of war, he was appointed, in September 1939, to the Ministry of Supply, in which he served throughout the war, rising to become Permanent Secretary, 1945-6. In 1946, he returned to academic life as Provost of Queen's College, 1946-8.

During the war he came to know several ministers, especially Ernest Bevin. He not only conducted much business with Bevin in the latter's capacity as Minister of Labour, but also Bevin felt a personal rapport with Franks as a fellow West Countryman. Franks listened amicably to Bevin's stories of TGWU activities in the Bristol docks.[2]

On 5 June 1947, US Secretary of State George Marshall pronounced his ideas on American aid for European recovery in a speech at Harvard University. These ideas, which produced the Marshall Plan, were in no sense in the shape of a plan in June 1947. Marshall stressed the need for the initiative to come from the European side. 'There must be some agreement among the countries of Europe,' said Marshall, 'as to the requirements of the situation ... it would be neither fitting nor efficacious for this government to undertake to draw up unilaterally a program designed to place Europe on its feet.'[3] Bevin took the political initiative in arranging a meeting with French Foreign Minister Georges Bidault, and beginning the process which resulted in the formation of the sixteen-nation CEEC (Conference on European Economic Cooperation). Much work was required, however, to transform Marshall's rather general and inchoate ideas into a specific plan. To chair the conference that was charged with this task Bevin called upon the Bristolean whom he had much admired in the wartime Ministry of Supply.

Franks was eminently well suited to chair the meeting in Paris of representatives of the sixteen participating nations. He was familiar with the practical details of matters of supply and the machinery of government bureaucracy. He was politically independent — throughout his life he remained an 'unreconstructed Gladstonian Liberal'.[4] In personality, he commanded respect as a man of keen intelligence, unimpeachable integrity and calm judgement. Franks regarded his assignment, namely, to chair the preparation of the CEEC report by September 1947, as a task for the Oxford summer vacation, not a long-term return to government service. His success in this assignment, however, was such that Bevin and Attlee allowed him only a brief return to his beloved Oxford before summoning him to a higher level of service in 1948 as Ambassador to the United States.

On 16 July 1947, Bevin made the opening statement to the CEEC and then left proceedings to Franks. Franks's main brief was simply to draw up in an orderly, factual manner the major needs of the economy of the participating European countries, to suggest how these needs could be fulfilled by the European countries themselves by means of inter-European cooperation, and to estimate the total sum of dollar aid required from the United States. Franks chaired the CEEC in businesslike fashion. An executive committee of six nations was established, and four subcommittees were set up to deal with Food and Agriculture, Fuel and Power, Iron and Steel, and Transport. It was clear, however, as Franks appreciated, that a factual estimate of economic needs could not be produced uninfluenced by political considerations.

Aside from rivalries among the European powers themselves, there was, above all, the delicate matter of the degree of supervision and control by the United States. Franks's more difficult task was to try to produce a report which was based, as far as possible, on a factual estimate of economic needs, rather than on political considerations and compromises. There was a potential difference of opinion between the estimates of Europe's needs by the CEEC and by the Nourse, Krug and Harriman committees, which advised Truman on American aid. Marshall had emphasized the essential element of European initiative, but Under-Secretary of State for Economic Affairs Will Clayton had referred to the need also for 'friendly advice' from Americans in drawing up the European economic recovery plan. To try to allay the suspicions that were rife among the European powers over American string-pulling in the background, Franks had a meeting with Clayton on 29 July. In response to Franks's question whether an American should assist with the draft of the final report, Clayton advised against using an American, since the part which he played could be misconstrued, but Clayton ambiguously added that there were people in the State Department with the right kind of experience, who might give useful help and advice when the time came.[5] Franks proceeded with the preparation of the report with little direct consultation with the Americans. There was constant awareness, however, of American views and wishes. On the matter of European unity, for example, American pressure was persistent that the work of the CEEC should lead not simply to an economic report, but to institutional arrangements linking the European nations together. With regard to a European customs union, for example, a matter viewed with a jaundiced eye in Whitehall, Franks reminded the executive committee that 'Mr Clayton has emphasized that any indication that can be given in the report that the first steps towards forming customs unions are being taken by certain countries, is likely to add greatly to the effectiveness and influence of our work'.[6]

In September 1947, when the CEEC report was drawn up, Bevin became disturbed that US representatives sought a postponement of the report, pending consideration of certain points raised by the US Government. He wrote to Marshall that 'the impression has been created that the work of the Conference has been unsatisfactory, and is now having to be done again under American pressure. This is, of course, not the case, but if the impression is allowed to persist it will do untold harm in the European countries'.[7] American influence, however, was not sufficient to scale down the figure of recommended dollar aid in the CEEC report, namely, $22.4 billion over four years, a significantly higher figure than the sums deemed feasible by the three American committees. Franks' approach was to publish a report which was a realistic estimate of Europe's economic needs, with an appreciation that political compromise would then be necessary to persuade the US Congress to appropriate such vast sums.

Franks had originally expected that his work would be completed with the submission of the CEEC report. He was called upon, however, to play a leading part in the next stage, namely, selling the programme in America. He led a CEEC delegation to the United States, met with administration officials and Congressional leaders, and travelled throughout the country speaking to Chambers of Commerce and other such organizations. Administration figures, who were caught between support for ERP (European Recovery Programme) and wariness of Congress, gave advice on tactics. Under-Secretary of State Robert Lovett, for example, told Franks that 'in supporting the recovery programme they were taking a calculated risk of some $20 billion . . . But if he were asked what corresponding risk the European countries were taking he would not know what to say'. Lovett suggested that to impress Congress evidence should be shown 'of some sacrifice of national customs and traditions'.[8] Franks emphasized the mutual economic advantages of ERP to the United States and Europe. This was not sufficient to persuade the Truman administration to support the CEEC report in its entirety. Instead of the $22.4 billion recommended in the CEEC report, the President submitted the ERP bill to Congress on 19 December 1947, requesting $17 billion over four years. But Franks could feel well pleased with his work in 1947. The vague concept of a programme of American aid for European economic recovery had been given specific shape. Moreover, the decisive initiative taken by Europeans had resulted in the United States responding to and amending the Europeans' plans drawn up in Paris, rather than the Europeans making alterations to American schemes. Franks realized that Marshall aid would not be given without any strings. But, as he told the Treasury Economic Planning Board, 'we need not fear political conditions in a simple-minded sense, such as a ban on nationalization . . . In general, it would not be necessary for us to consider a major modification of our policy in order to conciliate American opinion'.[9]

Franks returned to Queen's College, Oxford, in January 1948. His impressive performance in Paris and in the United States had been well noted, however, by Bevin and Attlee. When it was decided in the spring of 1948 that a replacement was required for Inverchapel as Ambassador in Washington, Attlee telephoned Franks to offer him the post.[10] Though surprised by the invitation, Franks was pleased to accept.

Franks arrived in Washington with six months to run before the presidential election of 1948. Like all other commentators, Franks assumed that the election would result in a change of administration. 'The Dewey-Warren ticket is an extremely strong one', he reported following the nomination of Thomas E. Dewey and Earl Warren as the Republican candidates for president and vice-president.[11] In September 1948 he wrote that 'only a miracle can now prevent Mr Dewey's election'.[12]

Franks also witnessed the growing difficulties of the Truman administration over the 'Red Scare', especially the allegations of Whittaker Chambers against Alger Hiss in the House Un-American Activities Committee in the summer of 1948. Franks was scathing in his criticism of the Un-American Activities Committee, and he contrasted 'the irresponsible airing of unproven accusations in Washington with the restrained procedure of the Royal Commission in Canada, which showed itself to be considerate of the rights of the individual and a scrupulous guardian of the reputations of the innocent'.[13] Nevertheless, he felt that 'there must be some fire behind the Bentley and Chambers's smoke, as indeed we know to be the case'. It was, therefore, regrettable, he felt, that this 'complex and delicate matter' was being dealt with by 'so irresponsible a body as the Un-American Activities Committee'. Yet, Franks was also critical of Truman's handling of the matter. 'President Truman has been maladroit,' he reported, 'in attempting to dimiss the whole matter as a political "red herring" '.[14]

Although he was dealing with an assumed lame duck administration which was in deep political trouble, Franks did not feel that he was marking time until a new administration came to office. The bipartisanship of American foreign policy at that time produced the assumption that the main lines of foreign policy would continue under a Dewey administration. Bevin was endeavouring, in 1948, to influence the main lines of American foreign policy, setting the United States on a course of international involvement to deter Soviet expansion. The Soviet threat to Norway in March, followed by the Czech coup in February, made Bevin increasingly eager to bring together the Western nations, including the United States, into closer alignment, although he was uncertain of the most suitable precise form. He wished more than simply a military alliance. He spoke of a 'spiritual alliance of the West'. It was at this time, when Bevin was groping with such ideas, that Franks was sent to Washington. It was also the time when the Berlin crisis acted as a catalyst for developing trends. As Franks noted later, 'Bevin had been sniffing around for a closer United States association, getting nowhere. The Berlin blockade unloosed everything. It created a new urgency, enabling the United States to take new initiatives'.[15]

Franks felt that American pride in the airlift strengthened American determination to face the Soviet threat, since it was apparent that 'a retreat under duress would constitute an incalculable blow to Western prestige'.[16] As weeks went by, Franks reported that the airlift was uniting America behind Allied containment of Soviet agression. 'Not even the Wallacites', he observed, 'have so far raised any claims for the Western Powers to get out of Berlin or otherwise to appease the Communists on this issue.'[17] On his arrival in Washington in May 1948, Franks reported that there was a 'momentary lowering of the temperature of United States discussion about the Russian problem'.[18] He felt that there still existed within the United States the division of opinion which had been present since 1945, namely, on the one hand 'those whose fervent wish for peace blinds them to reality' and on the other hand 'those on whom the way psychosis has such a deep hold that they instinctively reject any peaceful overture'. By the time of the Berlin crisis, a consensus was developing, however, for the policy which former Secretary of State James Byrnes had called 'patient firmness' — and which Franks termed 'not so patient firmness'.[19] Those who dissented had been reduced to an insignificant number on the political left, Franks thought, whom he dismissed as 'Henry Wallace's conglomerate following of Communists, idealists and crackpots'.[20]

Although Bevin's interest in 1948 was moving more towards military security, economic recovery remained a basic concern of British policy. Franks was back in Oxford in early 1948 when Congress debated ERP and voted for its implementation as from 1 April 1948. Franks faced, however, the myriad problems involved in the implementation of the Marshall Plan. Difficult negotiations took place over the bilateral US-UK treaty required as part of ERP. Moreover, Congress, with its Republican majority, had voted for a four-year programme but required annual decisions on appropriations, which involved hearings, questioning of witnesses, detailed examination of the use of aid, lectures by backwoods congressmen on the virtues of the use of private enterprise and the evils of socialism, and, at the end of the proceedings, cuts in the sums appropriated. It required all of Franks' patience and negotiating skill to ensure that the exasperating dealings with officials and Congress over ERP were conducted as smoothly as possible.

Franks advised calmness over ERP cuts in 1948 by the House of Representatives Appropriations Committee. He wrote that the Senate Appropriations Committee 'frequently restored the wilder and less practicable cuts and economies made by the lower chamber'.[21] Bevin was concerned that the bilateral treaty had been drafted with little consultation, and gave too great an impression of American domination. Franks worked on the text with American officials, and reported in June 1948 that 'we have at least, I think, considerably improved the text with which we were originally faced. I hope that in its present form, it will not prove too difficult in Parliament'.[22] Franks appreciated that administration officials were constantly wary of old-guard, anglophobic Republicans who controlled the purse-strings in Congress, such as John Taber, Joseph Martin and Charles Halleck. He warned that 'it would be unwise to discount too heavily the influence of the economizers, pruners and retrenchers in the 81st Congress'.[23] He therefore stressed the importance of subtle diplomacy. When Charles Dewey, for example, the secretary of the Congressional watchdog committee on ERP, went to London in July 1948, Franks pointed out that Dewey was a vain man who 'will have a good deal of influence in sweetening or poisoning the minds of his committee'. Franks therefore suggested that Dewey should be given an invitation to the Garden Party at Buckingham Palace and otherwise feted.[24] Franks accepted that submission to some Congressional impositions would be necessary, such as the ratio of loans to grants, and the use of 5 per cent of counterpart funds for strategic materials for the United States.[25]

The British, however, were so relatively successful in fending off the more restrictive impositions that were imposed that Paul Hoffman, director of ECA (Economic Cooperation Agency), told Franks that 'there was in his judgement a real risk that the knowledge or belief that the United Kingdom had persistently and successfully opposed ECA proposals on a whole succession of matters of importance would do great harm to our common objective during the critical period next year, especially as neither the sport of twisting the lion's tail nor the legend of ever-successful British diplomacy vis-à-vis United States negotiations was dead'.[26] At the end of the lengthy and tortuous negotiations both in OEEC and within the United States Government, ERP aid to Britain in 1948-9 was $1,263 million, a larger sum than to any other country. Franks could feel satisfied that, as the Economic Committee of the Cabinet concluded, 'the amount of dollar aid allocated to the United Kingdom was unexpectedly satisfactory'.[27]

Truman's surprising re-election created better prospects for closer Anglo-American relations than a Dewey administration. Above all, instead of John Foster Dulles, who would have been Dewey's choice as Secretary of State, Dean Acheson replaced the respected but aloof George Marshall. Franks had met Acheson on several occasions during the war, and they had established a good rapport.

Acheson records in his memoirs of his relationship with Franks:

> Not long after becoming Secretary of State, I made an unorthodox proposal. On an experimental basis I suggested that we talk regularly, and in complete personal confidence, about any international problems we saw arising ... The dangers and difficulties of such a relationship were obvious, but its usefulness proved to be so great that we continued it for five years. We met alone, usually at his residence or mine at the end of the day before or after dinner. No one was informed even of the fact of the meeting ... Later, comparing the relations between our governments during our time with those under our successors, we concluded that whereas we had thought of these relations and their management as a part of domestic affairs, they had regarded them as foreign affairs. The heart of the difference lay in the intimacy, the secrecy, and the complete confidence of Sir Oliver's and my relationship.[28]

It was a remarkable relationship between a secretary of state and the ambassador of a foreign country. It indicated that in the Truman-Acheson era Britain was not regarded as altogether a foreign country. The meetings took place on average once a week, and more frequently at times of crisis.[29] No record was kept of the Franks-Acheson conversations, as they were intended to be freewheeling discussions without the paraphernalia of aides, minutes and suchlike. Clearly, however, Franks' personal relationship with Acheson was an element of vital significance in the success of his ambassadorship and the effectiveness of British policy *vis-à-vis* the United States in these years.

The momentum towards Western union that had developed in mid-1948 with the Berlin crisis was interrupted by the presidential election and Marshall's departure. Franks worked quietly in late 1948 and early 1949, especially within the forum of the Washington Exploratory Talks on Security, on the particular issues which required resolution, leading to the signing of the North Atlantic Treaty on 4 April 1949. Franks was alert to matters of particular concern to the Americans. With regard to Italy, for example, Bevin favoured a treaty to be signed by the Brussels Pact nations, plus the United States and Canada, with other nations to accede later, but Franks stressed American pressure to bring in Italy as a founder member, and Bevin accepted this.[30]

From his arrival in Washington in May 1948 to the signing of the North Atlantic Treaty in April 1949, Franks enjoyed much success in bringing Britain and America together. In the spring of 1949, however, a deterioration in Anglo-American relations set in, mainly over economic issues, which rose to serious levels by September 1949. On 24 February 1949 Christopher Mayhew, Under-Secretary of State, made a speech in New York which, in its unfortunate wording, gave the impression that Marshall aid enabled Britain to engage in social programmes which would not otherwise have been possible. Paul Hoffman telephoned Franks early the next morning to express his grave concern over appropriations for the second year of the Marshall plan.[31] By mid-1949, recession in America and a worsening British balance-of-payments position, led to much gloomier Anglo-American relations than six months previously. Franks was recalled to London for talks, and he reported to the Cabinet Economic Policy Committee that 'the mood of Congress during July would be very uncertain and it was very important that the U.K. government should not take any action which might prejudice consideration of Congress of the Second Appropriation of aid under the European Recovery Programme'.[32]

The crisis atmosphere of gloom lifted after the Anglo-American-Canadian meeting in Washington in September, and the devaluation of the pound. By early 1950, Britain's recovery was back on course. Difficulties continued, however, over possible American interference in Britain's internal affairs by means of the leverage of Marshall aid, especially with the British general election in February 1950. When Hoffman came to Paris in January 1950, for example, to outline proposed penalties for failure of nations with regard to trade liberalization, Franks had a long talk with Hoffman and persuaded him to avoid references to penalties which would raise charges of dollar dictatorship and inject Anglo-American difficulties into the British general election.[33] Franks was not always so persuasive, however, and his difficulties grew with the decline of bipartisanship over foreign policy. Franks had been relieved when the Democrats won control of Congress in 1948, so that such figures as John Taber were replaced as chairman of committees by more sympathetic Democrats. Franks was saddened to find, however, that foreign policy became more partisan. 'Generally speaking', he reported, 'it can be said that Democrats are now the supporters of ERP and the Republicans its opponents'.[34] Franks was not concerned by narrow Congressional conditions on Marshall aid aimed at twisting the British lion's tail. When the House of Representatives voted in March 1950, for example, for an amendment to suspend Marshall aid to Britain unless Irish partition was ended, Franks confidently knew that the amendment would be eliminated at a later stage.[35] He was more troubled by the relative decline in the sense of common purpose in the Marshall Plan. He commented upon 'the supercession of the original altruistic ideal of the Marshall Plan by the motif of U.S. self-interest . . . The self-interest motif has, of course, always been present, but this year it has almost entirely ousted the altruistic'.[36]

The Korean War presented the most contentious and potentially disruptive issues in Anglo-American relations during Franks' term as Ambassador. His views on the larger issues were clear and consistent. He appreciated that the war accenutated differences between British and American policy on a number of Far East issues. It was vital, however, in his view, that such differences should not distract from the central matter, namely, that the United States had taken a resolute stand against aggression in Korea, and that Britain must show herself, in America'a hour of need, to be a dependable partner and ally.

When the Korean War broke out on 25 June 1950, Franks, warned that 'we must expect emotional reactions here which will have an immediate, and possibly important, effect on the U.S. government's attitude to several problems in the Far East'. In particular, he predicted that 'it is quite likely that we should be faced with some sudden decision on Formosa'.[37] Moreover, although Britain supported American condemnation of North Korean aggression, Bevin felt Truman's proposed statement unwise in its reference to the attack on the part of 'centrally-directed Communist imperialism'.[38] Bevin wrote to Franks that: 'It seems to us essential to give the Russians an opportunity of beating a retreat when confronted with this welcome manifestation of American power and determination. The Russians have so far made no statement of policy and have most carefully avoided identifying themselves with the North Koreans. We therefore most strongly urge that the statement be so worded as to omit any references to Soviet responsibility for the attack which however obvious is not susceptible to proof.'[39] Franks contacted Acheson and reported to Bevin that he 'was able to convey your message to Acheson and secure modifications which I believe meet your concern'. The reference to 'centrally-directed Communist imperialism' was omitted from Truman's statement.[40]

A matter of great anxiety to Britain was that Korea was a feint on the part of the Soviet Union to draw Western strength to a remote part of the Far East before a further Soviet assault was launched in Europe. Franks deliverd a personal message from Attlee to Truman on 6 July, expressing Britain's concerns and proposing that military and diplomatic representatives of Britain and the United States should meet to discuss further possible Soviet probes and the response which the two powers should make to them. Truman agreed to Attlee's suggestion, and assigned Philip Jessup and General Omar Bradley to liaise with their British counterparts.[41] Franks was pleased with the development of this close and exclusive Anglo-American partnership. Divisive issues on details of Korean policy, however, kept recurring. On 8

July, Bevin wrote that 'Mr Acheson should appreciate, and I put it to them very frankly ... Whereas the United States has the whole hearted backing of world opinion in the courageous initiative they took with the aggression in Korea, I do not believe that they could rely on the same support for their declared policy on Formosa'.[42] Britain wished to leave a possible face-saving exit to the Soviet Union, but felt that if the Soviets were asked to use their influence on the North Koreans to end this aggression, the Soviets were likely to raise the matters of Formosa and Chinese representation in the United Nations. Franks passed on Bevin's views to Acheson, who gave a blunt repudiation of Bevin's implication that American policy regarding Formosa was, among other matters, a stumbling-block to Soviet influence to bring peace in Korea.[43] Franks felt that the Formosa issue was satisfactorily dealt with by Truman's statement of 19 July which, as Franks wrote to Bevin, 'contains an important clarification of the U.S. position on Formosa which I think goes some way to meet our position in that it sharply distinguishes between the present temporary military necessity and the long-term disposal of the island'.[44] Above all, however, Frank felt that attention should be focused on the central issue of the resolute American action in defence of freedom, and that nit-picking examination of all aspects of Far East policy was unwise. He pointed out that 'the temperament of the American people is, when in doubt, to do something'.[45] While such impetuosity required in some respects British restraint, American action in Korea above all required British support. Franks advocated that such support should take the specific, substantial form of the commitment of British ground troops to Korea.

At the outbreak of the Korean War, the British Government decided that, in view of British commitments elsewhere in Asia, naval forces would be sent to Korea, but that it would not be possible to send land forces. The Chief of Staff's view on a token land contribution was that 'whilst they recognize and fully sympathize with the political arguments for this, they are technically opposed to it on military grounds'.[46] The Cabinet Defence Committee, therefore, decided on 6 July that 'no land or air forces should be made available for operations in Korea'.[47] With the rapid deterioration of the military situation in Korea, however, Franks became convinced that Britain must rally to America's aid in the more substantial form of British troops on the ground, even if small in number. Following United Nations Secretary General Trygvie Lie's request for member nations to send troops, on 15 July Franks sent a hand-written letter to Attlee, in Bevin's absence on holiday, arguing strongly for the commitment of British ground troops. He wrote that he was 'not making any suggestion about what our decision should be: that lies outside my province'. There was no doubt, however, about the decision that would logically follow from the arguments in his letter. He wrote that Anglo-American relations had greatly improved since two years previously. 'Then we were one of the queue of European countries', he wrote, 'Now ... we are effectively out of the queue, one of the two world powers outside Russia'. His strong feeling was that 'the Americans will to some extent — I know this to be true of the Defense Department — test the quality of the partnership by our attitude to the notion of a token ground force'. He stressed American apprehension over the grave military position, as the North Koreans swept all the way to Pusan. 'Now that it is evident that the ground operations in Korea will be difficult and prolonged,' Franks wrote, 'the importance of the token ground forces comes to the front. The Americans especially look to see what their partner can offer.' [48]

The issue became more acute on 20 July, when General Bradley expressly requested British land forces.[49] Bevin, who had returned to the Foreign Office, wrote to Franks on 22 July that 'from the military point of view, we would, of course, find it extremely hard to provide even a token force. But we realize that the question is at least in part, if not mainly, political'.[50] Bevin asked Franks for his assessment. In reply, on 23 July, in perhaps the most important telegram of his ambassadorship, Franks departed from his normal relatively bland, academically detached style, and advocated with great vigour that the dispatch of British ground troops in Korea was vitally important for the maintenance of close Anglo-American relations. 'I should expect the reaction of the United States to a negative decision to be deep and prolonged', he wrote. He felt that 'underneath the thoughts and emotions engendered at times by difficulties and disagreements between us, there is a steady and unquestioning assumption that we are the only dependable ally and partner. This derives from our position in the world over past decades, our partnership with them in two world wars, and their judgement of the British character. The Americans in Korea will be in a tough spot for a long time. They look round for their partner'. He argued that the Americans wished other nations would follow Britain's lead. More importantly, however, considerations of political psychology made it imperative for Britain to send troops. He argued that 'despite the power and position of the United States, the American people are not happy if they feel alone. This feeling is paradoxical, but it is real ... The American people will not understand it if they are alone on the ground in Korea. They will think it shows coolness to them or even disapproval of what they are doing. The U.S. administration is aware of this feeling and its vigour. It therefore moves the administration to look for assistance on the ground and once again they turn to Britain as the key'.⁵¹

At a meeting of the Defence Committee on 24 July, the Chiefs of Staff reconsidered the question of British ground troops in Korea and 'although in their view it was still militarily unsound, they recognized the strong political argument in its favour'.⁵² A decision to send a brigade to Korea was endorsed by the Cabinet on 25 July. The first British troops reached Korea by 29 August, and in due course there were two British brigades which, along with a brigade of Canadian and Australian troops, made up the 1st Commonwealth Division. Franks was pleased that British and American troops were fighting shoulder to shoulder in Korea. He referred to 'the dichotomy between the American view of the British they have helped in the last five years,' and the British they knew in each of the two World Wars. Once aggression had occurred in Korea, American opinion swung back from its post-war views about the economic weakness of Britain, and the efforts Britain was making to recover to the older view of Britain, from whom much should be expected and demanded'.⁵³ This was perhaps an overstatement of the effect on Anglo-American relations of the despatch of British troops to Korea. A refusal on Britain's part would certainly have had a devastating effect. Yet Franks went too far in suggesting that joint military participation in Korea restored a relationship somewhat akin to the Second World War bond. The delay in agreeing to send troops devalued the commitment to some extent. As Franks's successor, Roger Makins, noted in 1954, 'We gave the impression that our contribution was half-hearted, reluctant and late. We therefore never received the credit in the United States which our participation warranted, with resulting harm to Anglo-American relations'.⁵⁴ The Americans tended to take the presence of British troops in Korea for granted after a short time, and their presence made little impact on the consciousness of American public opinion. The greatest effect of the commitment of British troops to Korea, it might be argued, was that it made it more possible to ride the storms of bitter Anglo-American disagreement over the conduct of the Korean War during the autumn and winter of 1950–1.

Following the spectacular success of the American landing at Inchon in September 1950, and the subsequent retreat of the North Koreans, the fateful decision was taken to go beyond the objective of the restoration of the status quo in Korea, and to cross the 38th Parallel to reunite Korea. Although most of the later difficulties followed from this crucial decision, it was not a decision from which the British dissented. The Chiefs of Staff had given their view on 20 September that a top priority was to end the Korean conflict swiftly with the restoration of the status quo and withdraw troops to more important theatres. The Chiefs of Staff did not see any point in taking the risks involved in an attempt to reunite Korea.[55] Attlee and Bevin, however, felt that the crossing of the 38th Parallel by UN forces, and the subsequent reunification of Korea, with perhaps a buffer zone in the north between China and Korea, need not be seen as a threat by China and should not, therefore, lead to Chinese intervention. Bevin wrote that 'I must be misjudging Chou En-Lai's statesmanship if he and his government really intend to throw discretion to the winds, and to embark upon hostilities against the United Nations.' Attlee argued that the Chinese would welcome the removal of a Soviet client state in North Korea.[56] Franks was, therefore, instructed that 'we have no desire to take the very heavy responsibility of pressing the Americans to abandon any operations which may be contemplated north of the Parallel'.[57] The British, however, wished the advance northwards to proceed with caution. They became increasingly apprehensive over the precipitous nature of the sweep into North Korea of MacArthur's forces, which they viewed as unnecessarily provocative to the Chinese. Bevin felt that the offer of a buffer zone was the best hope of making a settlement with the Chinese. Franks reported, however, that Acheson had rejected this idea in a conversation on 23 November. Instead, MacArthur had been authorized to begin an offensive on 24 November which, it was felt, would end the war in a short time.[58]

When MacArthur's 'Home by Christmas' offensive brought about full-scale Chinese intervention and a débâcle for the United Nations forces, the bitter recriminations and accusations exchanged between the British and Americans led to the nadir of Anglo-American relations during Franks's ambassadorship, and tested to the full his skills in smoothing over differences. The British were aghast by the prospect of a lengthy war with the Chinese, and favoured concessions which, as Franks told Acheson, might bring about a swift settlement. In particular, they pressed the United States to agree to diplomatic recognition of communist China and the acceptance of communist China into the United Nations, as well as concessions regarding Formosa. Acheson became deeply incensed by the British position, and expressed American determination not to negotiate under duress.[59] The first essential, in the American view, was to stabilize the military position and, rather than offering concessions on the diplomatic front, to go on the offensive diplomatically, especially by passing a United Nations resolution condemning China as an aggressor, and by imposing economic sanctions on China. Franks reported that American officials 'of course realize that economic actions would involve us immediately in the most difficult problems'.[60] British trade with China through Hong Kong made Britain reluctant to introduce economic measures against China, not only for economic reasons, but also out of fear of provoking a Chinese assault on Hong Kong. The British were even more firmly opposed to a condemnatory resolution against China, which was, in their view, an expression of American moral self-righteousness which would antagonize the Chinese unnecessarily and make a negotiated settlement more difficult. Franks was instructed on 29 November 1950 that 'the introduction of a charge of aggression against the Chinese would have incalculable consequences, and we cannot be rushed into a grave step of this kind without further consultation and Cabinet consideration.'[61]

The deterioration in Anglo-American relations reached a crisis in early December, with Truman's careless remarks in a press conference regarding the possible use of the atomic bomb in Korea. Attlee's consequent visit to Washington calmed fears with regard to the atomic bomb, but little progress was made on other matters. Franks attended the sessions of talks between Truman and Attlee and reported that the British and American positions on most matters relating to China and a Korean settlement were at serious variance. Franks emphasized how Acheson, who dominated the talks, insisted on a refusal of concessions until the military situation improved, and deplored the hesitation and delay regarding the condemnatory resolution which the British and the Commonwealth countries had brought about. Franks reported that 'we were subjected to an uncomfortable half-hour's lecture on the deplorable effect that this delay would have on the United Nations itself and on American public opinion'.[62]

The condemnatory resolution became the touchstone of loyalty and support which the Americans insisted upon from their allies. The British, at first adamantly opposed, ultimately gave in and supported the resolution, which was passed in the United Nations General Assembly on 1 February 1951. Franks endeavoured to ensure that British yielding on the issue of the condemnatory resolution itself did not involve yielding on the more important implications of the resolution, namely, the possibility of negotiating a settlement to end the war. On 12 January, Franks reported that 'the Americans recognize that our objections to the word "aggressor" related to what may follow upon it, rather than to the statement of fact which it registers ... If the truth be known, they have very few ideas and have certainly not worked out the implications of those they have.'[63] His worry was that the Americans were not seriously trying to achieve a cease-fire. He received information leaked from a Senate Foreign Relations Committee briefing that a cease-fire proposal in January 1951 had been supported 'on the assumption that it would be rejected by the Chinese, and that the United States would thus gain support for its own resolutions declaring the Peking Government aggressors'.[64] He felt that Britain should appreciate how seriously Americans felt about the condemnatory resolution, while he hoped that support was gradually growing in the American administration for a moderate follow-up to China's condemnation as an aggressor. He stressed that 'in pursuing their present policy the administration, and in particular Mr. Acheson, are not actuated mainly by the desire to appease the Chinese lobby, but are acting on what they believe to be a vital moral principle, the neglect of which led to the destruction of the League of Nations and by indirect, but nonetheless, definite stages to the outbreak of the second World War.' [65] He felt that Britain should, therefore, yield on the issue of the condemnatory resolution, while Franks received assurances from Acheson and Assitant Secretary for Far Eastern Affairs Dean Rusk that the United States was prepared to hold comprehensive talks with the Chinese on all issues in the Far East. When the General Assembly passed the condemnatory resolution, Franks reported that 'there is little pressure for immediately following up the aggressor resolution with punitive action.' [66]

While British fears were allayed somewhat regarding the condemnatory resolution, British anger rose over General MacArthur's tactics, which torpedoed the prospects of opening negotiations and raised the possibility of an extended war against China. Following a Cabinet meeting on 23 January 1951, Franks was informed that the British Government was concerned over the series of controversial statements by MacArthur, but the Ambassador was not specifically instructed to raise the matter with the State Department. On 29 January, Franks was instructed to draw the attention formally of the State Department to MacArthur's statement of 28 January, that United Nations forces in Korea were fighting for a 'free Asia', and to make it clear that it was incompatible with MacArthur's position as United Nations Commander to make such controversial statements.[67]

Franks reported on 30 January that the State Department had agreed that 'this particular statement was ill-judged ... Unfortunately he [MacArthur] is a man who frequently allows himself an adornment of language which leads him outside the bounds of the subject'.[68] In March the British were outraged by MacArthur's statement calling upon the Chinese to accept United Nations terms, or accept the risk of an extended war on China itself. Franks took up the matter with Rusk, 'who made a completely clean breast of the whole incident. He said MacArthur's statement was unknown to anyone in Washington, and all the more unauthorized. The President wishes you to know that action had been taken at the highest level to ensure that this did not happen again'.[69] When MacArthur's letter to Representative Joseph Martin in early April led to his dismissal on 11 April 1951, the British Government wished to dampen suspicions that the British had pressed for his dismissal, since British protests over MacArthur's behaviour had become publicly known. On 14 April, Franks reported that 'the pro-MacArthur block is rather apt to blame us for his fall from power, and to attack the President and the State Department for being too much under British influence'.[70] The British were, of course, delighted at MacArthur's dismissal, but Franks warned that the American public reaction created a very dangerous political atmosphere in which Britain should tread warily. 'At the moment, the United States resembles a patient seized with violent convulsions,' he reported on 21 April. 'The prognosis is favourable, but a long period of tiresome convalescence is indicated.'[71]

With MacArthur's dismissal and the stabilization of the military situation in Korea, tensions in Anglo-American relations eased considerably. American allegations continued of Britain's wish to appease China. Even more so, American resentment continued over British trade with China. In May 1951, Franks reported that 'criticism of British trade with China, which has been a major source of friction here for some time, has grown in volume and acerbity'.[72] But, especially after the opening of Korea peace negotiations in June 1951, the bitter Anglo-American disputes of 1950-1 on Far Eastern matters receded. Other areas of disagreement continued, however, particularly economic and defence issues.

The Korean War acted as a catalyst for the growing feeling in the United States and Britain of the need for great increases in military spending in order to make containment credible. Acheson, in particular, had come to feel that the initial emphasis on economic recovery must be succeeded by greater emphasis on military expenditure. By 1950, the United States felt that British economic recovery was sufficient to justify the end of Marshall aid, and pressure was exerted on Britain to undertake a massive rearmament programme. The end of Marshall aid, combined with the economic effects of rearmament and a turn in the terms of trade against Britain, led to another serious financial crisis in Britain in 1951, which produced considerable strains in the Anglo-American relationship. Franks' experience in matters of aid and supply enabled him to use his talents to good effect to ameliorate the difficulties, and by the end of 1952, with British recovery from the 1951 balance-of-payments crisis, the relationship had greatly improved by the end of Franks's term.

Although the Marshall Plan had been devised as a four-year programme, 1948–52, in October 1950 Franks reported that Britain could not count on any more Marshall aid, other than what was in the pipeline through to the end of 1950.[73] Chancellor of the Exchequer Hugh Gaitskell wished the continuation of Marshall aid, as he felt that conditions in 1950 had been exceptional. Franks reported, however, that further Marshall aid would serve only to strengthen Britain's reserves, and that Congress was unwilling to continue aid for this purpose. The Cabinet therefore decided that amicable acquiescence in the American decision to terminate Marshall aid as from 31 December 1950 was the best approach.[74]

Franks was well aware that the American focus was shifting from economic to military matters. In March 1950, Franks wrote to Bevin that he had a long talk with Acheson who was groping for a means to build up the strength of the West. Acheson was not so appreciative of Britain's economic difficulties, Franks reported, and of the relationship between Britain's economic vulnerability and her potential military strength.[75] The views of Acheson and like-minded American officials found expression in NSC 68 in April 1950, which advocated a massive increase in the United States defence effort. Congressional support for such a programme was unlikely, however, until the outbreak of the Korean War in June 1950. In September 1950, Britain followed the American example and embarked on rearmament on a large scale, with a £3,600 million three-year programme, increased in January 1951 to £4,700 million. The programme was not directly conditional on American aid, but the British assumption was that the United States would give assistance to cope with any British dollar shortage that resulted from rearmament. The British assumption proved to be false, as American aid fell short of British expectations, while the diversion of British resources from exports to defence, combined with a turn in the terms of trade against Britain in 1951, left Britain in dire economic straits, and resentful towards the United States.[76]

Franks had little success in gaining a more sympathetic hearing for Britain from the United States Government, which argued that the matter could be resolved by burden-sharing within NATO, and which pressed for further effort in defence-spending by Britain. But Britain was disappointed with the NATO burden-sharing exercise. In September 1951, when Gaitskell came on a visit to Washington, the United States was still pressing for a greater British defence effort, even with the British economy in crisis. Franks reported Gaitskell's fury and his assertion that American plans for increased NATO defence-spending were 'absolute moonshine'. In practical terms, the British resolved the problem by obtaining aid from the Americans by indirect means as a supplement to direct aid, such as offshore purchases and increased charges for services for American bases in Britain. This involved, however, a considerable amount of haggling and wrangling. To a greater extent, the problem was solved by scaling down British rearmament when the Conservative Government came to office in October 1951, and by the retrenchment policies of the new Chancellor Rab Butler, which was, however, a painful solution for the British people. Throughout 1952 the problems continued, yet by June, when Franks returned to London for a visit, he was more optimistic. 'Franks came in like a breath of fresh air from the U.S.A.', Churchill's private secretary John Colville recorded. 'He thought everybody was too gloomy. We must edge our way out of the crisis ... Time was needed for remedial measures to take effect.' [77] The disputes over aid and defence policy in 1951-2 were stormy, and Franks needed to use his conciliatory powers between Acheson and Eden, who, although superficially very alike and whose memoirs contain fulsome mutual praise, had frequent bitter disagreements.[78] By the end of 1952, however, the British balance-of-payments crisis had eased, and by 1953 the British economy was less in need of American aid, allowing a firmer basis for a healthier Anglo-American relationship.

Franks was less successful in reconciling Anglo-American differences over atomic energy matters. As Margaret Gowing has shown, the Anglo-American relationship on atomic energy was almost in a different compartment from the relationship on other matters.[79] Congressional attitudes as reflected in the McMahon Act of 1946 made it abundantly clear that the United States was not willing to share atomic information with Britain to any important extent, despite Britain's wartime contribution in atomic matters. At a meeting of the Combined Policy Committee of representatives of Britain, the United States and Canada on 20 September 1949, George Kennan suggested that atomic bombs should be manufactured in the United States, and Britain furnished with a supply, rather than Britain building her own bombs. Franks rejected this proposal, arguing that the Modus Vivendi of 1948 had stipulated means of sharing information, and that this approach should be adopted.[80] The amount of information received as a result of the Modus Vivendi proved, however, to be very limited, while Britain had given up the American commitment of the Quebec Agreement of 1943 of joint agreement before use of an atomic bomb. Indeed, Britain did not even have agreement that the United States required British assent, or even consultation, for the use of atomic bombs from the American bases in Britain, which had been established in 1948. A crisis was reached in December 1950, with Truman's remarks about the possible use of atomic bombs in Korea and Attlee's consequent visit to Washington. The Americans rejected a British veto on the use of atomic bombs by the United States, but the matter of British consultation and consent with regard to the use of atomic bombs from bases in Britain, was opened for negotiation. At a meeting on 14 September 1951, Omar Bradley, chairman of the Joint Chiefs of Staff, agreed on the need for prior consultation and consent before the United States used atomic bombs from British bases, but no precise form of wording was agreed upon. In October 1951, Franks proposed a draft formula which stated that the question of the use of American bases in Britain in an emergency 'remains a matter for joint decision in the light of circumstances at the time'.[81] This formula was accepted by the Americans, and remained in force thereafter. Churchill, who was extremely critical of the Labour Government's inability to gain atomic information from the Americans, hoped to achieve more success on this matter. As Franks discovered when Churchill visited Truman in January 1952, although some further information was given to Churchill on America's strategic targeting, Churchill was no more successful than his predecessor in acquiring substantial amounts of information on atomic energy from the Americans. In 1952, Britain tested an atomic bomb which had been developed largely from British resources, and it was not until the late 1950s that the Americans made significant concessions to Britain on atomic energy matters.[82]

American unwillingness to supply information to Britain on atomic energy was greatly increased by evidence of lapses in British security. In May 1951, Guy Burgess and Donald MacLean fled to Moscow. Both Burgess and MacLean served in the Washington Embassy in Franks' term. MacLean had been in Washington since 1944 and left in August 1948, three months after Franks' arrival. In 1948, MacLean had been First Secretary and Deputy Head of Chancery, so that he knew everything of importance to the Embassy. Burgess was a Second Secretary from August 1950 to May 1951. To compound matters, Kim Philby was SIS senior representative in Washington from the autumn of 1949 to the summer of 1951. Franks, an academic on temporary duty as a diplomat, had little experience in vetting procedures and other such aspects of security, and it is understandable that he did not suspect officials who had been in service for quite some time. Nevertheless, as Ambassador, he had ultimate responsibility, and the failures of security on such a spectacular level in the Embassy in his time, had the result that his work as Ambassador was severely undermined by the relaying of information from the Embassy to the Soviet Union by MacLean, Burgess and Philby.

Franks's term as Ambassador came to an end in December 1952. Eden asked him to stay on, but he decided to return to England, mainly for reasons of his family's education. He was offered a variety of prestigious posts, including Secretary-General of NATO, Chairman of the Board of Governors of the BBC, and editor of *The Times*. Instead, he became Chairman of Lloyds Bank, 1954-62, and then returned to his first love, academic life, as Provost of Worcester College, Oxford, 1962-76. One historian has commented that 'Judged by the glittering promise of Franks in his forties, his subsequent career... appears somewhat muted.' [83] His fame in his post-ambassadorial career, however, came not from his main occupation, but the various reports which different British governments asked him to draw up on diverse matters, including the security services, Oxford University, and the Falklands War. Franks had become, as John Colville puts it, 'a man for all seasons'.[84]

Franks had served at a time of crucial importance in Anglo-American relations. The wartime partnership had dissolved, and serious divisions had arisen between the former partners over such matters as economics, the Far East, and atomic energy. The partnership was restored and the special relationship maintained, largely on account of the common interests of the two nations, especially their mutual need of one another in the containment of Soviet expansion. Nevertheless, although the lines of policy were determined by underlying interests, rather than by the decisions and actions of individuals, whether at the level of presidents, prime ministers, foreign secretary or ambassador, Franks' role was not inconsiderable in binding Britain and America together, and conciliating in the frequent times of strain and crises. His intelligence, independence and integrity gave him a quiet authority which won respect. His extraordinary personal relationship with Acheson gave him leverage and influence quite unusual for an ambassador. His understanding of both the British and American points of view produced, as the *Washington Post* put it, 'fertility in coming up with formulas and acceptable compromises'.[85] He had made a notable contribution to the main goal of his work, which, as he was quoted in the Foreign Office American Department some years later, was based on his belief that 'close and effective cooperation between Britain and the United States is the basic condition of an orderly world, the best chance of avoiding another world war, and our hope of peace.' [86]

Notes

1. P. Boyle interview with Lord Franks, 7 December 1985.
2. ibid.
3. *FRUS*, 1947, III, 239.
4. P. Boyle interview with Lord Franks, 7 December 1985.
5. FO 371/62415/UE 6606/168/53.
6. FO 371/62598/UE 7157/6328/53.
7. FO 371/62416/UE 8600/168/53.
8. FO 371/62683/UE 1014/9159/53.
9. FO 371/62749/UE 12624/10889/53.
10. P. Boyle interview with Lord Franks, 7 December 1985.
11. FO 371/68019/AN 2442/16/45.
12. FO 371/68019/AN 3487/16/45.
13. FO 371/68019/AN 2960/16/45.
14. FO 371/68019/AN 2984/16/45.
15. Oral History Interview 194, Oliver Franks, 16, Harry S. Truman Library, Independence, Missouri.
16. FO 371/68019/AN 2442/16/45.
17. FO 371/68019/AN 3384/16/45.
18. FO 371/68018/AN 2134/16/45.
19. FO 371/68019/AN 2442/16/45.
20. FO 371/68019/AN 2905/16/45.
21. FO 371/71756/UR 1875/7/98.
22. FO 800/515/US/48/42.
23. FO 371/71758/UR 2978/7/98.
24. FO 371/71760/UR 3988/7/98.
25. FO 371/71758/UR 3010/7/98; FO 371/71761/UR 5231/7/98.
26. FO 371/71762/UR 5514/7/98.
27. CAB 134/126/EPC (48), 33rd meeting.
28. D. Acheson, *Present at the creation*, 1969, 323-4.
29. P. Boyle interview with Lord Franks, 7 December 1985.
30. FO 371/79228/Z 1718/1074/72G.
31. FO 800/516/US/49/8.
32. CAB 134 EPC (49), 24th meeting.
33. FO 371/86969/UR 103/2 and 3.
34. FO 371/87044/UR 3132/63.
35. FO 371/87043/UR 3132/38.
36. FO 371/87044/UR 3132/63.
37. FO 371/84056/FK 1015/21.
38. CM (50), 39th Conclusions, Minute 4.
39. FO 371/84057/FK 1015/40.
40. ibid.
41. PREM 8/1405/Part I/T 52/50; PREM 8/1405/Part I/T 55A/50.
42. FO 371/84082/FK 1022/56.
43. FO 371/84086/FK 1022/111.
44. FO 371/84088/FK 1022/154.
45. FO 371/84093/FK 1022/241.
46. FO 371/84059/FK 1015/86.

47. CAB 131/8/DO (50), 12th meeting.
48. PREM 8/1405/Part I.
49. ibid.
50. FO 371/84090/FK 1022/198.
51. FO 371/FK 1022/222.
52. CAB 131/8/DO (50), 15th meeting.
53. FO 800/517/US/50/33.
54. PREM 11/666.
55. PREM 8/1405/Part 2/COS (50), 152nd meeting.
56. PREM 8/1405/Part 2.
57. FO 371/84100/FK 1022/401.
58. FO 371/84118/FK 1023/161.
59. FO 371/84119/FK 1023/196 and 197.
60. FO 371/84120/FK 1023/201.
61. FO 371/84119/FK 1023/182.
62. FO 371/92765/FK 1071/26.
63. FO 371/92767/FK/1071/69.
64. FO 371/90903/AU 1013/5.
65. FO 371/90903/AU 1013/6.
66. FO 371/90903/AU 1013/8.
67. FO 371/92816/FK 1096/67.
68. FO 371/92772/FK 1071/247.
69. FO 371/92813/FK 1096/9.
70. FO 371/90903/AU 1013/7.
71. FO 371/90903/AU 1013/18.
72. FO 371/90903/AU 1013/20.
73. FO 371/86983/UR 1027/3.
74. FO 371/87015/UR 284/38.
75. FO 800/517/US/50/8.
76. FO 371/86983/UR 1027/3.
77. J. Colville, *Fringes of power,* 1985, 652.
78. Acheson, op.cit., 578; A. Eden, *Full circle,* 1960, 200; A. Seldon, *Churchhill's Indian summer,* 1981, 389.
79. M. Gowing, *Independence and deterrence: Britain and atomic energy, 1945-52,* 2 vols, 1974, I, 241-3.
80. ibid., 285.
81. ibid., 317-18.
82. ibid., 413.
83. Seldon, op.cit., 631, note 83.
84. Colville, op.cit., 482.
85. *Washington Post,* 28 November 1952.
86. FO 381/114367/AU 1051/32.

7 William Strang and the Permanent Under-Secretary's Committee

Ritchie Ovendale

In February 1949 Ernest Bevin, the Foreign Secretary, agreed to the establishment of the Permanent Under-Secretary's Committee. Its function was to be similar to that of George Kennan's Policy Planning Staff in the United States which had been set up in 1947. The Permanent Under-Secretary's Committee was 'to consider long-term questions of foreign policy and to make recommendations' to the Foreign Secretary. Rather than concerning itself with the day-to-day affairs, the committee was to study long-term trends and their possible bearing upon the future formulation of British foreign policy. It met under the chairmanship of the newly appointed Permanent Under-Secretary, William Strang, and comprised one of the junior ministers and the Deputy and Assistant Under-Secretaries.[1] Throughout 1949 this Foreign Office committee met frequently and examined, against the background of joining the Cold War in Europe and Asia, how Britain could in future maintain its status as a great power. It is possible to argue that the decision had already been taken with the moves towards the formation of the North Atlantic Treaty Organization (NATO), and that Bevin, as early as February 1946, had opted for the Anglo-American alliance. But it should be remembered that when, on 5 March 1948, Bevin had presented to the Cabinet a paper entitled 'The Threat to Western Civilization' and had emphasized that resolute action had to be taken to counter the Russian threat, an unnamed member of that body had suggested that 'we should use United States aid to gain time, but our ultimate aim should be to attain a position in which the countries of Western Europe could be independent both of the United States and the Soviet Union'.[2] It was the Permanent Under-Secretary's Committee which in 1949 recommended that neither the Commonwealth alone, nor Western Europe alone, nor even the Commonwealth plus Western Europe would be strong enough, either economically or militarily, to stand on their own against the forces opposing them, and that the full participation of the United States was essential to sustain the free world which Russia was trying to undermine. Effectively the British Government, at the end of 1949, endorsed the conclusions of this committee that the prevailing policy of close Anglo-American cooperation in world affairs should continue, and that such cooperation would involve Britain's sustained political, military and economic effort. When, early in 1951, the principal of the Anglo-American special relationship as the corner-stone of British foreign policy was seriously challenged in Cabinet, a dying Bevin, assisted by Strang and Hugh Gaitskell, fought to sustain the policy decided upon by Strang's committee. What Britain had to do was to 'exert sufficient control over the policy of the well-intentioned but inexperienced colossus on whose cooperation our safety depends'.[3]

As chairman of the committee, Strang's influence was considerable. During 1949 he toured South East Asia, the Far East and the Middle East to see for himself those areas where Britain had an influence and which, it was thought, might be challenged by Russian penetration. His analyses of the situation in these countries was often reflected in the recommendations of the Permanent Under-Secretary's Committee. Noted for his self-effacement, Strang, along with Sir Esler Dening, did not have the usual background of a Foreign Official of the time.[4] Strang lacked the traditional background of the English public school. He was not a product of Oxbridge. Rather, he was a Scottish farmer's son who worked his way up through the ranks of the Foreign Office by sheer ability.

Around the time of his appointment as Permanent Under-Secretary, Strang was described by a journalist as being 'over six feet tall, slim, with a brown mustache, shy and correct', and, 'hardly the informal feet-on-desk type of diplomat instanced by Sir Oliver Franks, British Ambassador to Washington'.[5] Strang was widely regarded as a first class administrator, someone seen as being able to manage the Foreign Office machine at home and abroad and able to provide his Foreign Secretary with necessary information and advice for shaping policy. One of his subordinates commented that 'Strang never holds things up'. On his retirement in 1953, *The Times* observed that he 'coupled a capacity for hard work and very long hours with the analytical mind of a mathematician, which can cut swiftly and cleanly through a heavy file, or, where he is chairman of a committee, can focus upon the salient points for or against a policy, and present the results fairly, lucidly, and concisely'. Strang was regarded as both approachable and fair.[6] Writing immediately after his departure from the Foreign Office, Strang recalled that his years as Permanent Under-Secretary were the 'happiest years of a happy career'. In his own account of his role Strang described the real burden being that of 'making up one's mind what to decide or what to recommend'.[7]

Throughout his life Strang remained proud of his school and was pleased to be invited to speak to it on Founders' Day. He went to Palmer's School, Gray's, Essex, an early eighteenth-century foundation and which he himself described as 'one of the leading grammar schools in the country'. He was awarded an Essex County Major Scholarship to attend University College London, and read English. After graduating, he spent a year at the Sorbonne in Paris. The First World War intervened, and Strang served with the 4th Batallion Worcestershire Regiment on the Western Front. On being demobilized he sat for the higher examination for the Civil Service and headed the list of 500 candidates. He entered the Foreign Office, and in 1919 was appointed Third Secretary at Belgrade. Never heading an embassy abroad, Strang spent twenty-five of the thirty-four years of his service in the Foreign Office. He served on the embassy staff in Moscow in 1933 during the trial of the Vickers engineers accused of spying and sabotage. In September 1938 he accompanied Neville Chamberlain to Berchtesgarden, Godesberg and Munich. Lord Halifax sent him to Moscow in June 1939 to attempt to negotiate a treaty of mutual assistance with the Russians. During the Second World War he attended the Moscow Conference in 1943 and served on the European Advisory Commission, an inter-allied body set up to make plans for the post-hostilities period. In 1945 Strang was appointed Political Adviser to Field Marshal Sir Bernard Montgomery, the Commander-in-Chief of the British Occupation Forces in Germany, and from October 1947 served as Permanent Under-Secretary of the German Section of the Foreign Office.[8]

On hearing that he was to succeed Sir Orme Sargent as Permanent Under-Secretary, Strang suggested to Bevin that he should go on a tour of South and East Asia to see for himself a part of the world he only knew from reading and files. On the day that Strang took up his office he was on a flying boat between Singapore and Bangkok. His journey took him to Karachi, Delhi, Calcutta, Rangoon, Singapore, Kuala Lumpur, Batavia, Bangkok, Hong Kong, Shanghai and Tokyo. During his six-week tour Strang dined with Pandit Nehru, found General Douglas MacArthur charming and friendly in Tokyo, had tea with Thakin Nu, the Burmese Prime Minister, considered Batavia rather tawdry and thought that the Dutch could have made more of it, discussed the nature of Chinese communism at length with various officials, and was inspired by an intense feeling of pride in British achievement in Hong Kong. From the shores of Asia the significance of the battle for Berlin was enhanced. With the heartland already largely under Russian control, Strang became convinced that the seagirt periphery, the Rimland, stretching from Oslo to Tokyo, should be denied to communism and, if possible, defended against military attack. The area needed to be looked at as a whole. On his return he reported to Bevin that what was needed was not just a British but a Commonwealth policy, and that policy would have to be concerted with the United States. Britain had a part to play that could be played by no other power, but it could not be played alone; it would best be played by a combination of British experience and American resources.[9]

Strang's advice became that of the Permanent Under-Secretary's Committee, accepted British policy, was passed on to George Kennan and probably influenced his recommendations to President Truman, NSC 48/2, which became the basic American decision to halt the expansion of communism in Asia. The basis of the committee's discussion on South East Asia and the Far East was a paper by Esler Dening of the Far Eastern desk. On 23 March 1949 Strang suggested to Bevin that Sir Gladwyn Jebb should discuss issues raised in this paper which Kennan when in Washington.[10] In November 1949 the Foreign Office and the American Policy Planning Staff exchanged information on South East Asia. Kennan and his staff were allowed to read an edited version of the British papers drawn up by Strang's committee — the editing removing unfavourable references to the United States — and they commented that there was 'a remarkable similarity of view' in the British and American studies.[11]

The Permanent Under-Secretary's Committee drew up two papers on South East Asia and the Far East. Bevin agreed that initial versions of these papers should be circulated to the King, Attlee, the Chancellor of the Exchequer, the Lord President of the Council, the Minister of Defence, the Secretary of State for Commonwealth Relations, the Chiefs of Staff, Sir Norman Brook, and to the British Ambassadors in Washington, Paris and Cairo, to Sir E. Hall Patch, and the Colonial Secretary as well as to the Special Commissioner in South East Asia, Malcolm MacDonald.[12] They were presented to the Cabinet on 27 October, and later given a wider circulation.

Strang's committee argued that there was a real danger that the whole of Asia would become the servant of the Kremlin unless Britain exploited its special position in Asia to bring about a close collaboration between East and West. From the Persian Gulf to the China Sea no single power could dominate the region. Nor could any combination of powers resist Russian expansion. And no Asian power could bring about unity and cooperation. As Britain had come to terms with the new nationalist spirit in Asia it could use its political and economic influence to weld the area into some degree of regional cooperation. Most of Britain's former territories in the area were friendly independent members of the Commonwealth, and had been built upon a British foundation. Britain also had a peculiarly close relationship with those countries in South East Asia within the sterling area. The United States did not enjoy the same degree of prestige as did Britain, partly because it lacked the historical connections, partly because of its reluctance to play a leading part in South East Asia. Full development of the area, however, was only possible through American assistance, and the United States was reluctant to risk further losses after its experience in China. The committee thought that Britain was in the best position to build up a regional association in South East Asia in partnership with the West. Not only could Britain interest the United States, but it had means of influencing and coordinating the policies of the Asian dominions, and Australia and New Zealand. The immediate intention was to prevent the spread of communism and to resist Russian expansion. The long-term objective was to create a friendly system of partnership between East and West, and to improve economic and social conditions in South East Asia and the Far East. Working on the premise that the Far East comprised principally Japan, Korea and China — the first two being primarily an American commitment and the third a potentially hostile power — it was in South East Asia that Britain had to start promoting greater regional collaboration. Only later could the Far East be attached to any system that might emerge. Strang's committee argued that there were advantages in using a Commonwealth rather than just a British approach to achieve these aims, though the racial policies followed by South Africa and the resentment Asian countries felt over the 'White Australia' policy might endanger this. Furthermore, it was unrealistic to expect democracy to develop on the British pattern in the area: corruption and inefficiency would not vanish overnight. The masses of the peoples of Asia for many years would have little voice in government; universal suffrage was only likely to be exploited by the governing classes. The paper suggested that Britain should attempt to establish the nucleus of strategic cooperation between itself, Australia, New Zealand and the Commonwealth countries of Asia. This was essential before any wider region defence system could be contemplated. And then the cooperation could only be in the field of planning and exchange of views. Britain would have to supply the arms, and other commitments made any increase impossible. As so little could be done in the military fields the most profitable line seemed the economic one. A draft of the paper, amended at the request of the Colonial Office, referred to the problem of how to 'reconcile the insatiable appetite of India and the Colonial Empire' for economic assistance with Britain's slender resources and the need to develop South East Asia as a whole. Indeed, economic collaboration seemed to be 'the only form of greater unity' the countries of the area were likely to accept. It was hoped that this could lead to greater political and military cohesion. American participation was, however, essential and Britain's main objective should be to secure this.[13] The Russians presumably received a copy of these documents. It was decided to send them as a Foreign Office despatch to Nanking. That was passed to Guy Burgess of the Far Eastern Department. The despatch went missing.[14]

The Permanent Under-Secretary's Committee assessed the situation in the Middle East before its chairman saw the area for himself. Its assessment was ready by the end of April 1949; Strang toured the region between 21 May and 18 June. The committee, like Bevin's Middle East Conference of September 1945, stressed the economic aspect. The Middle East, and particularly the oil-producing countries, and Egypt with its cotton, was seen as an area of cardinal importance in the economic recovery of Britain and Western Europe. It was hoped that by 1951 82 per cent of Britain's oil supplies would come from there; in 1939 the figure had been 23 per cent. This should be the largest single factor in balancing Britain's overseas payments. If Britain failed to maintain its position in the Middle East the plans for Britain's economic recovery and future prosperity would fail.

The Middle East was strategically as crucial to Britain as it had been in 1945. Strang's committee pointed out that it shielded Africa, it was a key centre of land and sea communications and contained large supplies of oil. Above all, however, in the event of attack on the United Kingdom, it was one of the principal areas from which offensive air action could be taken against the aggressor. The strategic key to the area was Egypt; no alternative existed as a main base. If the Middle East were to be denied to an enemy in wartime, at least two conditions were necessary — certain peacetime facilities which included the maintenance of airfields and stores, and the goodwill of the inhabitants. It was also desirable that Britain should have the right of entry or reinforcement in case of apprehended emergency. Otherwise Britain might be obliged to enter or reinforce certain countries 'without right' or too late. The security of the Middle East was vital to the security of the United Kingdom.

The committee recognized, however, that it would be impossible for the British Government to hold the Middle East in a major war without the assistance of the United States. Britain and the United States could not be rivals in the area. The two countries should have a common policy. And, apart from Palestine, American policy had for some time been crystallizing on lines similar to those of Britain. There was a common approach to the problems of Greece, Turkey and Persia, to defence and to the promotion of social and economic advancement. Washington had undertaken to help London maintain its position in the Middle East.

Policy towards the Middle East had to be viewed in the light of the extension of communism in various parts of the world. Britain had overseen the emergence of the Middle Eastern countries to independence and self-government. But the transition from centuries of Turkish misrule to self-government under modern world conditions was difficult. Corruption, ineffiency and poverty were endemic. The standard of living of the mass of the people was appallingly low and the contrast with the wealth of the small and selfish ruling classes glaring. In spite of the contradiction between the principles of the Muslim religion and of communism, there were almost classic opportunities for communist agitation by the exploitation of hardship, chaos and discontent. To prevent the Middle East falling behind the Iron Curtain had to be a major objective of British policy and therefore merited a high priority in effort and contribution.

Strang's committee noted that Britain had treaties of alliance with Egypt (expiring in 1956), Iraq (expiring in 1957 with right of review in 1952) and Transjordan (expiring in 1968). These treaties provided for the stationing of certain minimum forces in peacetime, the right of entry in an apprehended emergency, and the provision of facilities in wartime. The treaties were not permanent, and the treaties with Egypt and Iraq expired on dates that were particularly awkward in terms of Russian preparedness. In the event of war, Britain had no alternative but to use Egypt as the main base. Cyrenaica and Transjordan 'can afford adjuncts but not a substitute'. Airfields in Iraq were important and desirable elsewhere, particularly in Saudi Arabia (there was an American airfield in Dhaharan) and in Cyprus. Air warning facilities, and possibly airfield and port facilities, were desirable in Syria and the Lebanon. The Americans wanted a fighter base in Tripolitania or Cyrenaica. A Middle East Pact, along the lines of the Atlantic Pact, or alternatively new treaties or agreements, would help to prevent the Middle East falling under communist domination.

Israel was a new factor. The Arab countries were united in their dislike and fear of Israel. The Arabs considered the creation of an independent state of Israel against the wishes of the majority of the former inhabitants as a major injustice and as an example of

Western imperial colonization on a grand scale. The creation of Israel was tending to promote Arab unity. Although Britain was criticized as being largely responsible for the creation of the state of Israel, the Arab states were, for the moment, turning towards Britain as being the only country likely to oppose indefinite Israeli expansion. Israel would have considerable strategic importance in the event of war. It should also be prevented from becoming communist. It was hoped that Israel would turn towards the West and not Russia, and have friendly relations with Britain and the United States. The committee wanted all of the Middle East, Greece, Turkey, the Arab countries, Iran, and Persian Gulf, Egypt and Cyrenaica, and Israel to be friendly towards Britain. But it stressed that if Britain were to secure the friendship of Israel at the expense of the Arab countries, Britain would lose economically and strategically more than it had gained. Britain had to be friendly to Israel, but not at the cost of losing the friendship of the Arab world. Strategically facilities in Israel would be no substitute for facilities in Egypt and the other Arab states.

In conclusion, the committee suggested that Britain needed to explore the possibility of a Near East and African pact. Dr D.F. Malan, the new Afrikaner Nationalist Prime Minister of South Africa, had mentioned that South Africa would join the Atlantic Pact if invited. Alternatively Malan had ideas of an African pact, including Britain, the United States, South Africa and the European countries with possessions in Africa. Strang's people, however, felt that the Middle East was the shield of Africa. Any African pact had to be accompanied or followed by a Middle East pact. It could be extended to include other African countries. This suggestion formed the basis of British policy in the Middle East, designed to deal with the Cold War, until the fall of Attlee's second Labour administration in October 1951.[15]

Strang had never handled Middle Eastern affairs before. Following the deliberation of the Permanent Under-Secretary's Committee he toured the area stopping in Tripoli, Benghazi, Cairo, Amman, Jerusalem, Tel Aviv, Beirut, Damascus and Tehran, as well as seeing the Prime Minister of Iraq during a brief refuelling stop at Baghdad. He felt that the Middle East lacked 'the teeming vitality of India or south-east Asia or the Far East'. He spoke to Kind Abdullah in Jordan, David Ben-Gurion in Israel, met Azzam Pasha, the Secretary-General of the Arab League in Cairo, saw in a refugee camp 'a small fraction of the great body of Palestine refugees, the tragic and pitiable counterpoint of the Jewish immigration into Israel', visited the temples at Baalbek in the Lebanon and crossed briefly into Syria.

On his return he reported to Bevin that the Arab states were weak, divided and lacking in a sense of direction. Their governments were unstable and corrupt and their social systems marked by extremes of wealth and poverty. Potential leaders were few, and the best of these in Strang's view — King Abdullah and Nuri Pasha — were discredited, old or tired. There seemed to be few younger or new leaders in the offing. The Arab states also faced the challenge of Russian communism along their northern borders and in the hearts of their people. In their state of unpreparedness they also faced an 'incalculable new challenge in the dynamic and expansionist state of Israel, vastly superior to them in intelligence, tenacity and purpose, planted among them by superior forces and skill, against a futile resistance on their part, the defeat of which has left them humiliated and resentful'. They were also burdened with 750,000 Arab refugees from Israel. In spite of everything, the Arab states had not lost faith in Britain: they had no on else to turn to and Britain was the best of a bad lot. Strang felt that 'if we would only make up our minds and tell the Arab States what we wanted, we would be astonished by the response'. Britain's first priority, however, had to be to settle its relations with Egypt.

Strang observed that intellectually a European was more at home in Israel than in any of the Arab countries. He found Tel Aviv 'a terrible place, noisy, tawdry, vulgar, but active, bustling, full of purpose. There is no stagnation here.' Seen in the mass under European skies and in an Eastern landscape, the Jews did not look out of place: 'For all their European culture, they remain an Eastern people, at home in Palestine. When one remembers that Zionism was distilled from the miseries of the ghettos of Eastern Europe and brought to fruition by the Nazi savageries, it strikes a sympathetic chord to see the Israelis walk as free men in a land of their own, however unjustly acquired.' Strang pointed to the Arab belief that Israel was a canker that threatened to spread from the Nile to the Euphrates (an idea deriving from a remark attributed to Ben-Gurion). There was little doubt, however, that Israel would aim at the economic domination of the Middle East.[16]

The committee's papers on South East Asia and the Far East, and the Middle East all emphasized the overriding significance of the United States for any future British foreign policy. In its detailed consideration of where Britain's future role lay the committee did give careful consideration to possible alternatives.

A paper entitled 'A Third World Power or Western Consolidation', produced in a fairly final form as early as the end of March 1949, examined the suggestion that the military alliance envisaged with the Atlantic Pact should be considered merely as a temporary phase, and that the real object should be to organize Europe into a 'Middle Power', co-equal with and independent of the United States and Russia. The supporters of this idea did acknowledge that for a considerable time Western Europe might have to lean heavily towards the United States and away from Russia. But it was suggested that an underlying aim of an organization of Europe should be 'the eventual creation of a system which would enable Western Europe, plus the bulk of the African continent, and in some form of loose association with other members of the Commonwealth to run an independent policy in world affairs which would not necessarily coincide with either Soviet or American wishes'. There was support for this idea not only amongst those in Britain who found American capitalism little more attractive than Russian communism, but also from those who disliked Britain being in a dependent position. In the United States the Planning Section of the State Department thought that the best way to consolidate the Western world was to build up another power unit with a strength equivalent to that of the United States and Russia. Isolationists also liked the idea. Some, particularly on the Continent, thought that this third power, even if weaker than the other two, could exploit its position as neutral in the same way as Belgium had done in 1914 and 1915, and Italy in 1939 and 1940.

Strang's committee, however, considered that there was little prospect that Britain would be able to unite the Commonwealth as a single power. Furthermore, any thought of a Third World power in Europe being able to resist Russia militarily by itself could be dismissed. Political cohesion of the Commonwealth countries with Western Europe was even less likely than with Britain. For the present, at any rate, the closest association with the United States was essential, not only to stand up to Russian aggression, but also in the interests of Commonwealth solidarity and European unity. It was usually possible to reconcile British and American views. There was, as yet, no evidence that partnership with the United States would involve Britain in a dangerous dependence on that country. Britain was more likely to find it difficult to reach a common approach with Western European countries. The United States was unlikely to embark on an aggressive policy, and if it did a British partnership with the United States would give Britain the opportunity to apply a break to American policy.[17]

Initially this paper had a circulation similar to the one on South East Asia and the Far East, and met with a favourable response. From Paris, Oliver Harvey thought it would be easier to influence the United States by a consolidation with that country rather than with the creation of a Third World power. Herbert Morrison argued that it was necessary to pursue Anglo-American cooperation. Philip Noel-Baker, the Secretary of State for Commonwealth Relations, reminded Bevin how difficult it was to get any firm commitment in advance from Commonwealth countries. The Minister of Defence, A.W. Alexander, accepted the conclusions and observed that a Third World power might just provide the Americans with the excuse for believing that a buffer state had been created.[18] The paper went to the Cabinet in October.[19]

The detailed paper surveying Anglo-American relations, present and future, was revised at various stages during 1949, particularly in the light of conversations in Washington. It was considered so sensitive that initially it had only a very limited circulation. In October certain ministers were allowed to see it, but at the end of November Bevin decided that for the present it was not to be circulated to the Cabinet as a whole.[20] Strang sent Bevin the first 'final draft' on 24 August 1949 with the warning that it was more controversial than the others. Bevin minuted: 'I will not circulate this.'[21] This version suggested that there need be no fundamental conflict of interest between Britain and the United States in any part of the world provided that Britain could achieve a position closely related to that of the United States, and yet sufficiently independent of it to be able to influence American policy in the desired direction. If Britain ceased to exist as a leading world power there would be a risk of major divergence, and the United States could withdraw from commitments in the Middle East, the Mediterranean and Africa. The United States could also decline to accept any responsibility in South and South East Asia and might limit its responsibility in the Far East and the Pacific.

The committee offered an analysis of the difficulties resulting from American traditions, and in particular the extent to which local minority groups often use their electoral importance to exert a disproportionate influence on national and international policies. The anti-colonial tradition also inspired a prejudice against 'imperialist' rule. This and a deep-seated isolationism made Americans reluctant to intervene in the affairs of other countries. Washington always hesitated to take responsibility for other nations or territories, and when it did assume this responsibility it demanded absolute control and imposed its own solutions. The problem of Israel occupied a special place in Anglo-American relations. Of the 10 million Jews in the world about 5 million lived in the United States and many were concentrated in the politically key state of New York. The committee observed: 'The sympathy of the strong Zionist element of American Jewry for the establishment of Israel and the political pressure which this element has been able to exert on the White House have imposed a considerable strain on relations with the United Kingdom, whose position in the Middle East would be fatally compromized if she were to lose entirely the friendship of the Moslem world.' It was hoped that this problem would diminish now that Israel existed, and since then British and American policy towards the Middle East had been virtually identical.[22] Other possible sources of political friction between Britain and the United States were the Irish problem and the anti-British feeling amongst the Roman Catholics who largely because of the influence of the Irish Americans viewed Britain as the largest Protestant power. There were difficulties in the field of economic relations. Though the two countries were seen as having similar international objectives, progress towards these appeared to many Americans to have been impeded by 'restrictionist policies and methods which have robbed the British economy of its competitive strength and sapped the will to work of the British people'. American suspicion of 'colonialism' also inspired a fear that Britain, through the sterling area, was exploiting the resources of the Commonwealth and the Colonial Empire for its own benefit. Strang's committee warned that if friction were allowed to increase or even continue in the economic field, it would threaten the basis on which strategic and political collaboration with the United States rested.[23]

The second revision of this version, at the end of 1949, argued that following the victorious wartime alliance, collaboration between Britain and the United States had been closer than ever before; the United States maintained closer relations with Britain than with any other country. In the military field the partnership had been maintained by the combined Chiefs of Staff organization. For the United States, Britain remained the principal military partner and ally, and the United States wanted that partnership to endure. British interests were likely to be best served by the maintenance and consolidation of the existing relations between the two countries. Any British attempt at self-sufficiency, even with the support of some Commonwealth countries, would entail 'a sharp contraction of political influence and material prosperity'. If it failed, Britain would be forced to beg once more for the benefits of association with the United States, not as an independent partner, but instead as 'a client existing on permanent doles from the American tax payer'. Strang's committee concluded that Britain had to continue to shoulder the political, economic and military burden of playing a leading role in world affairs, in close association with the United States, but not necessarily dominated by its policies. The Anglo-American partnership would for some time be an unequal one, and might eventually need a more formal expression. The inherent inequality could be ameliorated by Britain and the United States working closely in conjunction with other friendly states, such as the members of the Commonwealth, particularly in Asia and the Far East. Indeed it was in this region that Britain thought the alliance would be least effective. Here

American naïvety and selfishness seemed particularly evident. Inexperience could account for the narrowly conceived American policy towards China. The treatment of Japan, however, was an instance of the 'somewhat unimaginative tendency of the Americans to graft their own way of life on to rather improbable stock', and the insistence on restoring the low-cost Japanese economy on multilateral principles took little account of British economic interests. But an American 'stake' in the area was of great importance for the consolidation of Western influence. Although the United States was likely to maintain a line of strategic defence in the Pacific, the degree to which it would extend this westwards was dependent on the extent to which Britain and the other members of the Commonwealth would contribute. American sources were not unlimited, and the United States appeared unwilling to contemplate any major effort in South Asia. Therefore, Western resistance to the spread of Russian influence in the region depended largely on Britain. Strang's committee concluded, despite all the reservations, and this conclusion was acknowledged to be the corner-stone of British foreign policy: 'The interests of the United Kingdom therefore demand that her present policy of close Anglo-American cooperation in world affairs should continue. Such cooperation will involve our sustained political, military and economic effort.' [24]

Other issues considered by the Permanent Under-Secretary's Committee reflected this basic conclusion. It seems that the paper on 'British Policy towards Soviet Communism' remains closed to researchers. It urged the creation of a political, social and economic system stronger and more attractive than the Soviet system.[25] Federal union and customs union as viewed by the committee was unfeasible in the prevailing circumstances. It urged the promotion of a merger of the military functions of the Brussels Treaty Organization with those of the projected North Atlantic Treaty Organization and of its political and cultural functions with the Council of Europe.[26] Commenting on these papers, the Chiefs of Staff argued that the gravest disadvantage in the policy of working for a united Germany was the danger that it could lead to the withdrawal of all occupation forces, which would mean that American troops would go from Europe: a condition for a united Germany had to be that British and American troops should remain in Germany west of the Rhine.[27] In the final version of its paper on 'The Future of Germany' Strang's committee recommended that any agreement with the Russians had to contain adequate safeguards against Russian communist expansion and resurgent German nationalism; in particular, Germany should remain disarmed.[28] On the issue of a Channel tunnel the balance of Foreign Office views was against the scheme.[29]

Writing in the early 1960s about the activities of his committee Strang suggests that the papers were not designed 'for policy-planning purposes'. They were rather an aid to the senior staff of the Foreign Office, and forced the under-secretaries to pay attention to regions other than those for which they were responsible. He does acknowledge that Bevin followed the work of the committee with great interest, and that it was of general interest to some of his Cabinet colleagues.[30] Perhaps Strang is being unduly modest. The conclusions of the Permanent Under-Secretary's Committee on South East Asia and the Far East, and the Middle East were reflected in the British Defence Policy and Global Strategy Papers of 1950 and 1951.[31] The recommendation that Britain's role in the world depended on the Anglo-American special relationship, and that the idea of a Third World Force was impracticable, was confirmed early in 1951 during the Korean War at a time when several members of the Cabinet and sections of the establishment tried to break with the American alliance.[32] Strang's role throughout was considerable. On 13 March 1951, shortly before his death, Bevin wrote to Strang: 'I understand so well how much rests on your wise judgement and the sound advice you have given to Ministers from time to time, and I have been tremendously impressed by the care and earnestness with which you submitted your recommendations.' [33]

Notes

1. Public Record Office, London, FO 371/76384 W3113/3/500G, Strang to Bevin, 9 May 1949; William Strang, *The diplomatic career*, 1962, 110-12.
2. See R. Ovendale, *The English speaking alliance, Britain, the United States, the Dominions and the Cold War, 1945-51*, 1985, 45, 74.
3. FO 371/76386 W5573/3/500G, PUSC(51) Final second revise, Anglo-American relations present and future; Makins to Bevin, 9 November 1949; Ovendale, op.cit., 224-9, 278.
4. See Ovendale, op.cit., 285-7 for an account of the background of leading officials at that time.
5. Churchill College, Cambridge, Strang Papers, STRN 2/3, *Christian Science Monitor*, 27 May 1949.
6. Strang Papers, STRN 2/3, *The Times*, 12 November 1953.
7. William Strang, *Home and abroad*, 1956, 301, 281.
8. Strang Papers, STRN 2/3, *News Chronicle*, 1 December 1945; Strang, op.cit., passim.
9. Strang Papers, 2/3, unnumbered, Sir William Strang's tour in South

East Asia and the Far East, 27 February 1949; Strang, *Home and abroad*, op.cit., 239-50.
10. FO 371/76384, Strang to Bevin, 23 March 1949.
11. See Ovendale, op.cit., 165-6; for a different view see Robin Edmonds, *Setting the mould: the United States and Britain, 1945-1950*, 1986, 145.
12. FO 371/76385, Strang to Bevin, 26 August 1949.
13. FO 371/76386 W5572/3/500G, PUSC (53) Final, Regional cooperation in South East Asia and the Far East; Strang to Bevin, 16 October 1949; minute by Bevin, undated; PUSC (72) amendments to committee papers on South East Asia and the Far East in the light of comments received, 11 October 1949; W5572/3/500G, PUSC (32) Final, The United Kingdom in South East Asia and the Far East.
14. FO 371/76030 F17397/1055/61G, Green Division to Tucker, 27 January 1950.
15. FO 800/455, fos 191-6, PUSC (19), Final, Near East, Top Secret, 30 April 1949; see Ovendale, op.cit., 118-42, 245-70.
16. Strang Papers, STRN 2/3, E8752/1051/65, Sir William Strang's tour in the Middle East, 4 July 1949; Strang, *Home and abroad*, op.cit., 251-68.
17. FO 371/76384 W3114/3/500G, PUSC (22) Final, A Third World power or Western consolidation?; see also A. Adamthwaite, 'Britain and the world, 1945-1949: the view from the Foreign Office', J. Becker and F. Knippin (eds), *Power in Europe? Great Britain, France, Italy and Germany in a postwar world, 1945-1950*, Berlin, 1986, 17.
18. FO 371/76384, W3717/3/500G, Harvey to Strang, 22 June 1949; W3576/3/500G, Morrison to Bevin, 18 June 1949; W3643/3/500G, Noel-Baker to Bevin, 21 July 1949; W3941/3/500G, Alexander to Bevin, 7 July 1949.
19. FO 371/76386 W5573/3/500G, Strang to Bevin (draft), 15 October 1949.
20. Ibid., Makins to Bevin, 9 November 1949; minute, 23 November 1949.
21. FO 371/76385 W4707/3/500G, Strang to Bevin, 24 August 1949.
22. See R. Ovendale, *The origins of the Arab-Israeli wars*, 1984, 74-125.
23. FO 371/76385 W4707/3/500G, PUSC (51) Final, Anglo-American relations: present and future, 24 August 1949.
24. FO 371/76385 W4707/3/500G, PUSC (51) Final second revise, Anglo-American relations: present and future. On the post-1945 reltionship, see W.R. Louis and H. Bull (eds), *The special relationship: Anglo-American relations since 1945*, 1986.
25. FO 371/76385 W4657/3/500G, Harvey to Strang, 14 September 1949; Adamthwaite, op.cit., 18.
26. FO 371/76385 4640/3/500G. PUSC (48) Final, Western European international organizations, 17 August 1949.
27. FO 371/76386 W6137/3/500G, FO to Paris, Telegram no. 3026, 9 November 1949.
28. FO 371/76386 W6201/3/500G, PUSC (62) Final, The future of Germany.
29. FO 371/76386 W7265/3/500G, Channel Tunnel, 23 June 1949.
30. Strang, *The diplomatic career*, op.cit., 111.

31. See Ovendale, *The English-speaking alliance,* op.cit., 273-89.
32. ibid., 224-9.
33. Strang Papers, STRN 4/5, Bevin to Strang, 4 March 1951.

8 Development diplomacy: Sir John Troutbeck and the British Middle East Office, 1947-50
Wesley K. Wark

Strategic imperatives, vaguely formulated ideological aspirations for a new international order, force of habit, and fear all combined to pin the British to the Middle East as a vital sphere of influence after 1945. Great expectations vied with no less great anxiety in the British watch on the Middle East. This mix of passions was especially pronounced during the life of the first Labour Government of 1945-51. The Middle East emerged as a test case for Labour's new foreign policy, which sought both to sustain and transform the role of Britain as an imperial great power.[1]

Sir John Troutbeck, a passionate man himself, was to play a leading role, as head of the British Middle East Office (BMEO) from 1947 to 1950, in an innovative and ultimately unsuccessful effort at development diplomacy. This new instrument of diplomacy looked to the utilization of technical and economic aid to developing countries in order to stimulate regional stability and progress, and to secure Britain's foreign policy interests. The long-range goal in the Middle East was the creation of a new informal empire for Britain, to be built on the more secure foundations of economic, social, and finally military, 'partnership'.[2] Development initiatives were perceived as no mere adjunct to orthodox diplomacy at the outset of the post-war era, but were inspired by all the hopes and fears that Britain invested in the Middle East as a focal point for British recovery. Sir John Troutbeck and the British Middle East Office, the man and the institution, deserve study for their symbolic place and practical role in the evolution of post-war British foreign policy.[3]

As major determinants of British foreign policy in the Middle East, strategic imperatives, ideological aspirations, habit and fear naturally helped shape the creation of the British Middle East

Office and the definition of its mandate. For British defence planners, the Middle East was of vital strategic importance owing to a multitude of factors: the significance that the Suez Canal retained as a major imperial artery; the importance of the maintenance of bases for offensive and defensive action against a perceived Soviet threat; the logistical and manpower support that might be obtained from the region in the event of a great power conflict; and lastly as a shield for British interests in Africa.[4] All these were traditional calculations (if Russian was substituted for Soviet), but they were kept fresh by lessons from the Second World War. The riches of the oil fields in the Middle East, and British investment in and dependence on their output, added a new dimension to the calculation. The connection between this strategic assessment of the importance of the Middle East and the creation of the BMEO was indirect but strong. The burden of defence of the Middle East, so the argument went, would be reduced to manageable proportions if Britain could count on political and economic stability in the region and the maintenance of a Western orientation among the Arab states. Development diplomacy, managed by the BMEO, was to encourage both results.

The BMEO was also the brainchild of a Labour government that was searching for a way to give British foreign policy a more social-democratic spin. What this might amount to in practice was difficult to define, and the history of previous Labour governments in office offered little in the way of useful precedents. Labour's foreign policy in opposition in the 1930s was even less useful as a model for the post-1945 world.[5] In the end, the social-democratic aspirations of Labour's foreign policy were shaped principally by the powerful figure of the Foreign Secretary, Ernest Bevin. Bevin delighted in talking of basing British policy in the Middle East on 'peasants not pashas.'[6] His biographer tells us that Bevin had a long-running interest in questions of international economic development and sought ways to make social and economic betterment an intrinsic goal of British foreign policy in the Middle East.[7] His motives resist labelling as either altruistic or realistic — they were a blend of both. Bevin believed in the notion that common bonds united working-class societies and directed the BMEO to pursue the establishment of trade unions in the Middle East as a contribution to development.[8] In a more realist vein, Bevin held to the idea that British policy would find more friends and more understanding in the region if it could be firmly grounded in support for economic growth. The Middle East was seen as terribly poverty-stricken, backward and 'feudal' in its social order. The remedy was to be an aid programme that would accelerate progress and introduce modernity. The British Middle East Office partook of both the ideological generosity and naïvety of Labour's kindred vision of the Middle East masses and of the calculations of advantage that might accrue to Britain through development aid.

The siren calls of strategical imperatives and a Labour version of the 'white man's burden' were supplemented in the Middle East by what Elizabeth Monroe once amusingly described as the force of habit. 'Independence for India,' she wrote, 'should have reduced Britain's sense of responsibility for policing the classic passage through the Middle East. But habits die hard.'[9] The same judgement is supported, though from a different perspective, by Alan Bullock. Bullock calls attention to the strength of the contemporary expectation that Britain would continue to play a major role in the Middle East after 1945 because the area had been mapped out in red for so long. 'Britain's role in that part of the world was of such long standing that it was taken for granted by most Englishmen as part of the natural order, a belief confirmed by the effort the British had put into its defence during the war as the main theatre of British operations up to the invasion of Europe.'[10]

Historical continuity played a direct role in the creation of the BMEO. The Office had a wartime predecessor, the Middle East Supply Centre (MESC), with an impressive record of performance.[11] Set up in April 1941 as part of the proliferating British war effort under General Wavell's command, the MESC soon grew into a joint Anglo-American agency with enormous powers to organize and direct the economic and supply resources of the Middle East theatre. The original impetus behind the formation of the MESC had been to create a body that would have the power to allocate shipping resources, and especially to reduce demands for cargo space for consumer goods. The logic of events dictated that the MESC would eventually go much further: to transcend the strictly military dimension of their task by promoting regional production of war supplies and by treating the Middle East as a coherent economic market. By war's end the achievement of the MESC was considerable and Cairo, where it had its headquarters, had been transformed out of all recognition into a thriving commercial centre. The experience of the MESC suggested that technical guidance and aid could be effective in stimulating fast-paced growth in the Middle East, particularly if treated as a region with an interlocking trade potential.

But not all of the MESC experiment was to survive the coming of peace and the inevitable demobilization of war agencies. The staff drifted away to other occupations, and Anglo-American cooperation was brought to an abrupt halt at the end of the war.[12] Moreover, peacetime meant not only financial retrenchment and disengagement on the part of the allied governments, but also the flowering of a new and invigorated nationalism in the Middle East. The continuity that appeared to mark the life of the BMEO was thus partly deceptive. But the expectation lived on that the British Middle East Office should be able to achieve in peace a performance akin to that managed by the MESC in war. The BMEO was certainly not an automatic creation of imperial habit — indeed it represented a real innovation in the conduct of peacetime policy — but it was a captive from the beginning of the expectations rooted in the very different circumstances of the Second World War.

The final element in the British commitment to the Middle East was fear. There was a direct concern about the Soviet military threat to the region, and an indirect concern about the effects of communist propaganda and subversion. Other, more vague menaces were in the air. The British feared the prospect of a 'power vacuum' in the Middle East, especially if precipitate or large-scale British withdrawals from the area ever occurred.[13] The hoary 'Eastern question' was thus given a new face, in the form of British anxiety about which great power might try to usurp their position in the Middle East. The Soviet threat was uppermost in British minds, but there are signs of a considerable British distrust of American intentions and policy, over oil and Palestine in particular. Fears of this magnitude could scarcely be assuaged by an institution so small and so pacific as the BMEO was destined to be. Nevertheless the BMEO had its part to play in the drama of reassurance that the British required. The Middle East Office would win friends in the Middle East, bring the great Arabist tradition of Britain to bear to capture the hearts of Middle East peoples and prove the value of the British connection, and prevent the emergence of conditions in which communism might thrive. In this last sense, the BMEO was truly innovative, predating the Marshall Plan in Europe by three years although, of course, never enjoying the Marshall Plan's political clout or fiscal power.

Ernest Bevin had his own sharp vision of the importance of using British resources to create a new Middle East under British tutelage, one that linked the survival of social democracy at home to British success overseas: 'In the European scene ... we are the last bastion of social democracy. It may be said that this represents our way of life against the red tooth and claw of American capitalism and the communist dictatorship of Soviet Russia. Any weakening of our position in the Mediterranean area will in my view lead to the end of social democracy.'[14] Few probably shared this apocalyptic vision, but it was indicative of the great anxieties that underlay the postwar British approach to the Middle East.

The British Middle East Office owed its existence, in one sense, to the background forces enumerated above: the imperatives of grand strategy, ideological aspirations, imperial habits, and the fears and nightmares of a declining power. But these background forces required expression in the will and imagination of Whitehall and found them in the person of Ernest Bevin. It was Bevin who, in one of his earliest acts after his unexpected appointment as Foreign Secretary, called a conference of Middle East representatives to meet in London to discuss future policy. Bevin needed no time to learn the arcane ways of the Foreign Office; nor did he need to be educated in what constituted a good foreign policy by his staff. He knew the sort of policy that he wished Britain to pursue, at least in the Middle East.

Bevin took the chair at the conference on the Middle East and charged the assorted officials and proconsuls with the task of reviewing British foreign policy on the basis that Britain would continue to assert its predominance in the area and take overriding responsibility for its defence.[15] He also told the Cabinet, in advance of the conference, that he would use the sessions to discuss projects for economic development. 'I am anxious to promote schemes of economic development,' he stated, 'which would benefit the common people and I attach importance to measures of social advancement which would improve trade conditions.'[16]

The policy that emerged from the September 1945 conference set the course of British diplomacy in the Middle East for the remainder of the Labour Government's time in power. It was a policy firmly stamped by Bevin's outlook on what needed to be done to create an effective and lasting British presence in the Middle East, and to derive benefits from that presence. Bevin desired to erect an informal empire in the Middle East, with a social-democratic hue, in which economic development would play a key role. Specific recommendations followed from that basic policy. The Middle East was to be treated as a single region (as it had been by the Middle East Supply Centre in wartime), in order to allow coordination of economic and political initiatives; British influence was to be broadened by the creation of economic and social policies aimed at the betterment of the peoples of the Middle East and the establishment of improved markets for British trade; partnership in the economic sphere would be encouraged as a first step towards close military relations between Britain and the Middle East countries.[17]

The future of great power involvement in the Middle East was also surveyed in September 1945.[18] The United States was expected to launch a stiff commercial rivalry in the Middle East and British predominance would have to be vigorously defended. The conference noted that the Middle East market had been a British monopoly for 'generations' and warned against any concessions to the Americans. France's 'impossible' position in the Middle East required careful watching so that it did not lead to unnecessary embarrassments for the British. As for the anticipated Russian threat, the conference sounded what would become a characteristic 'Cold War' note. Soviet activities were viewed with the utmost alarm; the British assumed that Middle East societies would share this apprehension and draw correspondingly closer to the West. Development diplomacy was to be an important antidote to Soviet blandishments. The conference's conclusions on this point are worth quoting in full:

There are increasing signs of Russian political and economic penetration in almost all Middle East territories. These are viewed with extreme apprehension by the governments and peoples in these countries. The most effective counter to Russian advances is the economic and social betterment of the people whose lot under the existing social system makes them ready listeners to the propaganda of Communism.[19]

The British Middle East Office was set up in the autumn of 1945 and given the task of spearheading British development diplomacy by coordinating all economic and technical aid programmes in the region. The BMEO would function in an advisory capacity to promote schemes of agricultural development as a first economic priority and 'social betterment' programmes, including improved health services, 'the constitutional development of Trade Unionism', and 'above all, a review of the present system of land tenure'.[20] These directives were revealing. The governing philosophy was that the BMEO should be established to steer Middle East economies in the direction of improved economic performance, the redistribution of wealth (peasants not pashas), and, especially important from the British perspective, the wise use of the enormous sterling credits that had been accumulated by the region's governments during the war. Not only would Great Britain's troubles as a debtor nation thereby be eased, but in the long term a great market would be created. As the conference put it, 'If schemes of development are prepared and adopted, there should, therefore, be golden opportunities for the British exporter in the Middle East'.[21] Philanthropy and naked self-interest were thus nicely blended and the whole influenced by a wonderfully optimistic sense of the future prospects of the Middle East as a British sphere of influence.

The Cabinet approved the conclusions reached by the conference without dissent or major discussion.[22] Bevin reported that although Britain faced problems over Palestine, Egypt and the

Levant, these problems could be solved more easily if Britain could promote economic development and social reform. The way ahead seemed obvious.

The British Middle East Office, designed in 1945 as the steering mechanism for development diplomacy, was fitted into the foreign policy machine with agonizing slowness. From the beginning the BMEO was left to turn the British vision of a new Middle East into a reality with little in the way of resources and, surprisingly, few injections of Bevinite and Labour Party enthusiasm. The first director of the BMEO, Sir Arnold Overton, appointed in August 1945, played only a caretaker role and quickly discovered that his Office, rather than absorbing the vigorous establishment of the MESC, occupied only the shell of its magnificent headquarters at 10 Sharia Tolumbat in Cairo. The key personnel were already gone and little remained behind except a handful of economic surveys, pioneering ones, drawn up by visiting experts during the war. As Sir Arnold Overton put it, in his first annual report, 'it was necessary to start from scratch'.[23] He had to build up a new staff and decide on priorities for study and development guidance. Overton chose agriculture, public health, statistics, village improvement and telecommunications as the most pressing fields. Bevin's call for trade-union legislation and land tenure reform already looked utopian and was ignored by the Director. Even the task of creating a new team of experts to tackle these priorities proved slow and difficult. Not until the spring of 1947 was recruitment completed. Eighteen months had passed since the launching of the idea of development diplomacy. The team that was put together was professional, but miniscule. It consisted of only five persons, working under the direction of an ex-Colonial Office official, grouped in a 'Development Division' of the BMEO.[24]

Recruitment was not the only problem. Overton discovered that the BMEO, far from being welcomed as a British initiative by grateful Arab states, was distrusted and disliked, above all by the Egyptian Government, which refused to recognize its existence. This caused confusion and dismay in British circles, but did not shake British faith in their Middle East mission to the extent of forcing any reassessment of development diplomacy. The phenomenon was simply tagged as a problem: 'there is a good deal of suspicion that we mean to substitute economic domination for political and military domination,' Overton reported.[25] The obstacle of Middle East resistance was to be skirted by adopting a particular style of operations. The BMEO would henceforth eschew publicity, 'tread very warily', and 'concentrate on quiet work behind the scenes at the expert level.'[26] No substantive discussion of the wisdom or implications of this new style (very different from that of the MESC) was ever held.

Overton ended his first annual report with a cautionary note to the effect that while he was convinced that the BMEO was a sound idea, the British Government would have to be very patient, as results could only be expected over a period of years.[27] From being at the forefront of British policy towards the Middle East as laid down in September 1945, the BMEO, scarcely a year later, was deliberately slipped into the background shadows. When Overton prepared his final report on the BMEO in 1947, he catalogued the additional delays that had hampered the Office's work. Political instability and the backwardness of the Middle East were highlighted as hindrances to progress on the BMEO's part. The only positive thing that Overton had to say about development diplomacy was that he was sure the British would outlast the American commerical challenge, then beginning to mount, 'for psychological reasons'.[28]

One further development occurred in the history of the British Middle East Office in the interval before Sir John Troutbeck arrived as its chief in late 1947. Under pressure from the Chiefs of Staff, the Foreign Office proceeded to reorganize the BMEO in the spring of 1947 to give it political, as well as economic, responsibilities.[29] The military demands were occasioned by the need for coordinated political intelligence on the part of the Commanders-in-Chief in the Middle East. The military, harking back to the experience of the Second World War, thought that this political role could best be played from Cairo. Between 1945 and 1947 the BMEO did act as a channel for the communication of political intelligence from the Foreign Office and regional embassies, missions and consultants to the C-in-Cs. But this took the shape merely of the transmission of raw data, without interpretation, and the military were not satisfied with the arrangement. Accordingly, the terms of reference of the BMEO were changed. When Troutbeck came to head the office his duties were considerably expanded. The directive given to Troutbeck listed five principal functions of the BMEO, of which development and coordination of economic and social policy was only one. The rest concerned the duties of the head of the BMEO for providing political assessments of events in the Middle East to the Government in London and the military authorities on the spot.[30]

This was an important change, for it shifted the balance of the BMEO's function away from development diplomacy and towards regional political intelligence work and more orthodox diplomacy. This shift, seen within the Foreign Office as a necessary administrative adjustment and as a way of satisfying the military, was never considered in the light of its probable impact on the BMEO's original mission. It was a shift, however, that suited the incoming head of the Office, Sir John Troutbeck.

Why Sir John Troutbeck? On the face of it, he was not a natural contender for the vacant position of director of the British Middle East Office. He was a senior career diplomat, with an impressive Foreign Office record, but his Middle East experience was restricted to postings as a comparatively junior official in Istanbul and Addis Ababa in the late 1920s and early 1930s. Troutbeck was nearly two decades out of date on Middle East affairs. He certainly did not fit the bill proposed by the Permanent Under-Secretary, Orme Sargent, who specified that the new head of the BMEO should be a person 'Known and trusted in the Middle East'.[31] Troutbeck had spent the years from 1944 to 1947 engaged in German affairs in connection with the planning and execution of the peace treaty and occupation policy. He was no Orientalist and spoke none of the languages of the region. Perhaps most surprising of all, Troutbeck had no experience of economic development questions. He was, in these ways, an amateur. But Troutbeck had impressed Ernest Bevin with his work and judgement and was known to take a keen interest in the Palestine issue.[32] Bevin wanted a hand-picked Foreign Office man on the spot, whose good judgement he could trust and who would not be too 'colonial-minded'.

Bevin briefed Troutbeck personally on his new mission before Troutbeck left for Cairo in November 1947.[33] The Foreign Secretary reiterated to Troutbeck the maxims that he had originally laid down for the BMEO at the September 1945 conference. Bevin emphasized the importance of economic development, the use of economic solutions as a way to tackle political problems, and the value of development diplomacy as a weapon against Soviet propaganda. Clearly, Bevin's optimism about the BMEO remained strong in late 1947, despite the evidence of difficulties and the snail's pace of progress. The old formula 'peasants not pashas' was aired for Troutbeck's enlightenment, although it was no nearer realization in 1947 than it had been two years earlier. Indoctrinated in the faith, but without any new tools to carry out the job either in the way of finances or personnel, Troutbeck departed on his mission to Cairo.

One of Troutbeck's first acts upon arriving in the Middle East was to conduct a tour of parts of his new parish. His journey lasted from 12 November to 6 December 1947, and took him to Tehran, the Abadan refinery in the Persian Gulf, Baghdad, Damascus, Amman and Beirut.[34] Troutbeck was impressed by the work of the

BMEO, and enthusiastic about the way that the Office's experts had established close working relationships with the authorities in Iraq, especially, and also Iran. The BMEO had made slower headway in Syria, Lebanon and Transjordan. The problem that confronted the BMEO, he discovered, was less to gain acceptance and recognition for the British experts and their work than to find ways of having their development programmes put into practice. Troutbeck recognized that the execution of BMEO-inspired policy was being, and would continue to be, troubled by political instability in the region and by what he characterized as the 'romantic' approach taken to the subject by the authorities in countries such as Iran.[35] By 'romantic' he meant talk and enthusiasm devoid of practical action. There was also the evident lack of an infrastructure in the Middle East on which to build major economic development programmes. Some countries, such as Transjordan, were seen as so economically primitive as almost to defy development. Middle East nationalism, never defined directly as such, but rather labelled as suspicion and mistrust of foreigners, would also, Troutbeck understood, hinder progress. In Syria, for example, Troutbeck noted that the BMEO faced an 'exaggerated feeling of independence which is taking time to wear off.' [36] The Palestine question bedevilled everything, to the extent that Troutbeck could find no one in Amman who wished to talk to him about the mundane subject of economic development. To round off his impressions, Troutbeck noted that the American penetration of the Middle East was being held up by the way in which 'locally employed Americans get up against the inhabitants' as well as by the wayward operation of American foreign policy.' [37]

Troutbeck made several discoveries on his tour of the Middle East which were to be extremely important in the evolution of his views about development diplomacy. While his report to the Foreign Office on the standing of the BMEO in the region was highly favourable, he also gained the impression, that was later to grow into a conviction, that the idea of 'steering' the economies of the Middle East was not going to be easy and that there were no obvious methods by which this might be accomplished. Of even greater interest in Troutbeck's report was the way in which the new head of the BMEO read the evidence of his Office's impact. Troutbeck was far from fervent in his expression of hopes about the future of development diplomacy. What he did emphasize was the political payoffs that BMEO efforts appeared to have. Looking ahead, he argued that if the British relationship with the Arab states was to deteriorate seriously over the Palestine question, 'The B.M.E.O., with the British Council, may prove one of the few means of holding our position until things change for the better.' [38]

More realist in tone yet was his statement that 'Whatever success it [the BMEO] may achieve in the practical economic sphere, it seems to be proving a good political investment'.[39]

Sentiments such as these were not whole-heartedly in the spirit of the pronouncements of September 1945. Troutbeck's political antennae were more attuned to the power politics of the Middle East than to the issue of 'peasants not pashas'. But Troutbeck, at this stage, still held to Bevin's formula that economic progress in the Middle East might well provide the foundations for a stronger British presence. That he freighted this formula with greater concern for immediate political benefits than might have been the original intention was noticed by at least one official in London. When Troutbeck commented in his report that it was doubtful whether the Iranians would display warmer feelings towards the British as a result of the efforts that the Anglo-Iranian Oil Company was making with social programmes at Abadan, an anonymous official annotated in the margin, 'not the object of the game.'[40]

In his time as head of the BMEO, however, Troutbeck was eventually to turn the original formula of development diplomacy upside down. Instead of seeing economic aid programmes as a means of achieving a long-term influence for Britain in the Middle East, Troutbeck came to see the necessity of a political settlement and an established British role in the Middle East as a preliminary to any economic progress. In the course of this redefinition of the BMEO's mission, the original impetus behind economic aid programmes was finally dissipated, and Troutbeck himself plunged into the labyrinth of Middle East politics, spending little time on the role of coordinating programmes for economic and social improvement in the region. During his years as head of the BMEO he concentrated instead almost exclusively on the new tasks of political intelligence and regional assessments of Middle East policy that had been laid down for the office in the 1947 reorganization. Development diplomacy was spun off to the separate 'Development Division' which was increasingly left to plod along in relative obscurity.

The first retrospective report of the Development Division of the BMEO for the years 1946-8 made melancholy reading.[41] The expert staff of the division numbered only five (covering the fields of agriculture, forestry, statistics, entomology and animal husbandry). Two officials from the embassy staff at Cairo were added to the list (specialists in health and labour matters). Although the staff had covered many miles in the Middle East since March 1947, when recruitment was completed, and had engaged in herculean labours, the scope of their achievement was necessarily limited.

The Development Division chief, W.F. Crawford, acknowledged that his staff had spent much of their time in overcoming the suspicions that surrounded their work. While this effort had been successful, progress otherwise was slow. The conclusion to the report, submitted by Crawford, attempted to combine a bright note about future prospects with a bleak message about present conditions, as well as to draw attention to the BMEO's limited power to change things:

> The amount of development which has taken place in the Middle East is disappointing . . . More food must be produced for the increasing populations. This delay in development has been due to political, economic and financial troubles and to the fact that no spade work in research has ever been done. *It is not directly in the power of the Development Division to set right or make amends for any of these causes.* What the personnel of the division have accomplished is to get over the original mistrust, make friends on technical levels and have their opinion asked for, so that, as development takes place, they will be in a position to play a prominent part. There is no doubt that they are proving a valuable adjunct to British diplomacy in the Middle East.[42] (author's italics)

The very wording of the report, in fact, condemned the Development Division to peripheral status. An adjunct was an adjunct.

During 1948 and 1949 Sir John Troutbeck constructed his own ideas on the place of development diplomacy in British action in the Middle East. As these ideas evolved they grew more and more distant from the original inspiration behind Bevin's policy, but edged closer towards realism in the light of the political changes in the Middle East and the obvious limitations on British power. Palestine was, for Troutbeck, the climacteric. It was the chain of events from Britain's withdrawal from the Palestine mandate to the declaration of the state of Israel and the 1948 Arab–Israeli war which, more than anything else, brought Troutbeck's new view of the place of aid in British Middle East policy into clear focus.

Troutbeck believed intensely in the justice of the Arab cause over Palestine, was pro-Egyptian, strongly critical of many aspects of his own government's policy, fearful of the impact that Israel would have on the future politics of the region, and deeply sceptical about the wisdom of American foreign policy.[43] For Troutbeck, the breakdown of negotiations over Palestine before 1948, the nature of the war that ensued, and the difficult process of patching together a peace in the aftermath (in which he took direct part) held one irrefutable lesson. That lesson was that all hopes for economic and social progress in the Middle East were dependent on a solution to the Arab–Israeli conflict. Britain, he felt, had a major role to play in finding this solution, not least because it bore a major burden of historical guilt for the divisive conflict and in particular for the fate of the Arab population of Palestine.[44] Only after a political settlement had been achieved could Britain place realistic hopes in development diplomacy.

The strongest statement of Troutbeck's views on this point came in a 29 December 1949 letter written to Prime Minister Attlee, while Attlee was temporarily in charge of the Foreign Office. In it, Troutbeck called attention to the fact that Britain had long maintained the aim of improving the social and economic conditions of the Middle East, and that the United States, after President Truman's 'Point Four' declaration, had joined in that goal. He told the Prime Minister:

> We both proclaim that we wish for peace and stability in the Middle East as a foundation on which to build economic and social progress and so hold back the spread of communism. I cannot believe that these benefits will be secured in the absence of a firm political foundation. Conceivably, we may succeed in goading the Arab governments into setting up development boards, and the International Bank may be prevailed upon to advance them some money for their development schemes. But their hearts will not be in development while they are all the time looking over their shoulders at the Israeli frontier.[45]

Troutbeck used this conclusion to drive another, that the best way forward towards a peace settlement in the Middle East was for a 'Locarno' pact in the region, with Great Britain and the United States acting as guarantors of agreed-upon frontiers. The alternative to this admittedly radical step, Troutbeck felt, was awful to contemplate. Economic and social progress would remain a 'vain hope', disorder would prevail in the Middle East, and Britain would slowly but surely lose its predominant position in the region.[46]

Troutbeck's reflections on the Middle East situation in 1948–9 took other paths, in addition to the emphasis on peace as the prerequisite for economic and social progress. Experience gained at the BMEO, and the poor showing that the Arab states made in their brief war against Israel, convinced Troutbeck that the whole alignment of British development diplomacy had been based on false premises. He came to the view that the call for Anglo-Middle East partnerships in economic development was rooted in a misconception that Arab societies shared and comprehended the Western dream of progress. In a dispatch to the Foreign Office, Troutbeck wrote: 'I believe that to make real progress in economic and social development we may have to go deeper than we have yet contemplated. Basically, there is not much hope for progress until the Middle East peoples themselves have a burning desire for it (as the Jews for example have). It is that which we should try to instill in them.' [47] In addition to the establishment of a stable peace in the region, Troutbeck thus suggested a second major precondition for the success of development diplomacy — the fostering among the Arab nations of the Middle East of a Western ideal of progress.

Troutbeck was acutely aware that his analysis of the problems that Britain faced in the pursuit of development might well leave the Foreign Office floundering and that to play his role as guide through the intricacies of Middle East affairs it was necessary to come up with more concrete proposals. He believed that one way to restart the process of economic development after 1948 was to pour limited British resources into aid programmes that would immediately strengthen the Arab states, above all Egypt. Troutbeck saw Egypt as the bastion of the British position in the Middle East, the key to her strategical interests, and the path to conquering Arab sensibilities. Troutbeck urged the strengthening of Egypt and other Arab states within Britain's sphere of influence not through more economic aid programmes but through the provision of military assistance, in the form of training and arming Arab forces.[48] Such a move would provide a dramatic show of British faith in the Arab cause, act as an atonement for the mistakes of previous policies, and offer a necessary counter to what Troutbeck feared would be further aggressive expansion on the part of Israel. The head of the BMEO was prescient enough to see that a Middle East arms race held the potential to ruin all hopes for long-term development, and said so to the conference of Middle East representatives which Bevin convened in London in 1949.[49] But this awareness did not lead him to refute his views on the benefits of military assistance to Arab states. Nor did Troutbeck, the BMEO, or anyone else pause to reflect on the potential costs of narrowing economic assistance to the field of armaments and training. The economic distortions that this would inevitably introduce were, apparently, to be condoned given the urgency of achieving a military balance in the Middle East. In Troutbeck's evolving view of British development policy, military assistance and strengthening of the Arab states would have to augment great power peace plans, and the spread of Western ideals of progress, as preludes to genuine economic development.

Israel also figured prominently in Troutbeck's vision of the prospects for Middle East development diplomacy. His views on this subject were expressed most powerfully in a letter to Ernest Bevin on 24 January 1949, which sparked a debate in the Foreign Office and in the British Embassy in Washington.[50] Troutbeck saw

Israel as an inherently expansionistic state, not least because it was economically unstable. He did not believe that Zionist dynamism could be contained within the borders of the Israel established during 1948-9, nor did he believe that those borders would provide sufficient resources for Israel to satisfy a growing population. US policy was the wild card, and Troutbeck doubted whether the United States would be prepared to support Israel over the long haul as a permanent pensioner. He also wondered just how long American enthusiasm for Zionism would be sustained. Troutbeck's great concern was that Israel would at some time in the near future be faced with a choice between expansion, which he crudely referred to as the Israeli search for 'lebensraum', or collapse.

For all these reasons Troutbeck doubted that Israel would be able to find a way to live in peace in the Middle East. Nor did he subscribe to the view that an Israeli-sponsored form of development diplomacy might serve to pacify the region. He doubted that the economic dynamism of the state would bring any benefits to the Arab population of Palestine or neighbouring Arab states. In the immediate aftermath of the Deir Yassin massacre, Troutbeck wrote in great bitterness that Israeli control of an Arab population would bring not modernization, but 'the worst forms of oppression'.[51] This view was sustained in Troutbeck's mind by the experience of visiting the Gaza Strip in June 1949 and witnessing Arab refugee problems at first hand.[52]

Troutbeck's anti-Zionism was not cooly objective, as he himself had the courage to admit. It derived its strength not from any latent anti-Semitism but from a profound fear that Western policy towards the Middle East would be skewed by efforts made to support the 'dynamic' new state of Israel at the expense of the 'undynamic' Arabs.[53] Troutbeck wished instead to root British policy not in the rights and wrongs of the Arab–Israeli struggle, but in the definition of British national interest. Access to Middle East oil, protection of the Suez canal, and use of military bases in the region made the Arab States Britain's most important partner.

A final factor in Troutbeck's rethinking of British Middle East planning and policy came with his assessment of American policy. Troutbeck was critical of the American foreign policy process, which he believed was too susceptible to populist pressures and lent itself to incoherence. He succumbed to the allures of a rather typical view for the time, that the United States was essentially untutored in the ways of world power and terribly prone, in its naïvety, to wishful thinking. Troutbeck found all the proof he needed for the accuracy of these prejudices in American policy towards Palestine, which he believed had been ill thought out and irresponsible.[54]

Despite this scepticism about American conduct in the Middle East, Troutbeck came to believe by 1949 that an American role in both the political and economic spheres was vital and inevitable. He hoped that this role might be steered by the more knowledgeable and realistic British. This was a curious twist to the earlier policy of 'steering'; now it was the Americans, rather than the Arab states, that most needed to be guided. Troutbeck defended his own Office against the American penetration of the Middle East with vigour. He reacted with scarcely concealed hostility to a proposal made by Ernest Bevin in 1949 that American officials should be attached to the BMEO and that economic development programmes should be jointly administered.[55] He believed that too close an association with the United States would only work to damage the British image in the Middle East. Troutbeck, like many of his fellow officials in the region, believed that the British kept a special hold on the Arab imagination, one that the Americans would never obtain. His practical objection to Bevin's proposal — that the presence of American officials in the BMEO would hinder the political and military work of the Office (the supply of intelligence and guidance to the Middle East Commanders-in-Chief) and would compromise the activities of the Secret Intelligence Service (MI6), which shared the Sharia Tolumbat compound — was mere smoke.[56] Troutbeck's outlook was tinged with a certain anti-Americanism, never far from the surface, and outdone only by the persistent anti-Zionist theme in his reporting. He was a flesh-and-blood diplomat, never fearful of expressing his convictions to his masters in Whitehall.

Curiously, it was not until Troutbeck had left the British Middle East Office, to take up a new appointment as Ambassador to Iraq, that he solved a last piece of the Middle East puzzle for himself. It was only in Baghdad that he came to appreciate the true dimensions of Arab nationalism, an appreciation that had eluded him during his three years as head of the BMEO. It took the impact of Arab neutralism during the Korean War and exposure to the mercurial and loquacious Iraqi Prime Minister, Nuri Pasha, to convince Troutbeck that Arab nationalism was a genuine movement of long-term significance, rooted in a sense of Arab alienation from the West and in a desire to escape Western domination even if the costs of doing so were high.[57] This appreciation of the verities of Arab nationalism remained a missing dimension of Troutbeck's policy while in Cairo (where his contacts with senior Egyptian leaders were minimal) but became a crucial part of his views on development diplomacy once in Iraq and made him the wonder of junior members of his staff.[58]

Sir John Troutbeck was both an examplar and a prisoner of the thinking and forces that tied the British to an effort to retain their great power status in the Middle East after 1945. His strategical obsession was with the retention of British predominance in the region on the basis of an Anglo-Arab partnership, centred on Egypt, that would secure the Canal, oil and bases. Ideological aspirations played a not inconsiderable part in the policies urged by this man, whom William Roger Louis described most fittingly as 'a quintessential Englishman with an outraged sense of justice.' [59] Troutbeck saw a powerful moral case for Britain in securing the rights of Arab states in the Middle East against the pressures of Zionism and the American presence. Frequent historical analogies, especially comparing the wrongs of British policy in the Middle East in the late 1940s with similar wrongs committed under the name of appeasement in the 1930s, enlivened his prose and underscored his belief in a British mission. There is no convincing sign that Troutbeck shared or even particularly understood the social-democratic spin that Bevin had wanted to put on British Middle East policy. Troutbeck believed in Anglo-Arab partnership but was no fighter for a policy based on 'peasants not pashas'. It was beyond his realist ken. He did serve the idea of development diplomacy as best he could but in doing so altered it out of all recognition.

Experience of Middle East politics led him to reverse the established formulas of development diplomacy, by putting forceful British action and the achievement of political calm in the region ahead of aid programmes. The habits of empire also shaped his policy. Troutbeck came to share the habitual outlook on the Middle East of many of the proconsuls in the region. He was of the generation that never questioned the right or capability of Britain to act as a post-war great power in the Middle East and held firm to the comforting belief in the special place that the British enjoyed in the hearts and minds of Middle Eastern societies.

Fear breathed urgency into his counsels. Troutbeck was alarmed by the expansionist tendencies of Israel, the irresponsibility of American policy, and above all by the spectre of eternal disorder and war that he beheld for the region. Nothing rings more true than Troutbeck's remark to Prime Minister Samir of Transjordan in late 1947, on the eve of the outbreak of the Arab–Israeli conflict, that 'he had lived through two world wars and had no desire to live through another.' [60] But ultimately it was his fear of the implications of the loss of British influence in the Middle East that dictated his outlook and brought him to a position as champion of one wing of the Foreign Office debate on the Middle East. For

Troutbeck, British relations with Egypt were the key and he was prepared, if need be, to let the rest 'go hang'.[61]

His passionate views on the Palestine issue apart, Troutbeck's most significant contribution to Middle East diplomacy in his tenure as chief of the BMEO was his re-evaluation of the potentialities of development diplomacy. Exemplar and prisoner that he was of the larger determining influences on British foreign policy, when it came to ideas on development and its role, Troutbeck was his own man. Certainly Troutbeck was not interested in economic aid to Middle East countries for its own sake, nor did he show any interest in involving himself in detail in the work of the lowly Development Division of the BMEO. He counted himself a realist and was determined to place development diplomacy within the larger context of power politics in the Middle East and to subordinate the role of social and economic betterment to the achievement of political stability. There was more 'pasha' than 'peasant' in his policy. But in his evolving views on development diplomacy, Troutbeck realized some major truths about British foreign policy. In essence, he came to see the original Bevinite inspiration for Middle East policy as mistaken and untimely. The force of unanticipated events and the unexpected degree of political upheaval in the region, particularly occasioned by the Palestine problem and the frigidity of Anglo-Egyptian relations, forced a deflection of priorities away from development. Even without war, political instability and vehement nationalism, Troutbeck came to see that the Middle East was not willing or able to respond to British initiatives on development and aid. In his darkest moments, Troutbeck was capable of issuing jeremiads about the Middle East that rivalled in tone those of the redoubtable Sir Robert Vansittart in full cry against the German threat in the 1930s.

But Troutbeck did have a programme, one that rested its hopes not in development but in a great-power-imposed peace in the Middle East and the construction of a strong Anglo-Arab partnership founded on Egypt. This policy proved in the end no more realistic or capable of achievement than had Bevin's original pursuit of development diplomacy. Fortunately, perhaps, Troutbeck retired in 1954 at the mandatory age of 60 from his post as Ambassador in Iraq before witnessing the final destruction of such hopes in the Suez débâcle.

Standard critiques of British Middle East development policy suggest that the failures that the British experienced were a result simply of the lack of finances and adequate resources. Alan Bullock, for example, writes that 'Bevin ... at the end of 1945 succeeded in establishing a Middle East Office in Cairo which carried out the advisory and technical services of the war-time Middle East Supply Centre. But Britain's inability to provide any large-scale financial support for development schemes meant that this most promising and original element in the concept of partnership never achieved more than a marginal effect.' [62] That lack of resources hindered the work of the BMEO is irrefutable. The last of the major reports produced by the Development Division during Troutbeck's tenure as head of the BMEO made even more melancholy reading than the first.[63] The staff of expert advisers had been reduced from seven to six, owing to the death of V.K. Maitland (forestry and soil conservation) in the wilds of Persia while on a survey. Work was increasingly being held up by the inability of the BMEO to employ highly qualified people on temporary contracts, or to coordinate the activities of the Division with the international agencies that were beginning to flourish in the region. The prestige of the BMEO remained high, its officials believed, but no comments were offered whatsoever on the likely progress of its work, or the impact of its efforts on British foreign policy goals.[64] The Development Division, by 1950, was taking the 'long view' and had settled into its role as a minor agency of the Government. This did not prevent it from coming under attack in Parliament as a wasteful appendage of the Cairo Embassy.[65]

But lack of resources was far from the whole story behind the failure of development diplomacy to satisfy the great expectations placed in it in September 1945. As Sir John Troutbeck had the cleverness to discover, the assumptions on which development diplomacy were based were badly flawed. Troutbeck's tenure at the BMEO suggest that even busy officials immersed in the day-to-day conduct of British affairs could appreciate that Bevin's drive for a Middle East partnership, sustained by social and economic aid, and dependent upon an assumption about Britain's ability to steer events singlehandedly, was incapable of fulfilment. At the apogee of his career, Sir John Troutbeck fought a losing battle to make his own Middle East dreams come true. What defeated him was the fact that the days of British informal empire in the Middle East, even in social-democratic guise, were over.

Notes

1. Useful accounts are to be found in: Elisabeth Barker, *The British between the superpowers, 1945-1950,* Toronto, 1983; Alan Bullock, *Ernest Bevin: Foreign Secretary, 1945-1951,* 1985; William Roger Louis, *The British Empire in the Middle East, 1945-1951,* 1984; Elizabeth Monroe, *Britain's moment in the Middle East, 1914-1956,*

1963; Kenneth O. Morgan, *Labour in power, 1945-1951,* 1984; Ritchie Ovendale, *The English speaking alliance: Britain, the United States, the Dominions and the Cold War, 1945-1951,* 1985; Ritchie Ovendale (ed.), *The foreign policy of the British Labour governments, 1945-1951,* 1984; Howard M. Sachar, *Europe leaves the Middle East, 1936-1954,* New York, 1972; and D. Cameron Watt, *Succeeding John Bull: America in Britain's place, 1900-1975,* 1984.
2. CP(45) 174, 17 September 1945, CAB 129/2. (All references are to documents held in the Public Record Office, Kew.)
3. Extended treatment is given by Louis, op.cit., to Troutbeck's ideas on Middle East politics but this otherwise valuable standard work has little to say on the subject of the British Middle East Office or the themes of this essay.
4. A worthwhile discussion of defence issues can be found in Barker, op.cit., and in Ovendale, op.cit., chapter 5.
5. See M.A. Fitzsimons, *The foreign policy of the British Labour Government,* Notre Dame, 1953.
6. Bevin to Halifax (Washington), 12 October 1945, FO 800/484/PA/45/13.
7. Bullock, op.cit., 114.
8. CP(45) 174, 17 September 1945, CAB 129/2.
9. Monroe, op.cit., 159.
10. Bullock, op.cit., 113.
11. The Middle East Supply Centre deserves extended study. See Martin W. Wilmington, 'The Middle East Supply Centre: a reappraisal', *Middle East Journal,* **VI**, Spring 1952, 144-66.
12. ibid., 161. Wilmington wrongly sees America as the sole culprit in the breakdown of post-war cooperation.
13. This was the argument that Bevin used to effect in defeating Attlee's proposal to consider a British withdrawal from the Middle East. See Bullock, op.cit., 155, 350-1.
14. Quoted in Barker, op.cit., 39.
15. 'Middle East policy', CP(45) 174, 17 September 1945, CAB 129/2.
16. 'Middle East policy', CP(45) 130, 28 August 1945, CAB 129/1.
17. CP(45) 174, 17 September 1945, CAB 129/2.
18. ibid.
19. ibid.
20. 'Annex, Part 1: British Economic policy in the Middle East', op.cit. ibid.
21. ibid.
22. CM(45) 38, 4 October 1945, CAB 128/1.
23. Overton, 'Note on the British Middle East Office', 4 July 1946, FO 371/61500, E8795/44/65.
24. CP(48) 211, 'The Development Division of the British Middle East Office', 30 August 1948, in FO 371/68388, E10090/120/65.
25. FO 371/61500, E8795/44/65.
26. ibid.
27. ibid.
28. Overton to Middle East Official Committee, informal minutes of mtg.,

10 June 1947, FO 371/61499, E5377/44/65.
29. Reorganization was discussed in the following Foreign Office files: E1141/44/64, 27 February 1947, FO 371/61498; E2305/44/65, 13 March 1947, FO 371/61498; E4601/44/65, 16 May 1947, FO 371/61499.
30. The BMEO's new directive was spelled out for Troutbeck in E10394/44/65, 27 October 1947, FO 371/61501.
31. Sargent to Bevin, 16 May 1947, FO 371/61499, E4601/44/65.
32. Troutbeck note, 8 October 1947, FO 371/61501, E10395/44/65.
33. Troutbeck minute, 4 November 1947, FO 371/61501, E10401/44/65.
34. Troutbeck sent a lengthy, but informal, report on his tour to the head of the Egyptian Department in the Foreign Office, M.R. Wright, 31 December 1947, FO 371/68387, E436/120/65.
35. ibid.
36. ibid.
37. ibid. Foreign Office officials hastened to assure themselves that Troutbeck was not urging any change in Anglo-American relations in the Middle East.
38. ibid.
39. ibid.
40. The official was probably Wright, see note 34 above.
41. CP(48) 211, 'The Development Division of the B.M.E.O.', 30 August 1948 in FO 371/68288, E10090/120/65.
42. ibid.
43. For Troutbeck's general views, especially on Palestine, see Louis, op.cit., who provides extensive discussion.
44. Troutbeck to Wright, FO, 3 March 1949, FO 371/75064, E3158/1052/65.
45. Troutbeck review of Middle East, to Attlee, 29 December 1949, FO 371/82181, EE1017/1.
46. ibid.
47. Troutbeck minute, 12 April 1949, FO 371/75085, E5082.
48. ibid.
49. Minutes of Middle East Conference, 21 July 1949, FO 371/75072, E9043.
50. Troutbeck to Bevin, 24 January 1949, FO 371/75054, E3518/1026/65; Oliver Franks (Washington) to Bevin, 17 February 1949, FO 371/75054, E2480/1026/65G. Louis op.cit., provides an excellent discussion of this debate on 614ff.
51. Troutbeck to Wright, 18 May 1948, FO 371/68386, E8738.
52. Troutbeck to Bevin, 16 June 1949, FO 371/75343, E7816.
53. Troutbeck to Bevin, 24 January 1949, FO 371/75054, E3518/1026/65.
54. ibid. There is an interesting discussion of American 'sentimental anti-colonialism' in this period in Watt, op.cit., 108. See also Louis's (op.cit.) informed conclusion about Troutbeck, 743.
55. Troutbeck to Bevin, 9 June 1949, FO 371/75054, E7480/1026/65G.
56. ibid. There is a beguiling sketch of the SIS in Cairo in Anthony Verrier, *Through the looking glass: British foreign policy in an age of illusions*, 1983, 90.
57. Troutbeck to Morrison, 13 June 1951, FO 371/91185, E1024/35/G.

58. Anthony Parsons, *They say the lion: Britain's legacy to the Arabs: a personal memoir,* 1986, 8.
59. Louis, op.cit., 576.
60. Troutbeck to FO, 3 December 1947, FO 371/61502, E11449/44/65.
61. Troutbeck to Bevin, 24 January 1949, FO 371/75054, E3518/1026/65.
62. Bullock, op.cit., 250.
63. BMEO to Bevin, 24 November 1950, FO 371/81926, E1052/24.
64. ibid. It is also worth noting that Development Division reports were no longer considered important enough to circulate to Cabinet.
65. House of Commons debates (Hansard), 14 November 1949, cols. 172-73; F.J. Erroll, MP, letter to Attlee, with FO response, 15 November 1949, FO 371/75069, E14297/1054/65.

Index

Abadan, 236, 238
Abdullah, King, 121-142, 144-147, 219-220
Acheson, Dean, 17, 21, 195-196, 198-199, 202-207, 209
  speech in Cleveland (May 1947), 24
Adamthwaite, A., 2
Addis Ababa, 236
Advisory Committee on Atomic Energy, 14
Afghanistan, 63
Al-Arrash, 125
Albania, 22
Alexander, A. W., 222
Algiers, 98, 104
Amin Al-Husseini, Haj, 129, 138, 142, 150
Amman, 122, 128, 134, 136, 140, 143, 145-147, 150-151, 219, 236
Anders, General, 157
Anderson, Sir John, 12, 14, 160
Anglo-Iranian Oil Company, 238
Anglo-Soviet Treaty of Alliance (1942), 23, 42, 48, 175
Aqaba Gulf, 141
Arabia, 127
Arab League, 128-132, 141, 143-146, 150
Arab Legion, 126, 131-132, 140-141
Atlantic Pact, *see* NATO
Atomic Energy Commission, 18
Attlee, C., 1, 9, 10, 14-15, 19-20, 22, 24-25, 29, 33, 55, 59, 87-89, 91, 100, 110, 161, 170, 190, 192, 198-199, 202-203, 208, 215, 219, 240
  efforts to maintain atomic partnership, 14
  and British Empire, 60-61
  views on foreign and defence policy, 68
Auriol, Vincent, 117,
Australasia, 66
Australia, 177, 216
Austria, 21, 23-24, 53, 68, 72
Azerbaijan, 72
Azzam Pasha, 131-132, 219

Baalbek, 219
Baghdad, 123, 236, 243
Balfour, Sir John, 25, 41
Balkans, 43, 52, 56, 59, 65, 90; *see also* individual countries
Baltic republics, 46
Bangkok, 214
Barclay, Sir Roderick, 39-40
Barrington-Ward, R. M., 45
Batavia, 214
Bateman, Charles, 161, 181-182
Bedales, 39
Bedell Smith, Walter, 87
Beeley, Harold, 129-130
Beirut, 219, 236
Belgium, 14, 18, 28-29, 99, 105, 221
  Communist Party of, 27-28
Belgian Congo, 10, 14, 31
Belgian Government, 10
Belgrade, 214
Benelux, 172
Benghazi, 219
Ben Gurion, David, 219-220
Berchtesgaden, 214
Berlin, 52, 172, 173, 175, 193-194, 196, 214
Berlin, West, 173-174, 182
Berlin, Sir Isaiah, 44, 62, 65, 79, 91
Beriya, Lavrenty, 73
Bernadotte, Count Folke, 146
Bethell, Lord, 161
Bevin, E., 1-4, 9, 18-19, 22-26, 28-31, 33, 39, 57, 59, 62, 64-68, 70, 78-81, 83-85, 88-89, 98, 101-

104, 106-107, 109, 111-115, 117, 128-135, 137, 140-141, 145, 160-161, 165, 168-172, 175-176, 179, 189-190, 192-194, 196, 198-200, 202, 206, 212-215, 219, 222, 225, 229, 231-232, 236, 238, 241, 243-245
speech to Press Association, 24
view of Frank Roberts, 40
Bidault, Georges, 102-103, 109, 110, 112, 190
Bierut, Boleslaw, 157-158
Blum, Leon, 110-111, 113
Board of Trade, 26, 101, 113-116
Bohlen, Charles, 25
Bolitho, Hector, 136
Bradley, General Omar, 198, 200, 208
Bremen, 43
Breslau, 175
Bridges, Sir Edward, 29
Brimelow, Thomas, (Lord Brimelow), 60, 62-63, 65, 69-70, 81, 84-85, 89-90, 161, 168
Bristol, 189
Bristol Grammar School, 189
British Council, 237
British Empire, 55, 66, 70, 77
British Legion, 133-134
Brook, Sir Norman, 215
Brooke, General Sir Alan, 49
Brown, Lord, (George Brown), 3
Brussels Pact, 115, 172, 196, 224
Buckingham Palace, 195
Bulgaria, 22, 24, 41-42, 52-53, 65
Bullock, Lord, 1, 230, 245
Burgess, Guy, 162, 208-209, 217
Burma, 177
Burrows, Bernard, 136
Butler, Sir Nevile, 18
Butler, R. A. B., 207
Byrnes, James, F., 14, 21, 30, 64-65, 70, 163, 194
Stuttgard speech, 163

Caccia, Harold, 81-82
Cadogan, Sir Alexander, 2, 43, 54, 60, 70
Cairo, 219, 230, 234-236, 238, 243
Calcutta, 214
Campbell, Sir Ronald, 18
Canada, 16
Catharine the Great, 74
Cavendish-Bentinck, Victor, 158,

160-162, 164
Central Eastern Europe, 167
Central Europe, 44, 55, 59, 82
Ceylon, 177
Chamberlain, Neville, 214
Chambers, Whittaker, 193
Chiefs of Staff (British), 12, 16, 49, 68, 81-82, 85, 87, 89, 100, 134-135, 137, 140, 199, 201-202, 224, 235
Chiefs of Staff (United States), 16-17, 208
China, 24, 177, 202, 204-205, 216
China Sea, 215
Chou En-Lai, 202
Churchill, Sir Winston, 9, 11-12, 32, 47, 49, 52, 54, 59, 69-70, 98-101, 104, 123-125, 147, 156-158, 160, 163, 189, 208
Churchill-Stalin agreement (October 1944), 41-43, 158
Clark Kerr, Sir Archibald (Lord Inverchapel), 20-21, 40-42, 44, 46-49, 52-53, 55, 60, 64, 81, 157
Clayton, Will, 21-23, 25, 191
Colombo Conference, 10
Colville, Sir John, 39, 207, 209
Combined Development Trust (CDT), 13-15, 29
Combined Policy Committee (CPC), 11-15, 29-30
Committee of Three, 31
Commonwealth, 9, 10, 14-16, 27-28, 50, 77, 81, 113, 115, 189, 216, 221, 223-224
Conference on European Economic Cooperation (CEEC), 190-192
Connally, Tom, 17
Congress (United States), 13
Cooper, Lady Diana, 101, 117
Council of Europe, 224
Council of Foreign Ministers (London 1945), 55-56, 58-59, 62, 160
Crawford, W. F., 239
Cripps, Sir Stafford, 1, 25, 114
Crocker, Major, 133
Crossman, R., 2
Cunningham, Sir Alan, 132
Curie, Joliot, 28
Cyprus, 218
Cyrenaica, 218-219
Czechoslovakia, 21-24, 53, 56, 156, 167, 168, 171

Daily Worker, 181
Dalton, Hugh, 1-2, 25, 68
Damascus, 122-124, 219, 236
Danube, 174
Davis, Dwight F., 10
de Gaulle, General Charles, 98, 103, 106-107, 109
Declaration on Liberated Europe, 41, 58
Defence Committee, 31
Deir Yassin, 242
Delhi, 214
Delmer, Sefton, 164
Dening, Sir Esler, 213, 215
Deutscher, Isaac, 162
Dewey, Charles, 195
Dewey, Thomas E., 193, 195
Dhaharan, 218
Dodecanese, 72
Dominions, 9, 28, 77
Douglas, Lewis, 17-18, 31, 174
Dulles, John Foster, 195
Dunkirk Treaty, 111-112, 115, 117

East Central Europe, 162
Eastern Europe, 21-22, 24-25, 41-44, 46-48, 51-56, 59, 165, 172, 174, 220
Eastern Mediterranean, 44, 55, 65-67, 83
Economic Commission for Europe (ECE), 24, 26
Economic Cooperation Agency (ECA), 195
Eden, Sir Anthony, 11-12, 39, 43, 45-50, 52, 54-55, 59, 99-101, 105-106, 125, 156, 160, 206, 209
Egypt, 56, 68, 71, 126-127, 138, 140, 142-143, 145, 157, 217-220, 233, 241, 245
Einstein, Albert, 167
Eire, 113
Eisenhower, General Dwight D., 16
Elbe, 168
Euphrates, 220
European Advisory Commission, 214
European Recovery Programme (ERP), 19, 25, 27, 29-30, 192, 194-195, 197

Faisal, Amir, 122-123
Falklands War, 209

Far East, 55, 67, 83-84, 177, 198, 204, 209, 213, 216, 221-223, 225
Fawzi, Al-Qawqji, 132
Finland, 22-23, 53
Finletter, Tom, 19
Food and Agriculture Organization, 19
Formosa, 198-199, 202
Forrestal, James, 28-29, 31
France, 27-28, 46, 72, 82, 86, 89, 98, 105-109, 113-116, 123, 156, 168-169, 172-173
  claim to atomic patents, 11
  Communist Party of, 28
Franco, General Francisco, 114
Franks, Oliver, 5, 26, 213
French West Africa, 10
Fulton, Missouri, 69, 163

Gaitskell, Hugh, 206, 213
Gaza Strip, 143, 145-146, 242
Germany, 24, 42, 48, 50, 68, 71-74, 78, 80, 82-83, 100-102, 105-112, 114, 116, 156, 168-169, 172-173, 177, 182, 214, 224
Glasgow University, 189
Glubb Pasha, 121, 125-126, 128, 132, 134, 136, 141, 148, 151
Godesberg, 214
Goldie, Colonel, 133
Gomulka, Wladyslaw, 157
Gouin, Felix, 107
Gousenko, Igor, 14-15
Gowing, Margaret, 32, 207
Grabski, Stanislaw, 163, 165
Greater Syria, 124-126
Greece, 21, 23-24, 41-44, 52-53, 55, 61-62, 65-67, 71-72, 105, 170, 172, 175, 218-219
Grocholski, Count, 164
Gromyko, Andrei, 178
Groves-Anderson memorandum, 14-15
Groves, Gen. Leslie R., 14-15
Gush Etzion, 133

Hagana, 133-134
Haifa, 133
Halifax, Lord, 11-13, 15, 33, 170, 214
Halleck, Charles, 195
Hall Patch, Sir Edmund, 25, 215
Hamburg, 43
Hancock, Patrick, 161

Hankey, Robin, 70, 81, 84-85
Harriman Committee, 26, 191
Harrison, Geoffrey, 40, 176, 178
Harvey, Oliver, 107-109, 116, 221
Harwell, 15
Hejaz, 123, 142
Henderson, Sir Nicholas, 3
Hickenlooper, Bourke, 17, 29-30
Hiroshima, 9
Hiss, Alger, 193
Hilter, Adolf, 4, 70, 99, 144
Hoffman, Paul, 195, 197
Holland, 99
Hong Kong, 203, 214
Hopkins, Harry, 51
Hungary, 22, 24, 52-53, 63, 72, 169
Hussein, Sharif, 123
Hyde Park Aide Memoire, 12-14

Ibn Saud, King, 125
India, 56, 61, 66, 71, 177, 217, 230
Indian Ocean, 66
Indonesia, 67, 72
International Bank, 19, 22-23, 240
International Labour Organization, 10
International Monetary Fund, 19, 22
International Trade Organization, 19-20
Iran, *see* Persia
Iraq, 123, 125, 135, 139-140, 148, 218, 243, 245
Israel, 141-145, 218-220, 222, 238, 240-242, 244
Istanbul, 236
Italy, 21, 23-24, 28, 72, 169, 171-173, 196, 221
Ivan the Terrible, 74

Jabel Druz, 125
Jaffa, 133
Japan, 50, 73, 174, 216, 224
Jebb, Gladwyn (Lord Gladwyn), 54, 60, 160, 173-174, 176, 215
Jericho, 146-147
Jerusalem, 122, 124-125, 133-134, 140, 142, 219
Jessup, Philip, 198
Jewish Agency, 129, 132-133
Joint Intelligence Sub-Committee (JIC), 44, 81-83, 85
Joint Planning Staff, 49
Joint Staff Mission, 11, 13

Jordan, *see* Transjordan

Karachi, 214
Katyn, 46, 156
Kelly, Sir David, 179-180
Kennan, George F., 17, 30-31, 70-71, 78-80, 207, 212, 215
  view of Frank Roberts, 40
Kenny, W. John, 19
Kerak, 122-123
King, W. L. Mackenzie, 14
Korea, 174, 198-203, 205, 208, 216
Korean War, 198-199, 201, 205-206, 242
Krug Committee, 191
Kuala Lumpur, 214

La Follette, Robert M., 26
Lapie Pierre-Olivier, 110
Lawrence, T. E., 122, 124
League of Nations, 2, 156, 204
Lebanon, 100, 102-103, 123, 125, 139, 143, 218, 237
Lenin, Vladimir Ilyich, 62
Levant, 54, 72, 102-103, 105, 108, 234
Libya, 55
Lie, Trygve, 199
Lilienthal, David, 16, 29
Litvinov, Maxim, 156
Lockhart, Sir Robert Bruce, 43-45, 47-48, 51, 53, 63, 70
London Committee, 19, 25-26
Lloyd, Selwyn, 40
Louis, Wm. Roger, 244
Lovett, Robert, 30, 192
Lublin Committee, 157

MacArthur, General Douglas, 202, 204-205, 214
MacDonald, Malcolm, 215
Maclean, Donald, 13, 21, 23, 29-30, 32, 208-209
  succeeds Makins on CPC, 17
  his defection, 33
McMahon, Act, 1946 (United States), 15, 18, 207
Macmillan, Harold, 8, 10-11, 33, 39
McNeil, Hector, 25, 181
Madrid, 156
Maitland, V. K., 246
Makins, Sir Roger, 5, 48, 201
Malan, Dr D. F., 219
Malaya, 172

INDEX

Malenkov, Georgi, 73
Malik, Yakov, 178
Manchuria, 88
Mao Tse-Tung, 177
Marshall, Gen. George, 12, 23, 29, 31, 191-192, 195, 197
  his view on Commonwealth, 16
  June 1947 speech, 24-25, 169, 189
Marshall Plan, 9, 22, 25-27, 30-31, 105, 112, 177, 179, 189, 194, 197, 205-206, 231
Marshall aid, see Marshall Plan
Martin, Joseph, 195, 205
Marx, Karl, 45
Massigli, René, 111-112
Matthews, H. Freeman, 23
Mayhew, Christopher, 197
Mecca, 122-123
Mediterranean, 58, 66, 68, 129, 145, 222, 231
Meir, Golda, 134
Middle East, 11, 44, 55, 61, 65-67, 71, 75, 77, 81-84, 100, 116, 121-122, 126-127, 130, 135, 137, 139, 142, 144, 148, 150-151, 213, 217-220, 222-223, 225
Middle East Supply Centre (MESC), 230, 232, 234
Mikolajczyk, Stanislaw, 157-158, 160-161
Ministerial Committee on Atomic Energy, 18, 29
Modzelewski, Zygmunt, 161
Molotov, Vyacheslav M., 45, 49, 58, 64, 68, 73, 112, 160, 164-165, 169, 171, 176, 178
Monro, Sir Gordon, 29
Monroe, Elizabeth, 135, 151, 230
Montgomery, Field Marshal Sir Bernard, 40, 43, 89, 180, 214
Morrison, Herbert, 221
Munich, 214
Musa Al-Alami, 132

Nablus, 149
Nanking, 217
NATO, 105, 144, 196, 206, 212, 218-220, 224
Nehru, Pandit, 214
Neisse, 159, 163-164
Nenni, Pietro, 171
New Statesman, 2
New York, 222

New Zealand, 216
Nicholson, Harold, 116
Nile, 220
Noel-Baker, Philip, 221
NKVD, 159, 162, 166
North Korea, 202
North West Africa, 10
Norway, 99, 176
Nourse Committee, 191
Nuri Pasha, 135, 220, 243

Oder, 159, 163-164
OEEC, 195
Official Committee on Atomic Energy, 16, 18, 27
O'Malley, Sir Owen, 49, 53
Oslo, 215
Overseas Negotiations Committee, 19
Overton, Sir Arnold, 234-235
Oxford, 190, 194
Oxford University, 189, 209

Pacific, 222, 224
Palestine, 121-122, 125-132, 134-135, 137-141, 143-144, 147, 151, 172, 218, 231, 233, 236, 239-240, 242, 245
Palmer's School, Essex, 214
Paris Council of Foreign Ministers (1946), 88, 107
Parker, Ralph, 45
Paterson, Robert P., 13
Patton, Gen. George S., 43, 51
Pearson, Lester, B., 15
Pentagon, 17
Persia, 24, 42, 44, 54-55, 61, 66-67, 71-72, 75, 81, 84, 90, 157-158, 172, 218-219, 237, 246
Persian Gulf, 67, 84, 215, 219, 236
Peterson, Sir Maurice, 2, 40, 66, 81, 89, 164-165
Peter the Great, 74
Philby, Kim, 208-209
Philby, St. John, 124
PINCHER, 17
Poland, 22-24, 41-42, 44, 46, 53, 72, 90, 156-167, 169
Polish Socialist Party, 163-164
Polish Workers' Party, 156
Potsdam (Berlin) conference, 53-54, 61, 90, 101, 159-160, 164
Prague, 178
Pravda, 23, 69, 170, 181

Pusan, 200

Quebec Agreement, 12-16, 27, 29, 207
Queen's College, Oxford, 189, 192

Ramadier, Paul, 112-113
Rangoon, 214
Red Sea, 68
Revers, General, 114
Rhine, 108, 168, 224
Rhineland, 106
Roberts, Frank, 5, 31
Romania, 22, 42, 52-53, 63-65, 157, 178
Roosevelt, F. D., 12, 99
Rowan, L., 19
Rugby, 39
Ruhr, 25, 43, 56, 72, 102, 107-112
Rusk, Dean, 204
Russia Committee, 10, 85, 160, 176-177, 180

Saar, 107, 110
Salisbury, Lord, 1
Samaria, 141
San Franciso, 12
Sargent, Sir Orme, 1, 2, 33, 42-45, 47-49, 51-55, 59, 63-65, 68, 70, 77, 81-82, 87, 109, 111, 159, 168, 174, 214, 236
Saudi Arabia, 145, 218
Scandinavia, 172
Schuman Plan, 115
Senate Joint Committee, 17
Sengier, M., 28
Shanghai, 214
Sharett, Moshe, 134
Shuneh, 145
Singapore, 214
Smith, Walter Bedell, 39-40
Smuts, Field Marshal Jan, 28-29
Sochi, 66
Sofia, 178
Sorbonne, 214
South Africa, 15, 27-29, 216, 219
South East Asia, 84, 177, 213, 216-217, 221-222, 225
South Eastern Europe, 21-22, 41, 61
Southern Europe, 23
Spaak, Paul-Henri, 28, 104
Spain, 72, 164
Stalin, Marshal Josif, 4, 23, 41, 44-46, 53, 55, 59-61, 66, 73, 75, 83, 88, 101, 156-159, 163, 167-168, 174-177, 179-180
Stettin, 167
Stimson, Henry L., 12
Straits, 52, 55, 67
Strang, W., (Lord Strang), 39, 46, 181
Strasburger, Henryk, 162
Suez Canal, 127, 229, 242, 244
Sunday Express, 5
Sykes-Picot agreement, 123
Syria, 100-103, 123, 125-126, 138-139, 143, 145, 148, 218-219, 237

Taber, John, 195, 197
Talal, Prince, 136
Tangier, 54
TASS, 180-182
Tawfiq, Abu Al-Huda, 128, 130-132, 142, 145
Taylor, A. J. P., 3, 175
Tehran, 68, 219, 236
Tehran conference, 61
Tel Aviv, 219-220
TGWU, 189
Thakin Nu, 214
Thomas, Lord, 4
Thorp, Willard, 22
Tiberias, 133
Times, 45, 213
Tito, Marshal Josip Broz, 53, 55, 167, 174, 177
Tokyo, 214-215
Toukan, Jamal, 149
Transjordan, 121-131, 134-136, 138-144, 147-148, 150-151, 218, 237
Trieste, 53, 72, 167, 169
Trinity College, Cambridge, 39
Tripoli, 219
Tripolitania, 55-56, 58, 218
Truman Doctrine, 16, 24
Truman, Harry S., 12-14, 17, 19, 28, 51, 191-192, 196, 198-199, 203, 208, 240
Turkey, 21, 24, 42, 44, 53-56, 61-63, 65-67, 72, 75, 81, 172, 218-219

United Kingdom Atomic Energy Authority, 10
United Nations Organisation, 2, 9, 13-18, 20, 23-24, 26-27, 29, 52, 62, 68, 89, 100-101, 103-105,

122, 128-129, 132, 134, 136-140, 146, 199, 202-203
commission on nuclear control, 15
Security Council, 67
United Nations General Assembly, 161
United Nations Relief and Rehabilitation Administration (UNRRA), 19-21
United States Atomic Energy Commission (USAEC), 16, 29
University College, London, 214

Vandenberg, Arthur, H., 17, 30
Vansittart, Lord, 104, 180, 245
Venezia Giulia, 53
Vienna, 172
Vinson, Fred, 22
Vyshinski, Andrei, 41, 67, 178

Wallace, Henry, 88
War Department (United States), 15
Warner, Christopher, 2, 3, 47-48, 57, 59, 62, 70, 81-82, 85-86, 88, 90, 159, 161

Warner, F. A., 174
Warren, Earl, 193
Washington Declaration, 15
Washington Post, 209
Wavell, General Sir Archibald, 230
West Bank, 140, 142-143, 145-151
Western Europe, 21, 23, 44, 54, 61, 77, 90, 98, 101, 105, 113, 115-116, 171, 179, 182, 217, 221
Western Union, 170, 172
Williams, Francis, 2
Wilson, Field Marshal Sir Henry Maitland, 11, 13, 16
Worcester College, Oxford, 209
World Bank, 21-22
World Federation of Trade Unions, 75, 173

Yalta, 41, 47, 51-52, 58, 81, 157
agreement, 12, 40-43, 90, 161, 164
conference, 46
Yugoslavia, 39, 53, 72, 174, 176

Zeeland, M. Paul van, 10
Zefat, 133
Zilliacus, Konni, 175, 179